The Globalization of Israel

GLOBALIZING REGIONS

Globalizing Regions offers concise accounts of how the nations and regions of the world are experiencing the effects of globalization. Richly descriptive yet theoretically informed, each volume shows how individual places are navigating the tension between age-old traditions and the new forces generated by globalization.

Australia by Anthony Moran

Global Hong Kong by Gary McDonogh and Cindy Wong

On Argentina and the Southern Cone by Alejandro Grimson and Gabriel Kessler

The Koreas by Charles Armstrong

China and Globalization: The Social, Economic, and Political Transformation of Chinese Society by Doug Guthrie

Morocco by Shana Cohen and Larabi Jaidi

Global Ireland: Same Difference by Tom Inglis

The Netherlands by Frank J. Lechner

Forthcoming:
Global Iberia by Gary McDonogh

Global Indonesia by Jean Gelman Taylor

Global Iran by Camron Michael Amin

The Philippines by James Tyner

Turkey by Alev Cinar

Brazil and Globalization by Fiona Macaulay and Mahrukh Doctor

The Globalization of Israel

McWorld in Tel Aviv, Jihad in Jerusalem

URI RAM

Routledge
Taylor & Francis Group
New York   London

Routledge
Taylor & Francis Group
270 Madison Avenue
New York, NY 10016

Routledge
Taylor & Francis Group
2 Park Square
Milton Park, Abingdon
Oxon OX14 4RN

© 2008 by Taylor & Francis Group, LLC
Routledge is an imprint of Taylor & Francis Group, an Informa business

Printed in the United States of America on acid-free paper
10 9 8 7 6 5 4 3 2 1

International Standard Book Number-13: 978-0-415-95304-7 (Softcover) 978-0-415-95303-0 (Hardcover)

Library of Congress Cataloging-in-Publication Data

Ram, Uri.
    [Globalizatsyah shel Yisra'el. English]
    The globalization of Israel : McWorld in Tel Aviv, jihad in Jerusalem / Uri Ram.
        p. cm. -- (Globalizing regions)
    Includes bibliographical references and index.
    ISBN 978-0-415-95304-7 (pbk.) -- ISBN 978-0-415-95303-0 (cloth)
    1. Globalization--Israel. 2. Post-Zionism. 3. Postmodernism--Social aspects--Israel. 4.
Israel--Social conditions. 5. Israel--Economic conditions. I. Title.

HN660.Z9G56713 2007
303.48'25694--dc22
                                                                        2006102525

Visit the Taylor & Francis Web site at
http://www.taylorandfrancis.com

and the Routledge Web site at
http://www.routledge.com

Contents

Preface: It Could Be Any City

The front-cover photo depicts the new business district in Tel Aviv, along the Ayalon Highways, which is walking distance from where I live. The initial reaction of the Routledge staff to the photo was somewhat disapproving, because, as I was told, the photo "is not particularly recognizable as Israel" and "looks to us like it could be any city." I was delighted. I couldn't have phrased a better motto for a book that shows Israel to be a capitalist society in the global era. Of course there are things that are "recognizable as Israel" in the book, but it argues, on the whole, that they inexorably take the shape of "any city" in our globalizing world.

Globalization of Israel offers a new paradigm for the study of contemporary Israeli society. It argues, in a nutshell, that under the impact of globalization, Israel is being bifurcated into two polar opposites—capitalism versus tribalism, or "McWorld" versus "Jihad"—that contradict and abet each other dialectically. It argues, furthermore, that this bifurcation overlaps to a significant extent with socioeconomic divisions on one hand and with political-cultural divisions on the other hand. The winners and the losers of globalization render their distinct class experiences into divergent cultural identities, and neoliberal economics and neonationalist politics grow simultaneously, if contradictorily.

The book is a culmination of a long period of my grappling with questions that emerged in the 1990s, when the consequences of globalization began to be sensed in Israel, though the theory of globalization was barely familiar there. What puzzled me most was the dichotomous nature of the changes that swamped Israel: postmodernity in Tel Aviv versus neofundamentalism in Jerusalem; high-tech industrial parks in the center versus sacred sites of veneration in the peripheries; an exclamation of constitutional revolution versus an adherence to ethnonationalistic principles. During the 1990s the Israeli economy underwent an informational revolution and a neoliberal turn, Israeli society underwent deep class polarization, Israeli popular culture underwent "McDonaldization," Israeli political culture underwent Americanization, and Israeli national ideology became a bone of contention between die-hard Zionists and radical critics. All the while Israel and the Palestinian Liberation Organization signed the Oslo Accord; Yitzhak Rabin, Israel's prime minister, was assassinated; a second Palestinian intifada broke out; and the Oslo Accord crumbled. The analytical challenge I undertook was to weave all this into a systemic comprehensive sociological account. *Globalization of Israel*, with the "bifurcation model" at its core, is the fruition of this endeavor. On a normative level, the book also represents my anxiety as an Israeli in the face of the moral quandary of my society, which results from the growing discrepancy between the country's democratic posture and its ethnonationalist practice. This issue is tackled head-on by the concept of post-Zionism that is articulated throughout the book.

My work on such a long-term complicated project was made possible by the loving support of my wife, Nava Schreiber, and of our son, Ilya Ram. Ben Gurion University and its Department of Sociology and Anthropology (formerly the Department of Behavioral Sciences) provided a permanent academic setting for my work. My indebtedness to the inspiration that I have received from the works of many colleagues and friends is expressed in the bibliographical list. Gili Baruch and Eran Fisher, two students of mine, provided extremely helpful comments throughout the maturation of this project. The New School for Social Research and its Department of Sociology—of which I am a graduate—have extended their hospitality to me in the years 2000 to 2001 and 2006 to 2007. Part of the research for this book was made possible by a grant from the Ministry of Science of the Government of Israel (1999–2001), and the research for Chapter 3 was aided by a grant from the Burda Center for Innovative Communications at Ben Gurion University (2000). I am grateful to the United States Institute for Peace, in Washington, D.C., for a generous grant that enabled a year of research and writing (2000–2001). The content of this book and the opinions expressed in it do not necessarily reflect those of the United States Institute for Peace or any of the other institutions mentioned previously. I want to extend my gratitude also to Yitzhak Binyamini and Idan Zivoni, editors at Resling Publishers in Tel Aviv, whose enthusiastic welcoming of a former Hebrew version of this book (2005) helped me with the compilation of the distinct parts of my research into an integrated book. Finally I want to thank the editors at Routledge who accepted the manuscript and accompanied its production into the final product that it is.

Some of the chapters of this book are revised and updated versions of articles that had been previously published in scholarly journals, and I thank the publishers for their permission to return to these texts and rearticulate them in this book. The detailed list of acknowledgments appears after the preface. An article that I published in the journal *Constellations*, edited by Andrew Arato and Nancy Fraser (Vol. 6, no. 3; Blackwell, 1999), under the title "The State of the Nation: Contemporary Challenges to Zionism in Israel" is not reproduced here, but it served as the launching of some of the ideas developed in the book. The same applies for a chapter that I published in the book *The New Israel*, edited by Gershon Shafir and Yoav Peled, under the title " 'The Promised Land of Business Opportunities': Liberal Post-Zionism in the Glocal Age" (Westview, 2000).

Acknowledgments

Permission was granted for the reproduction of articles of mine as a basis for revised and updated chapters in this book:

Chapter 4: "Citizens, Consumers and Believers: The Israeli Public Sphere between Fundamentalism and Capitalism," *Israel Studies* 3, no. 1 (1999): 24–44.

Chapter 5: "Glocommodification: How the Global Consumes the Local—McDonald's in Israel," *Current Sociology* 52, no. 2 (2003): 11–31.

Chapter 6: "Post-Nationalist Pasts: The Case of Israel," *Social Science History* 22, no. 4 (1988): 513–45.

Chapter 6: "Historiosophical Foundations of the Historical Strife in Israel," *Journal of Israeli History* 20, nos. 2–3 (2001): 43–61.

Introduction: The Globalization
Paradigm in Israel Studies

The twentieth century came to its ending with the demolition of the Berlin Wall in 1989. The twenty-first century got to its opening with the downfall of the World Trade Center in New York City in 2001. The demolition of the Berlin Wall symbolized the end of the totalitarian regimes of the previous century (though remnants of them prevail) and inspired hopes for a new century of global freedom and abundance, in which the best aspirations of Western modernity would finally be realized. Francis Fukuyama called it the "end of history" (Fukuyama 1992). But a backlash to Western complacency had been already lurking in Riyadh, Kabul, Teheran, and elsewhere in the Muslim world and soon instigated the September 11th attacks on New York and Washington and ushered the "clash of civilizations," as it was dubbed by Samuel Huntington (Huntington 1998).

The two diametrically opposing approaches to globalization—the "end of history" and the "clash of civilizations"—tap significant dimensions of it, yet in delineating a stiff binary of the past versus the future and of Western or Northern modern *us* versus the Eastern, or rather Southern, underdeveloped or traditional *them*, they are implicated by ahistoricity, essentialism, and simplicity. Neither of these approaches can therefore grasp in its entirety the intricacy of the dialectic of globalization, the way in which it is a self-contradictory process, which accommodates both an "end" and a "clash," both an "us" and a "them." We thus prefer in this book the approach to globalization that is encapsulated by the image of "McWorld versus Jihad" that was offered in a book of that title by Benjamin Barber (Barber 1995). Following Barber we propose to perceive globalization in a somewhat Hegelian manner as a contradictory dynamic totality that conjoins two negations: "McWorld" versus "Jihad," the one with and against the other, as two dimensions of the very same process of globalization, and for that matter two dimensions of it that are inimical to democracy, the one being hypercommercial, the other being hypercommunal.

The concept of globalization has been at the cutting edge of the humanities and the social sciences for a decade and a half now. This book ponders whether Israeli society undergoes globalization, how much it is affected by globalization, and how it responds to globalization. Such questions have rarely been asked with regard to Israel, and it is high time that they were and that answers are sought for as well. This does not imply that unique and local factors—culture, history, and institutions that are distinctively Israeli—are ignored. No two societies are alike, not even societies that are a part of a regional block or share a common type of regime; this is even more apparent in the case of Israel, which is rather a new historical innovation and is rather alien to its region. Yet the perspective offered here does stipulate that the unique and local factors are analyzed in juxtaposition with and as functioning within the wider, external context. The book thus offers a new sociological perspective in Israel studies—the globalization paradigm—a paradigm that defines in large the contours of our era.

Israel is frequently discussed in conjunction with the Israeli–Arab conflict and its recurrent wars, with the occupation of the Palestinian territories, or with terrorist attacks on it. Without downplaying the centrality of the colonial, national, and militaristic dimensions of Israeli reality, this book aims to direct the spotlight elsewhere—toward Israel as a capitalist society in the era of globalization. The book suggests that in the past twenty years or so Israel has undergone an extensive and intensive process of globalization, which fundamentally affects its economy, society, culture, and politics, and therefore that the paradigm of globalization is essential to the understanding of contemporary Israel, including the aspects mentioned previously.[1] The book argues more specifically that the effect of globalization on Israel is two pronged. Under the impact of globalization, societies become simultaneously more universalistic and more particularistic, more constitutional and more "tribal" (or communal). Globalization is a dialectical process that generates simultaneously both (neo-) liberalism and (neo-) fundamentalism—and Israel is a case in point.

BIFURCATION: BETWEEN MCWORLD AND JIHAD

"McWorld" signifies the world of universal consumer brands, and "Jihad" signifies the world of communitarian holy wars (not just the Muslim variety or even necessarily a religious variety). Unlike in the "end" and the "clash" perspectives, the McWorld versus Jihad perspective depicts not a plain dichotomous inversion but rather a unitary contradictory complementation. Although the promiscuity and decadence of McWorld is the target of Jihad's moral rage and identity fury, Jihad's fundamentalist message is fueled and shaped by the same developments that cast McWorld. Likewise, although McWorld glitters itself with sparks of progress and rationality, it in fact shares Jihad's disrespect for individual "pursuit of happiness" with its crass commodification and ghastly exploitation.

McWorldist consumerism and Jihadist fundamentalism are thus but two different expressions of the same process of globalization. As put by Barber, "Progress moves in steps but sometimes lurched backwards in history's twisting maze. Jihad not only revolts against but also abets McWorld, while McWorld not only imperils but also recreates and reinforces Jihad. They produce their contraries and need one another" (Barber 1995, 5). Furthermore, McWorld and Jihad are not the tags of distinct social groups or world regions but rather dimensions of globalization that are intermixed, so that at certain points they almost collapse into what was termed "McJihad" (Mitchell 2002).

Finally, Barber's approach is preferable to both Fukuyama's and Huntington's not merely because it is dialectical but also because it is critical, as we just saw, not only of the presumed "other"—the bearer of Jihad—but rather also of the "self" of the West—the originator of McWorld. He warns that the blend of McWorld and Jihad jeopardizes democratic culture, especially the institution of the public sphere, where citizens can communicate and deliberate policies: "More than anything else, what has been lost in the clash of Jihad and McWorld has been the idea of the *public* as something more than a random collection of consumers or an aggregation of special political interests or product of identity politics" (Barber 1995, 286). And he proceeds to explain the distinction between the concept of the democratic public on one hand and the concepts of premodern faith politics and postmodern consumption politics on the other hand: "The voice of civil society, of citizens in deliberative conversation, challenges the exclusivity and irrationality of Jihad clamor but is equally antithetical to the claims of McWorld's private markets to represent some aggregative public good. Neither Jihad nor McWorld grasp the meaning of 'public,' and the idea of the public realized offers a powerful remedy to the privatizing and de-democratizing effects of aggressive tribes and aggressive markets" (287). Jihad is a trend of particularism and of exclusion. It moulds blood communities based on hatred and intolerance. McWorld is a trend of universalism and of inclusion, but one that is based on markets that are indifferent to public needs or to elementary social justice. In other words, Jihad is based on solidarity lacking universalism (with authoritarian and repressive hierarchy even within its own core groups), whereas McWorld is based on universalism lacking solidarity (thus on formal equality but not actual equality).

In the vocabulary of Jürgen Habermas, both McWorld and Jihad "colonize" the public sphere of potential rational communication (Habermas 1989). In the terms of Manuel Castells, the same contemporary dialectic appears as a one between the "network" and "identity" (Castells 1997). In this book we refer to McWorld and Jihad interchangeably as the "global" and the "local" poles of the axial tension of our epoch.

Since the 1990s the dynamic dialectics of the global and the local have been taking place on a planetary scale. We argue in this book that such a dialectical dynamic also takes place inside Israel, metaphorically between Tel Aviv as a site of McWorld and Jerusalem as a site of Jihad.

Israel is straddled geopolitically between McWorld and Jihad, between being a protégé of the United States and being situated in the Middle East, the heart of world Islamic resistance to the United States. Yet we argue further that not only is Israel situated globally between McWorld and Jihad but Israel also undergoes inside it the same bifurcation and tension between the capitalist and tribal dimensions of McWorld and Jihad that take place in the world at large. A dialectical struggle between a global, capitalist, civic trend and a local nationalist-religious trend takes place within Israel.

The McWorld–Jihad or global–local dialectics is the source for the confusing impressions that any observer may gauge from Israel in recent years. On the one hand Israel is a stable parliamentarian democracy, it is highly advanced economically, and it is a Western-style consumer society; on the other hand it is a state of occupation, apartheid, and social deprivations and a place where a separation between church (i.e., synagogue) and state hardly obtains. The two major and large cities of Israel—Tel Aviv and Jerusalem—each undertakes a nonproportional share of McWorld and Jihad, respectively. To extend the metaphor, we note that the dialectic may take place in between them, on highway number 1 that separates—and bridges—the two cities, which are only a forty-five-minute drive away from each other.

From this perspective, although Israeli society undergoes socioeconomic "marketization," it also undergoes simultaneously cultural-political "tribalization." We argue further that in the case of Israel, the McWorld versus Jihad tension is rendered into a tension between the Jewish facet of its identity and the Israeli facet of its identity. The official Zionist ideology of Israel depicts it in terms of a "Jewish and democratic"

Israeli nation-state. We argue that globalization bifurcates the "Jewish–democratic" unison and splits the "Jewish" and the "democratic" dimensions into a Jewish–Jihad trend—which we term "neo-Zionism"—and an Israeli–McWorld trend—which we term "post-Zionism." We also argue that this bifurcation overlaps to a significant extent with the class polarity, so that significant portions of the winners of globalization tend to become more "global" whereas significant portions of the losers of globalization tend to react more "local."

The sociological literature on Israel enlists manifold cleavages in it: nation, class, religion, ethnicity, gender, and ideology cleavages, to name just the major ones. It is maintained in the present work that much of this divergence in fact coalesces along the McWorld–Jihad or global–local watershed. Analyzing Israeli society through the prism of the globalization paradigm as offered here thus sheds light on the most important changes in Israeli society in the past two decades: the simultaneous development, from the same source, of two interwoven yet conflicting political cultures—the culture of the market and the culture of identity. In this way a social reality that seems otherwise chaotic and formless acquires some measure of coherence, at least in theoretical terms.

Our interpretation of Israel as elucidated previously may be depicted in terms of a heuristic "bifurcation model," which consists of two steps. One step is a transition between two successive historical processes: from centripetal modernization (state formation, nation building, economic developmentalism, etc.) toward a centrifugal globalization (flexible production, multiculturalism, etc.). The second step is a bifurcation along the two dialectically opposing poles of globalization—McWorld versus Jihad or the global versus the local. If we imagine

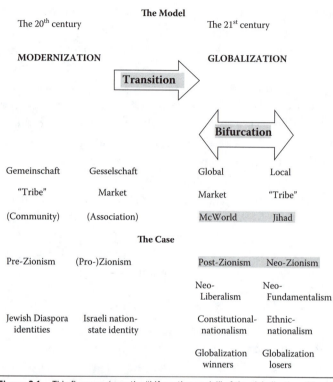

The Model

The 20th century   The 21st century

MODERNIZATION   **GLOBALIZATION**

Transition

Bifurcation

Gemeinschaft	Gesselschaft	Global	Local
"Tribe"	Market	Market	"Tribe"
(Community)	(Association)	McWorld	Jihad

The Case

Pre-Zionism	(Pro-)Zionism	Post-Zionism	Neo-Zionism
		Neo-Liberalism	Neo-Fundamentalism
Jewish Diaspora identities	Israeli nation-state identity	Constitutional-nationalism	Ethnic-nationalism
		Globalization winners	Globalization losers

Figure 0.1 This figure portrays the "bifurcation model" of the globalization of Israel.

modernization also as a process having two dialectically opposing poles—tradition versus modernity or, in classical sociological terminology, Gemeinschaft versus Gesellschaft—then the
overall transformation of Jewish–Israeli society since its very
inception in the last decades of the nineteenth century until our
own days in the first decade of the twenty-first century may be
portrayed as in Figure 0.1. The model of bifurcation includes
thus: step 1, a transition from the process of modernization
to the process of globalization, and step 2, a yet unresolved

tension and oscillation between the two poles of the globalization process, the global and the local. The two arrows in the graph and especially the double-edged arrow of "bifurcation" mark the "you are here" red circle of this book—a transition from modernization to globalization and a dialectical tension between global winners–McWorld–post-Zionism and global losers–Jihad–neo-Zionism, which is at the core of our analysis of the globalization of Israel.

So this book is engaged with exploring the meaning of the bifurcation model in the case of Israel in the past two decades or, better yet put, with exploring the meaning of Israel in the past two decades by the projection of this model on its seemingly chaotic reality. What does it mean to say that Israel passed a transition from modernization to globalization, and what does it mean to say that Israel is currently bifurcating and fluctuating in tension between the global and the local? Answering these questions is the challenge of this book.

GLOBALIZATION: BETWEEN DURKHEIM AND MARX

McWorld and Jihad are two facets of globalization. But what is globalization? The reality of globalization is too complex and the literature about it too huge to be summarized here.[2] The following comments are thus meant only as a launching pad toward the more substantial discussion of the issues, which is offered in the balance of the book.

Approaches to globalization differ. One famed way of classifying them was offered by David Held and his associates. This classification divides the scholars of globalization into three camps: "hyper-globalizers" "sceptics," and "transformationalists" (Held et al. 1999). Hyper-globalizers regard globalization as an economic and technical juggernaut that reshapes human societies by creating a unified global market. Sceptics view what they sometimes call "globalony" as a much-exaggerated talk about processes that are not that new and not that omnipotent. Transformationalists are those in between who recognize the epochal impact of globalization yet think it is susceptible to modification by local responses and policies.

As useful as this classification might be, it shrouds a more fundamental theoretical distinction regarding the causes and effects of globalization, a distinction between two schools that may be traced back to Emile Durkheim and Karl Marx. The Durkheimian school regards globalization in terms of systemic evolution and social development, whereas the Marxist school regards globalization in terms of capital accumulation and social conflict. In short, whereas for Durkheimians globalization signifies a new stage of *modernity*, for Marxists it signifies a new stage of *capitalism*.

In the spirit of Durkheim's argument about the origins of social change in the heightened "volume" and "density" of social interaction (Durkheim 1947), and furthermore in the spirit of Talcott Parsons's articulation of social development as a process of functional differentiation and social reintegration (Parsons 1951), the mainstream approach to globalization depicts it mainly as a process that is rooted in the transformation of the spatial-temporal boundaries of society. Globalization is thus about attributes such as stretching, intensification, speeding up, velocity, and impact of social transactions. From suchlike perspective David Held and his associates define globalization as follows:

A process (or set of processes) which embodies a transformation in the *spatial* organization of social relations and transactions—assessed in terms of their extensity, intensity, velocity and impact—generating transcontinental or interregional flows and networks of activity, interaction and the exercise of power. (Held et al. 1999, 16)

They thus characterize globalization around the *stretching* of social, political, and economic activities across frontiers; the *intensification*, interconnectedness, and flows of trade, finance, migration, messages, and so on; the *speeding up* of global interactions and processes; the increased *velocity* of the diffusion of ideas, goods, information, capital, and people by the development of a worldwide system of transportation and communication; and the deepening *impact* of all the above "such that the effects of distant events can be highly significant elsewhere and specific local developments can come to have considerable global consequences [so that] the boundaries between domestic matters and global affairs become increasingly fluid" (Held and McGrew 1999, 1).

Likewise Anthony Giddens considers globalization as a change in the scale of human interconnectedness, which is defined as "disembedding": "the 'lifting out' of social relations from local contexts of interaction and their restructuring across indefinite spans of time–space" (Giddens 1990, 21). The dynamism of modernity stems from the ability to create relations between present and absent agents by bureaucratic systems based on print documentation, whereas the enhanced dynamism of globalization (associated with postmodernity or high modernity) stems from the ability to turn physically absent agents to virtually present ones through means such as audiovisual communications based on digital data processing and satellite communication technology. Giddens therefore describes globalization as "the bracketing of time and space by social systems" (22) and as "the intensification of worldwide social relations which link distant localities in such a way that local happenings are shaped by events occurring many miles away and vice versa" (64).

With a noted preference to the Durkheimian interpretation of globalization—and with a focus on economics—and yet in quite an informative way, the United Nations (1999) *Human Development Report 1999* gives a succinct response to the question "Globalization—What's Really New?" that provides a useful snapshot of at least some components of globalization, as shown in Table 0.1.

The Marxist approach to globalization leans back on Marx's fundamental notion of capitalism as a self-dynamized, world-changing process of accumulation of capital. Of a resounding echo in regard to globalization are passages such as the following from the *Communist Manifesto*, which anticipated the economic, social, cultural, and political attributes of globalization (Marx and Engels 1848/1998), albeit without taking account of the potential for a backlash in the form of reactionary Jihadism:

> Modern industry has established the world market, for which the discovery of America paved the way. This market has given an immense development to commerce, to navigation, to communication by land. This development has, in turn, reacted on the extension of industry; and in proportion as industry, commerce, navigation, railways extended, in the same proportion the bourgeoisie developed, increased its capital, and pushed into the background every class handed down from the Middle Ages. …

Table 0.1 Introduction to Globalization

Globalization—What's Really New?

Some argue that globalization is not new and that the world was more integrated a century ago. Trade and investment as a proportion of gross domestic production were comparable, and with borders open, many people were migrating abroad. What's new this time?

New Markets

- Growing global markets in services—banking, insurance, transport
- New financial markets—deregulated, globally linked, working around the clock, with action at a distance in real time, with new instruments such as derivatives
- Deregulation of antitrust laws and proliferation of mergers and acquisitions
- Global consumer markets with global brands

New Actors

- Multinational corporations integrating their production and marketing, dominating world production
- The World Trade Organization—the first multilateral organization with authority to enforce national governments' compliance with rules
- An international criminal court system in the making
- A booming international network of nongovernmental organizations
- Regional blocs proliferating and gaining importance—European Union, Association of South-East Asian Nations, Mercosur, North American Free Trade Association, Southern African Development Community, among many others
- More policy coordination groups—G-7, G-10, G-22, G-77, Organization for Economic Cooperation and Development

New Rules and Norms

- Market economic policies spreading around the world, with greater privatization and liberalization than in earlier decades
- Widespread adoption of democracy as the choice of political regime
- Human rights conventions and instruments building up in both coverage and number of signatories—and growing awareness among people around the world
- Consensus goals and action agenda for development

continued

Table 0.1 (continued) Introduction to Globalization

New Rules and Norms

- Conventions and agreements on the global environment—biodiversity, ozone layer, disposal of hazardous wastes, desertification, climate change
- Multilateral agreements in trade, taking on such new agendas as environmental and social conditions
- New multilateral agreements—for services, intellectual property, communications—more binding on national governments than any previous agreements
- The Multilateral Agreement on Investment under debate

New (Faster and Cheaper) Tools of Communication

- Internet and electronic communications linking many people simultaneously
- Cellular phones
- Fax machines
- Faster and cheaper transport by air, rail, and road (box below)
- Computer-aided design

Declining Cost of Transport and Communications (1990 US$)

Year	Sea Freight (Average Ocean Freight and Port Charges per Tone)	Air Transport (Average Revenue Passenger Mile)	Telephone Call (Three Minutes, New York to London)	Computers (Index, 1990 = 100)
1920	95	—	—	—
1930	60	0.68	245	—
1940	63	0.46	189	—
1950	34	0.30	53	—
1960	27	0.24	46	12,500
1970	27	0.16	32	1,947
1980	24	0.10	5	362
1990	29	0.11	3	100

Source: IMF (1997a); United Nations, *Human Development Report 1999* (p. 30, Box 1.1, and Table 1.1).

The bourgeoisie cannot exist without constantly revolutionising the instruments of production, and thereby the relations of production, and with them the whole relations of society. Conservation of the old modes of production in unaltered form, was, on the contrary, the first condition of existence for all earlier industrial classes. Constant revolutionising of production, uninterrupted disturbance of all social conditions, everlasting uncertainty and agitation distinguish the bourgeois epoch from all earlier ones. All fixed, fast-frozen relations, with their train of ancient and venerable prejudices and opinions, are swept away, all new-formed ones become antiquated before they can ossify. All that is solid melts into air, all that is holy is profaned, and man is at last compelled to face with sober senses his real conditions of life, and his relations with his kind. ...

The bourgeoisie has through its exploitation of the world market given a cosmopolitan character to production and consumption in every country. To the great chagrin of Reactionists, it has drawn from under the feet of industry the national ground on which it stood. All old-established national industries have been destroyed or are daily being destroyed. They are dislodged by new industries, whose introduction becomes a life and death question for all civilised nations, by industries that no longer work up indigenous raw material, but raw material drawn from the remotest zones; industries whose products are consumed, not only at home, but in every quarter of the globe. In place of the old wants, satisfied by the production of the country, we find new wants, requiring for their satisfaction the products of distant lands and climes. In place of the old local and national seclusion and self-sufficiency, we have intercourse in every direction, universal inter-dependence of nations. And as in material, so also in intellectual production. The intellectual creations of individual nations become common property. National one-sidedness and narrow-mindedness become more and more impossible, and from the numerous national and local literatures, there arises a world literature.

The Marxist approach does not contravene the social physic of the Durkheimian approach, i.e., the space-time theme discussed above, but in shifting the focus from *modernity* to *capitalism* it also shifts the focus from system differentiation and integration to social power and domination. Thus David Harvey grants the "time–space compression" and the enhanced technologically enabled interconnectivity yet locates this within the imbalanced and unequal set of capitalist social relations in general and within the context of a huge overhaul in the way that capitalist accumulation encroaches over world human and material resources (Harvey 1989). Globalization is largely identified with a new stage of capitalist—especially American—imperialism (Harvey 2003) and with neoliberalism, the aim of which is to circumvent the constraints and controls of the previous nation-state and Fordist regime of accumulation (Harvey 2005).[3] William Robinson is adamant that globalization is labeled "global capitalism" and divulges that "globalization can essentially be seen as the near culmination of a centuries-long process of the spread of capitalist production around the globe and its displacement of all pre-capitalist relations, bringing about a new form of connection between all human beings around the world" (Robinson 2004, 3).

Globalization is ultimately explained, in this view, not by the technological advancements in themselves but by the immanent hanker of capitalism to access new sources of labor and raw materials and new outlets for its products. Thus "new patterns of accumulation opened up by globalizing technologies both require and make possible economies of scale that are truly global and require a more generalized commodification of world economy" (Robinson 2004, 9). Globalization thus signifies a transition from an inward-oriented national capitalism toward outward-oriented transnational capitalism, in which there is not only an international circulation of products (as was the case already previously) but also rather a functional integration of the production process across borders.

This book concurs with the view that globalization is the new stage of capitalism in the intersection of the twentieth and twenty-first centuries (without embracing any of the economistic, teleological, and even eschatological features that have stuck on to Marxist theory throughout the twentieth century). Globalization follows the former stage of capitalism, which endured roughly from World War I to the 1970s, a stage that was variably defined as monopoly capitalism, corporate capitalism, organized capitalism, state capitalism, and Fordist capitalism (in this count, the period between 1492 and 1789 is marked as mercantile capitalism and the period between 1789 and 1917 is marked as industrial capitalism or liberal capitalism). Global capitalism is thus associated with new methods by which capitalism currently operates, such as flexible accumulation or post-Fordism, and with manifold political and cultural consequences, from postnationalism and postmodernism to ethno-nationalism and neo-fundamentalism.

In more concrete historical terms the coming of global capitalism is associated with the end of the cold war and the demise of the Soviet Union (1989), the concomitant fall of organized labor and of socialism as an ideological alternative, and the passing of third world liberation struggles. Out of this new constellation the United States emerged as the ultimate world power, at least until new challenges to its imposed empire started to loom around the beginning of the third millennium, whether in the form of competing economic and strategic blocs (the European Union, Southeast Asia, etc.) or in the form of Islamic resurgence.[4]

The new Marxian concept of globalization that was articulated from the mid-1990s on is a successor of the concept of World-System that has been devised and elaborated by Immanuel Wallerstein and his associates since the 1970s (Wallerstein 2004). The World-System is the capitalist "society" writ large, as it evolved since the early sixteenth century, when the west European, and later North American, powers expanded their rule across the globe and created colonies and empires that served their enrichment and development on the expense of the subjugated societies in Africa, Asia, and Latin America, which were subjected to impoverishment and underdevelopment (Wallerstein 2003).

In this perspective economic development, societal structures, and forms of governance are seen as results of the structural relations and relative functional locations of subunits in the system rather than as the result of immanent developments in any of the subunits in themselves. In this way the intra-societal Marxian conception of class structure that consists of capital, labor, and middle class is expanded by world-system analysis into a global scope, in the form of core states, peripheral states, and semiperiphery ones, respectively. Later Marxist approaches to globalization differ basically only in viewing the chain of accumulation by exploitation less in terms of a linear hierarchy among coherent territorial national units and more in terms of flexible social and economic networks dotted by nodal fixes.[5]

* * *

As is already implied by the McWorld versus Jihad depiction, the concept of globalization embraces an inherent antagonism. This is made explicit by the complementary term *glocalization* that literally consists of a combination of the terms *global* and *local*. It too may be viewed from a Durkheimian perspective or alternatively from a Marxian perspective.

The *Oxford English Dictionary* defines *glocalization* as the process of "telescoping global and local to make a blend" or as "the fact of adapting products or services that are available all over the world to make them suitable for local needs."[6] As in the Durkheimian approach in large, so also in the case of glocalization, such definitions assume reciprocal equilibrium and thus give the impression of equity on both sides in producing the final blend or in adjusting the two to each other. The Marxian concept of glocalization rather shows the global factor (McWorld) to be the prime and active mover, relative to a reactive and derivative local factor (Jihad).

Overall globalization–glocalization is a process of deconstruction or of disassemblage of modern institutions and beliefs. In this sense globalization has been associated with two major cultural currents: postmodernity in the 1980s and postcoloniality later on. These cultural articulations challenge and subvert the epistemological and moral assumptions that underlie Euro-American claims to rationalism, humanism, and universalism, which served to legitimate Western supremacy.[7] These are centrifugal trends that reverse, or undo, the centripetal outcomes of modernity and generate others, differences and particularisms.

One renowned graphic way to describe it is to refer to the transition from a "melting pot" of unification, or universalization or standardization, into a "salad bowl" of pluralization, or particularization or differentiation.[8] In economics the simultaneous move may mean a transition from hierarchy to networks, in society it may mean a transition from system to complexity, in culture it may mean a transition from essentiality to hybridity, and in politics it may mean a transition from ideology to identity. Yet again, although postmodernism and postcolonialism may have deconstructive and subversive qualities, from a Marxist perspective they too are considered as part and parcel of the "cultural logic of late capitalism," to cite a well-famed work of Fredrick Jameson (Jameson 1991), or as the cultural effects of global and flexible capitalist conditions, to refer to a famed work by David Harvey (Harvey 1989).

We thus deploy in this book a two-pronged dialectical concept of globalization. It consists of global "metatrends" that undermine and reshape modern institutions and beliefs, especially the nation-state and the bureaucratic institutions, from the "top down," through technological, financial, media, interregional, and commercial transnational systems, and local "infratrends" that undermine and reshape these institutions and beliefs from the "bottom up," through ethnic, religious, racial, nationalist, regional, and cultural subnational identities. The global trends represent hypercapitalism (McWorld), the local backlash trends adhere sometimes—certainly in the Israeli case—to neofundamentalism (Jihad). This glocal intertwining of opposites is the reason for the ostensibly chaotic condition typical of our time—an unprecedented homogenization is taking place to create one human society (not harmonious or egalitarian but uniform as a structural condition) whereas all the while an unprecedented heterogenization of human societies into separate and sometimes separatist identity groups is also taking place. The perplexing result is that the demise of boundaries and identities affected by the global trend (post-Zionism in Israel) generates reactive local trends and the surmise of rigid boundaries and entrenched identities (neo-Zionism in Israel).

Both McWorld and Jihad are far from being heartwarming: the new networks are indifferent (in theory if not always in practice) to gender, color, race, creed, and culture, which is supposedly more democratic. However, they lack commitment to members (socialism) or, at least, to voters (liberalism), which is less democratic. The new communities are, in contrast, communities of identity that give voice to "other" groups, the oppressed, repressed, and marginalized, which is supposedly more democratic. But they are also exempt from the universal commitment to the equality of any person regardless of gender, color, race, creed, and culture and from commitment to individuals as such—their freedom and happiness—which is once again less democratic, and significantly so. With the rise of McWorld and Jihad, as Barber rightly maintains, democratic and egalitarian civic society is in peril. All this—we maintain—obtains in Israel.

ISRAEL: BETWEEN TEL AVIV AND JERUSALEM

From the perspective of the globalization paradigm that is suggested here, the recent transformations of Israeli society ought to be analyzed not merely as internal mutations, stemming from unique and local circumstances, but also within the framework of the larger societal constellation called globalization.

The chapters of this book deal with the repercussions of globalization on Israel and with Israeli responses to globalization, and while doing so they also address the analytical and normative issues that globalization involves.

The present chapter launches the major thesis of the book about the globalization paradigm in Israeli studies. The chapter outlines the McWorld versus Jihad approach to globalization and relates why it is preferable to both the "end of history" and the "clash of civilizations" approaches. It then distinguishes between an integrative Durkheimian approach and a conflictual Marxist approach to globalization. The chapter outlines, above all, the bifurcation model that renders the globalization paradigm applicable to the case of Israel. The balance of the chapter presents in an anticipatory manner the structure of the book and the themes of its chapters.

This book starts with a discussion of the economic aspects of the globalization of Israel and gradually passes to its social, political, and cultural aspects. Each of the chapters is focused on a certain facet of the overall process and centered on a key concept. Each chapter analyzes an emblematic manifestation of the conceptualized process in Israel and also elucidates the major theoretical issues pertaining to the chapter. All this is in the following order: the globalization paradigm in Israeli studies (Introduction), globalization (Chapter 1), polarization (Chapter 2), post-Fordization (Chapter 3), Americanization (Chapter 4), McDonaldization (Chapter 5), postnationalization (Chapter 6), and finally a brief conclusion.

Chapter 1, "Globalization," delineates three major socio-economic components of the globalization of Israel: on the economic plane—a postindustrial revolution, that is, the radical transformation of the economic structure of Israel from import-substitution, labor-intensive, traditional, domestic-oriented industries into knowledge-intensive, high-tech, export-oriented industries; on the social plane—a bourgeois revolution, that is, the rise to power of a new class of business-men and professionals, the resulting radical transformation of macroeconomic policies from Keynesian state intervention into privatization, deregulation and neoliberalization; and on the individual everyday-life plane—a consumerist revolu-tion, that is, a radical transformation from an economy of prudence to one that celebrates opulent consumerism.

Whereas Chapter 1 offers a conceptual and empirical anal-ysis of the said transformations, the next chapter dwells on further social, cultural, and political consequences of these transformations, and the chapter that follows it recounts the overall transformation on a higher level of abstraction, where it is shown and explained to be an outcome of globalization and more specifically of the transition from national Fordism to global post-Fordism.

Chapter 2 addresses the social polarization that globaliza-tion generates. It examines the repercussions of the socio-economic revolutions discussed in Chapter 1 on three social categories and thus recounts the predicament of the middle class, the ascent of the business and professional class, and the plight of the laboring classes.

The chapter examines also the political implications of the new class polarization in Israel. The decline of the nation-state as the core of collective identity and the bifurcation of identity into postnational and neonational political cultures are tied to the globalization of Israel and to the development of an advanced or postindustrial economy, a bourgeois hegemony, and a consumer society. The political–cultural impact of globalization is argued to be class differentiated. The winners of the globalization process, the upper classes, welcome the integration in the global system and thus lay the foundation for the market culture and inadvertently also for post-Zionism. The losers of the globalization process, the lower classes, tend to react by adherence to the local principles of ethno-nationalism and thus provide fodder for the culture of neo-Zionist "tribalism." The middle classes are perplexed by these two trends that overwhelm them—economically from above and culturally from below. Thus we show how the new interests and identities that emerge translate ultimately into political tendencies.

Chapter 3, on post-Fordism, establishes the class-based Marxist model of globalization that is adopted in the book. This model recasts the transformations wrought by globalization that are discussed in the previous chapters in terms of a transition from a national Fordist to a global post-Fordist capitalist regime of accumulation and regulation; that is, the shift from the typical post–World War II triangular social pact of labor–state–capital into an imbalanced situation where capital becomes mobile and flexible and labor loses its national-territorial political power base. We analyze the contours of the epochal transition in Israel from national to global capitalism, with a focus on one major outcome of this transition—the new pattern of wealth distribution, namely, the rise in inequality. A short presentation of this trend worldwide antecedes the analysis of the case of Israel, and both sections are followed by an account of the transition from the national-Fordist model of capitalism to the transnational post-Fordist one.

The following chapters deal with the effects of globalization on the political culture in Israel. Chapter 4 deals with the Americanization of the political culture in Israel, as it is expressed by the decline of political parties and by the rise of two alternative political modes: commercialization and communalization.

In the past Israel was a par excellence political parties polity. Parties had preceded the state, created it, and led it. The parties set up economic projects, established social institutions, and generated cultural movements. Today parties exist only as loose frameworks in the electoral and parliamentary context. They do not function any longer as bearers of distinct ideologies or programs. We analyze this transition of Israeli political culture from a modern European model, of programmatic political parties that represent collective social interests, into a postmodern communal and commercial media-based Americanized political culture. This process is illustrated in the chapter along two points in time: the elections of 1996 and of 2006.

Chapter 5 addresses the implications of globalization on Israeli popular everyday culture, and in its center stage is the concept of McDonaldization. Among social scientists, the global–local encounter has spawned a continuous polemic between "homogenizers," who believe that globalization generates a worldwide universalization of culture, and "heterogenizers," who believe that particular, local, or indigenous cultures survive or even thrive. In this chapter we argue that such dichotomous framing compels a flattened adjudication of what is in fact a double-layered outcome. Globalization has diverse effects: it homogenizes on the structural level (the McWorld effect), and it heterogenizes on the symbolic level (the Jihad effect). In this view global technological, organizational, and commercial flows do subsume and appropriate the local idiom, or consume it, so to speak, yet this happens with no necessary abolition of local symbols, cultures, or habits. It is indeed the peculiarity of contemporary structural globalization that it not only enables but also may at points even encourage local symbolic idioms.

To establish this argument, at least as the case of Israel goes, this chapter analyzes the process of McDonaldization of Israeli culture. Since McDonald's first arrived to Israel in 1993, it has been involved in a variety of symbolic encounters, of which two are closely examined in the chapter: first, the encounter between McDonald's, as the epitome of global fast food, and the veteran local version of fast food, namely, the falafel; and second, the encounter between McDonald's, as a symbol of global-American consumer culture, and local national identity and ideology, as it evolved around the McDonald's branch located nearby a fallen soldiers memorial site (in the Golani Junction in northern Israel).

Chapter 6 continues the line of argument from the previous chapters and focuses on the issue of national identity and postnationalism. As in the spheres of political culture and popular culture, in the sphere of national identity globalization is a two-pronged process, creating both McWorld and Jihad effects. In the two recent decades Jewish–Israeli mainstream nationalism—Zionism—is challenged by two opposite perspectives: a postnationalist perspective, which tilts toward global cosmopolitanism, and a neonationalist perspective, which tilts toward local tribalism.

Chapter 6 examines the fundamental assumptions of the three major alternative foci of collective identity that are presently available in Jewish Israel: nationalism, postnationalism, and neonationalism. It differentiates them by analyzing their respective answers to three questions: the temporal question—

"when" is the nation, to which the answer is given either in terms of the past (remembrance) or in terms of the present (forgetfulness); the spatial question—"where" is the nation, to which the answer is given either in sacrilegious terms (the "Holy Land") or in terms of pragmatic territorialism (sovereignty); and the gatekeeping question—"who" is the nation, to which an answer is given either in terms of French-type *jus soli* republicanism or in terms of German-type *jus sanguinis* Volkism.

One

Globalization

This chapter delineates three major socioeconomic components of the globalization of Israel: on the economic plane, a postindustrial revolution; on the social plane, a bourgeois revolution; and on individual everyday-life plane, a consumerist revolution. The aim is not to produce a comprehensive description of Israeli economy or society as such but rather to highlight three of the most dynamic aspects of the socioeconomic globalization of Israel or, to put it more graphically, to depict the three spearheads of Israeli globalization. Whereas this chapter offers a conceptual and empirical presentation of the said transformations, Chapter 2 dwells on further social and political consequences of these transformations, and Chapter 3 recounts the overall transformation on a higher level of abstraction, where it is shown and explained to be an outcome of globalization and more specifically of the transition from national Fordism to global post-Fordism.

THE POSTINDUSTRIAL REVOLUTION

The economic forefront of the globalization of Israel is a postindustrial revolution that has taken place in it since the 1990s.[1] Postindustrialization means not deindustrialization but rather a transition from labor-intensive material industries to knowledge-intensive informational industries and the expansion of services (Bell 1976; Castells 1996; May 2002). This revolution ushered Israel into the category of the world's wealthiest nations. The most common measure of a country's economic development and wealth is its gross domestic production (GDP) per capita. Measured on the basis of exchange rate (2003 current prices), Israel's GDP per capita in 2005 was $17,209; measured on the basis of actual purchase value (a measure called purchasing power parities—PPP) it was $23,037. By these measures Israel's economic sturdiness is situated somewhat above that of Greece ($15,700 and $20,400, respectively) and somewhat below that of New Zealand ($19,800 and $23,200, respectively), and it is about 60 percent that of the United States ($37,600 in both measures) (Central Bureau of Statistics [CBS] 2005, 807, Table 28.7).

The postindustrial revolution consists of at least the following four ingredients: a growth in the service economic sector on account of the industrial sector, a particular growth in the financial services sector compared to all others, a growth in the volume of foreign commerce relative to the product, and the growth of the information and communication technologies (ICT) sector. The sectorial structure of employment in the Israeli economy fits the postindustrial characterization: a negligible 2.1 percent of the workforce is employed in agriculture, 5.4 percent in construction, 17 percent in industry (including utilities), 13.6 percent in commerce, and the other

61.9 percent in business, personal, and public services (including transportation) (CBS 2005, 3–4, Table 2.20). The share of commerce and services in the output of the business sector rose from about 37 percent in 1980 to about 58 percent in 2003 (*Bank of Israel Annual Report* [BIAR] 2005, 9, Diagram A-4).

We dwell mainly on the latter of the four ingredients, the ICT sector, which has been the foremost catalyst of the growth and the globalization of Israeli economy since the 1990s. In the words of the Bank of Israel, the ICT sector "is a significant component in the integration of the local economy with the global economy" (BIAR 2004a, 105).[2] Needless to say, the developments in this sector are intertwined directly and indirectly with the rest of the economy, especially with sectors such as finance and communications.

The volume and productivity of the ICT sector in Israel is outstanding. Between 1990 and 2002 the product of the sector increased at an average annual growth rate of about 13 percent compared to 5 percent growth rate in the business sector as a whole. Its product grew in this period from New Israeli Shekels (NIS) 8.7 billion to about NIS 36 billion.[3] The product per employed person in the ICT sector is close to three times higher than that of the business sector as a whole: NIS 346,000 compared to NIS 141,000, respectively.[4] Over the period the product per employee increased by 3 percent in the overall economy, 9 percent in the business sector, and 53 percent in the ICT sector.[5] According to the Bank of Israel data, this is a higher output than in the United States (BIAR 2002, 41). The ICT sector accounted in the same period for 33 percent of the total increase in the business sector product (CBS 2003a, 2). The share of the ICT product in the economic product in Israel is considerably higher than in other developed countries:

Table 1.1 The Share of ICT Branches in Israeli Economy (in Percentages, on the Basis of Fixed 1995 Prices)

The Share of the ICT Branches in the:	1990	1992	1995	1998	2000
GDP of the private sector	8.1	8.6	10.8	16.2	20.2
GDP of the entire economy	5.0	5.5	7.1	10.8	13.6
Export	14.0	16.3	16.5	24.4	30.0
Employment, overall	3.5	3.5	4.0	4.7	6.0
Employment, private sector	4.9	4.9	5.5	6.5	8.2

Source: Central Bureau of Statistics (2001).

Note: ICT = information and communication technologies, GDP = gross domestic production.

about 17.5 percent in 2001 compared to less then 9 percent on the average in the European Union countries and 11.4 percent in the United States (BIAR 2004a, 107–8).

Table 1.1 presents some basic data on the volume of ICT branches in the Israeli economy for selected years in the 1990–2000 decade.

The turn to high-tech industry marks the third phase in the development of industry in Israel. Israel's first wave of industrialization took place in the 1950s and 1960s, and it was in textile manufacturing and other consumptive staples (Levi-Faur 2001). A second wave of industrialization took place in the late 1960s and 1970s and was associated with armament and aviation industries and created Israel's large military–industrial sector (Peri and Neubach 1984; Lifshitz 2003). The third is, as said, the postindustrial wave that has taken place since the 1990s.

In fewer than five decades, Israel had experienced in condensation the full path of modern industrialization of the past two centuries, from the mechanical and textile revolution in the first third of the nineteenth century, mostly in England, through the chemical and electrical revolution centered in Germany and the United States in the late nineteenth century, to the electronic and then digital revolution that developed initially in the United States and spread to western Europe, Japan, and Southeast Asia in the second half of the twentieth century and at an intensified pace since the 1990s. Important to notice is that although the first and second waves of industrialization in Israel were state initiated and guided, and the second wave was also state owned and operated, the third wave of industrialization is by and large a private entrepreneurial initiative. Nevertheless it must be emphasized that even this economic development is sponsored and supported by the state and even more so is fed by state-made resources, especially in the form of "human capital" that has been created in Israel's universities, armament industries, and the advanced units of the Israeli military.[6]

The leading component in the postindustrial revolution in Israel is, as said, the ICT sector, a knowledge-intensive branch of production, which turned obsolete much of the labor-intensive, traditional industrial sector. Alongside these two sectors there is a sector classified as "mixed." The advanced industries weigh close to 28 percent of the output and more than 34 percent of the export, the mixed industries weigh close to 35 percent of the output and more than 42 percent of the export, and the traditional industries weigh close to 39 percent of the output and 17.4 percent of the export (BIAR 2002, chap. 1; BIAR 2004a, 45–56). The traditional branches of industry are relatively labor intensive, low in productivity, and directed predominantly to the local market (87 percent of the product); the advanced branches, in contrast, are knowledge intensive, highly productive, and directed predominantly to external markets (54 percent of the product) (BIAR 2002, 49; CBS 2001, 23). The share of the ICT sector in the export from Israel grew from 14 percent in 1990 to 26 percent in 2002, which amounted to the value of about $11 billion. Although the total export of goods and services from Israel increased in this period by a factor of 2.3, the export of electronic components and electronic communication equipment rose by a factor of 7, and computer and related services, research and development, and start-up companies rose by a factor of 10 (CBS 2003b, 3).

The decline of the traditional industries has been imminent. The integration into the global market was involved with the reduction of tariffs and customs on many consumer goods and with free trade agreements with foreign countries, where labor is cheaper (such as Mexico, Poland, Hungary, and Turkey). The outcome was a drop in the prices of the products of the traditional industries, the contraction of part of them, and the relocation of production lines of another part of them (more is discussed on this in Chapter 2). And so although middle-class consumers enjoyed the reduced purchase prices of apparel and other imported products, the lower-class workers in the "development towns," where these industries made the backbone of mass employment, saw the plunge of both their pay and their jobs. Thus between 1994 and 2005, the number of employees in the textile industry fell from 43,500 to 18,700.[7] In contrast the number of employees in the ICT branches—clustered in the country's richest central areas—multiplied during the 1990s by 2.7, reaching 148,000 by the year 2000 (BIAR 2002, 49; CBS 2001, 19). Overall the traditional industries decreased from 46.4 percent of industrial output and of industrial employment in 1975 to around 29 percent of industrial output and about 39 percent of industrial employment in 2004. The textile industry declined in this period from 12.2 percent of industrial output to 4.1 percent and from 19.6 percent of industrial employees to 7 percent (Ministry of Industry, Trade, and Labor [MITL] 2004). In 2004 textile accounted for 4.6 percent and food and beverages accounted for 2.5 percent of Israeli export, whereas metals and machinery accounted for 15.4 percent and electronics accounted for 38.9 percent (MITL 2005, 12).

An enabling condition of the postindustrial revolution in Israel is its high level of human capital; that is, of education and skill. Israel enjoys an exceeding proportion of educational and technical expertise: approximately 28 percent of the population has university degrees, and there are 135 engineers and scientists to every 10,000 manufacturing employees, compared to 80 in the United States, 75 in Japan, and 55 in Germany. Israel ranks second behind Switzerland in academic papers per capita and third behind Switzerland and Sweden in citations per capita (Fontenay and Carmel 2002/2004, 8). Between the 1970s and 1990s, there was a rise in employment rates of academic and scientific professions, free professions (managerial and technical), and service professions. There was simultaneously a drop in clerical professions, skilled farm labor, and construction and unskilled manual labor. The share of jobs in the professional categories mentioned previously rose from about 35 percent in the 1980s to about 52 percent in the 1990s (CBS 1998b, Employment and Wages, 29, Chart 18). The growth of high professional categories is correlated with the rise in the educational level of the workforce (or rather a part of it). The average number of school years for all industry rose from 8.2 (elementary school) in the 1960s to 11.7 (high school) in the early 1990s (BIAR 1995, 11, Chart B). The share of engineers and technicians in the workforce rose from 5.7 percent in the 1970s to 16.8 percent in the early 1990s (BIAR 1995, 11, Chart B). The share of industry employees with more than thirteen years of education (higher education) rose from 17 percent in 1980 to 25 percent in 1990 and up to 40 percent in 1997. The share of employees with academic diplomas rose from 2.3 percent in 1970 to 12.2 percent in 1997 (CBS 1998b, Employment and Wages, 46).

The professional–educational profile of the high-tech branches is exceptionally high, which explains their unique contribution both to the GDP and to the rise of income disparities among wage earners. Of ICT employees, 31 percent are professionals or technicians and 29 percent are academicians or managerial, compared to 15 percent and 20 percent, respectively, for the entire economy. The share of employees with higher education and diplomas in ICT branches is 73 percent, compared with 50 percent for all other sectors (CBS 1998b, Chart 6).

Instrumental in the vibrancy of the high-tech sector has been the emergence of the "venture capital" infrastructure in Israel. The first such fund, called Athena, was established in 1985 with an initial fund of $29 million. By 2000 there were more than one hundred venture capital funds managing investment in the value of $7.3 milliard (Fontenay and Carmel 2002/2004, 30). Israel equals the the Silicon Valley in venture capital per capita (cited in Fontenay and Carmel 2002/2004, 6). The vibrancy of the sector is perhaps best attested by the burgeoning of yet another type of economic operation—the start-up venture. Start-ups are usually innovated by energetic and talented computer technicians and programmers, of the kind that were called "symbolic analysts" (Reich 1992) and "the creative class" (Florida 2003). The common ambition is to concoct a software application that will eventually make the company marketable on Wall Street or be purchased by an American corporation. The "from rags to riches" story of several ventures, such as Mirabilis, Butterfly, and Chromatics— all sold to American investors for tens of millions of dollars— has caught the imagination of many young Israelis. In the late 1990s four thousand start-ups, financed mostly by local and foreign venture capital, were active in Israel (Greenwood 1998, 179–80; *Red Herring* 2000). Israel was ranked fifth in the world in the number of start-ups and first in start-ups per capita (Arazi, quoted in Kipnis 2004, 1). A 2006 database on the ICT branches enlists more than 4,700 Israeli high-tech companies.[8] Even if these numbers are somewhat inflated, they still tell a tale.

The role of American and multinational corporations in the success story of the Israeli high-tech sector is decisive. Motorola was first to open an R&D center in Israel, and it employs there some four thousand employees. IBM operates in Israel its largest lab outside the United States, with some four thousand employees, and Intel operates in Israel its largest R&D center outside the United States, and together with its production facilities there it employs some five thousand Israelis. Other corporations that in various times had bases in Israel are Microsoft, National Semiconductor, Digital, Lucent, and more. One estimation is that forty-three of the world's fifty largest technology corporations operate a development center in Israel.[9] In many cases American firms bought Israeli firms: Computer Associates bought Memco, GE Medical Systems bought ElGems, BMC bought New Dimensions, and Sun,

Cisco, Applied Materials, and other firms also acquired Israeli firms (Fontenay and Carmel 2002/2004, 22). The volume of purchase of Israeli high-tech companies by foreign ones is gigantic. In 1998 foreign companies purchased twenty Israeli start-ups in the sum of $3 billion (Steinberg 1999). According to one estimate, between 1995 and 2003 one hundred fifty Israeli high-tech groups were acquired by American corporations, in the sum of $25 billion, and according to another estimate, between 1997 and 2004 foreign companies purchased Israeli ones in the sum of $15 billion.[10] The penetration of Israeli businesses into the U.S. market is also noticeable. Israel has more companies listed on the U.S.-based stock exchange than any country besides the United States and Canada. More than one hundred Israeli high-tech firms are listed on the U.S. and European equity market, primarily NASDAQ (Fontenay and Carmel 2002/2004, 28). Incidentally, according to "Forbes 500," eight Israeli companies are in the top two thousand companies in the world for 2004 (Maor 2004).[11]

From the 1990s on, electronics and computerization are the economically strong links in Israel's globalized networking. Yet this link also bears cultural implications. On the eve of the Jewish New Year in 1998, the *Haaretz* daily started publishing a series named "Virtual Israel," where the high-tech industry was portrayed not merely as the leading export industry in Israel but as a "Dreamland" (Green 1998). In 2006 the dream of swift enrichment through an ingenious start-up still resonated in the psyche of young Israelis, who fantasize about being the next Gil Shweid—a next-door guy who at age twenty-one established the Checkpoint start-up and who today, fifteen years later, ranks as number eight in the list of the wealthiest persons in Israel, with a fortune of $860 million (Ben Yehuda

2006; *The Marker* 2006). This dream is widely nourished by the media, as in a *Ma'ariv*'s daily special supplement titled "Israelis Who Made It," that is, Israelis who made a lot of money from high-tech entrepreneurship (*Mamon* 2003).

Much of the operation of the high-tech sector is clustered in "technology parks" such as Matam in the city of Haifa and in smaller centers in Migdal Haemek and in Jerusalem, yet the mainstay of the industry—86 percent of Israel's high-tech firms—is located in the greater Tel Aviv area (Kipnis 2004, 188), and the city has thus acquired the attributes of a global city (Alfasi and Fenster 2004; Kipnis 2004). High-tech parks prospered around it, and it became a hub of the new global networks. *Newsweek* magazine designated Tel Aviv as one of the ten leading high-tech centers in the world (*Newsweek* 1998; Kipnis and Noam 1998; Felsenstein, Schamp, and Shachar 2003). Tel Aviv became the business capital of Israel, where more than 55 percent of headquarters of the country's manufacturing firms are located (Kipnis 2004, 188). The postindustrial flourishing of Tel Aviv propelled a change in the city's physical layout. Although up to 1960 buildings were not permitted to rise higher than three to four stories, in 1965 the first tall building, of thirty-six stories, was built in the city's business district (Shalom Tower), and today there are more than seventy-five office and residential buildings of twenty stories or more (Kipnis 2004, 188–89). All this also turned Tel Aviv into one of the world's most expensive cities, and according to the *Economist* magazine, it came to be only 13 percent cheaper to live in than New York City (*Ynet News*, August 22, 2004). In Tel Aviv and its vicinity, and in the gentrified neighborhoods and posh country suburbs around it, a bubble of an Israeli glocal culture is nourished by the uprising high-tech elites (Baruch 2002). As economic geographer Baruch Kipnis put it, "Last, but not least, Tel Aviv, a secular, cosmopolitan city, is the main center of 'creative industry' including music, theatre, dancing, visual arts, innovative medicine, and other scientific areas, to name but a few. Many of these have been actively involved in the global arena and have a world fame" (Kipnis 2004, 188; on these aspects of Tel Aviv, see also Maoz 2005, 141–223).

The role of multinational corporations, mostly American based, in Israeli globalization is not limited to the high-tech sector only. According to one estimation, at the end of the 1990s, foreign-based companies owned 51 percent of the twenty largest companies in Israel (ownership worth $19 billion out of a total combined value of $37 billion) (Nasi 1999). All in all, foreign investment in Israel rose dramatically during the 1990s—from about US$1.4 billion to US$11.7 billion (Ministry of Finance 2003).

In 2006 Israel's CBS measured for the first time the economic activities of foreign multinational enterprises in Israel and of Israeli multinational enterprises in Israel.[12] The data bespeak for the very substantial integration of Israel into the global chain of production and exchange. Israeli affiliates of foreign-controlled companies account for 16.4 percent of the manufacturing output and 6.6 percent of the output of the economy as a whole, 10.8 percent of employed persons in manufacturing and 3.4 percent in the economy as a whole, and 19.8 percent of value added in manufacturing and 10.4 percent in the economy as a whole. Yet these figures include the traditional industries and services, where foreign intervention is indeed low. As shown in Table 1.2, the figures are significantly higher in the mixed industries and even more

Table 1.2 Volume of Multinational Enterprise Activities in Israel (Israeli Affiliates of Foreign Companies), 2003 (Arranged by the Order of Output Column)

Name of Industry	Multinational Enterprises from Output (%)	Multinational Enterprises from Employed Persons (%)	Multinational Enterprises from Value Added (%)	Multinational Enterprises from Export (%)
Total	**6.6**	**3.4**	**10.4**	**25.1**
Small Volume: Traditional Industries and Services				
Other industries	0.3	0.2	0.7	8.1
Real estate, and renting of machinery and equipment	0.4	0.9	1.1	—
Construction	1	0.2	0.7	—
Transport and communication	1	1.1	1.4	—
Manufacturing n.e.c.	1.3	2.4	3.9	0.4
Other business activities	2.4	1.1	1.9	—
Wholesale trade	6.7	4.1	12.5	—
Transport equipment	6.8	6.8	8.6	8.9
Plastic and rubber	8.1	3.8	8.7	14.1
Metal products, and machinery and equipment	8.7	4.9	6.3	22.3
Textile and wearing apparel	10.1	7.5	11.3	36.2
Paper, publishing, and printing	10.2	4.6	8.1	30.2
Hotels and accommodation services	10.2	4.3	7.6	—

continued

41 **Globalization**

Table 1.2 (continued) Volume of Multinational Enterprise Activities in Israel (Israeli Affiliates of Foreign Companies), 2003
(Arranged by the Order of Output Column)

Name of Industry	Multinational Enterprises from Output (%)	Multinational Enterprises from Employed Persons (%)	Multinational Enterprises from Value Added (%)	Multinational Enterprises from Export (%)
Total	**6.6**	**3.4**	**10.4**	**25.1**
Medium Volume: Mixed Industries				
Electric motors and electric distribution apparatus	11.8	5.8	14.2	28.4
Food, beverages, and tobacco products	12.1	10.7	13.6	14.8
Chemicals and chemical products	14.9	12.3	14.1	9.8
Nonmetallic mineral products	18.9	11.8	16.1	49.9
Basic metal	19.4	13.1	24	42.2
Large Volume: Advanced Industries and ICT				
Equipment for control and supervision, and medical and scientific equipment	25.9	18.6	24	30.8
Computer and related services	38.6	20.8	38.7	19.8
Research and development	40	31.5	42.5	14
Electronic communication equipment	49.3	45.6	53.3	42.8
Electronic components	66.2	30.3	80.6	83.4

Source: Based on Central Bureau of Statistics (2006d, Tables 3.2.1, 3.2.2, 3.2.3, 1.2.2).
Note: ICT = information and communication technologies.

so in the advanced ICT industries, where figures are as high as 66 percent of output of the manufacturing of electronic components, close to 46 percent of employed persons in the manufacturing of electronic communication equipment, more than 80 percent the value added in the manufacture of electronic components, and more than 83 percent of the export of electronic components.[13]

Of no lesser significance is the volume of economic activities of Israeli-based and Israeli-owned multinational companies that have subsidiaries abroad. Such companies account for 33.8 percent of the output of manufacturing and 11.3 percent of all economic output in Israel, 23 percent of employed persons in manufacturing and 5.2 percent in the economy as a whole, and 38.7 percent of the value added in manufacturing and 14.8 percent in the economy as a whole. Yet again the figures vary dramatically between industries. Multinational Israeli companies account for 20.8 percent of the output in the food and related industries, 23.4 percent in electronic components, 25.4 percent in metal and related products, 36.4 percent in plastic and rubber products, 41.8 percent in electric motors and distribution apparatus, 48.6 percent in textile and apparel, 54.4 percent in electronic communication equipment, 57.5 percent in supervision and medical and scientific equipment, and 66.2 percent in chemicals and chemical products.[14]

THE BOURGEOIS REVOLUTION

The term *bourgeois revolution* is used here in an allusion to the historical theme of the rise of a class of private entrepreneurs, businessmen, industrialists, and financiers but also of managers, professionals, and technicians—directors, engineers, software programmers—who tip the scale of the balance from a pre- or a non- or quasi-capitalist social structure into a full-fledged capitalist one. Such a transformation occurred in Israel during the 1990s, and it is all the more palpable on the background of the quasi-socialist and collectivist history of this society, in which Labour has been the "natural" party of governance ever since the times of agricultural communes in the 1920s and up to the times of the military–industrial state conglomerate in the 1970s. The bourgeois class in question, the "new bourgeoisie," is a class that emerged under the auspices of the Labour governments but became independent and potent from the 1980s and 1990s onward.

The bourgeois revolution took place in conjunction with the economic changes discussed previously, that is, the postindustrial revolution, even though it is not restricted to the specific industries in question. The postindustrial revolution was shaped hand in hand with a fundamental shift in the relationship between the state and the business sector and, as a consequence, in the relationship between capital owners and waged employees. This shift may be described as a shift of the center of gravity of social power from the public sector and the government to the private sector and, more pointedly, the business corporations, and subsequently as a loss of power to organized labor. The new postindustrial elites occupy a halfway point between the position of "waged labor," from which its members usually start their careers, and the position of "ownership of capital," to which they usually aspire. The special lure of their venture is its suspension in between the "earth" of a present that demands work around the clock and the "sky" of expectations for a lavish future and early retirement, a state of mind that reflects a classical case of "contradictory class location," wherein exceptional proficiency generates professional autonomy and generous remunerations (Wright 1982). This midway point serves as virtual bridge on which some young Israelis can experience—or at the least can aspire to experience—steep class mobility and thus serves also as an obstruction that hides the reality in which the new race to the top for some in fact leaves a much larger number of others in a race to the bottom (more on this in Chapter 2).

Until the 1970s the Israeli economy was by and large dominated by two sectors: the public sector, which comprised the economic enterprises of the Federation of Labour, and the governmental sector. These sectors were responsible by estimation for more than half of the GDP (Aharoni 1991). Though there always has been a private sector in the Israeli economy, which was the domain of the old petite bourgeoisie, it was politically and economically subsidiary, dependent on government support, and susceptible to bureaucratic regulation. Throughout, the government and the Histadrut were dominated by the same elite—that of the Mapai historical party—and despite occasional brawls over economic and social benefits, this coordination worked relatively smoothly (Maman 1997). In addition to the distinction between the two sectors in the Israeli economy, the public and the private, and with partial parallel to it, there was also a distinction between the two economies in Israel: the "big economy," which was composed mainly of public enterprises, with few initial private holding companies, and the "small economy" of a multitude of dispersed middle-size and small-size enterprises (Nitzan and Bichler 2002; Maman 2002).

In the 1980s a process started of reversal of the distribution of economic weight between public and private, together with an extensive privatization of the public branch of the big economy. Public assets were being sold in the market, and private holding companies started to amass assets and to attract investment from abroad. A constant rise in the share of the private sector ensued. Between 1985 and 1993 the share of employees in the private sector grew from two-thirds to three-quarters of the overall workforce and the share of the private sector in the GDP rose from 47 percent to 62 percent (BIAR 1995, 117, Chart B 41). The financial sector was also revolutionized "from a situation where the government regulates most economic activity, to a situation where wide areas are highly competitive and regulation is limited" (Ministry of Finance, Government of Israel. The Supervisor of the Financial Market, Insurance and Savings. 1997). Since the 1980s the share of government-directed investment dropped from 85 percent of all investment to a mere 15 percent (Aharoni 1998, 138).

This change in the balance of power between public and private is epitomized by the term *privatization* that entered the Israeli lexicon in the 1980s. Yet privatization is not simply a definite economic policy but something that should rather be understood, as Petras and Veltmeyer argue for the Latin American case, as a "counter-reform movement against historical trends and part of a general effort to subvert the welfare state, mixed economies and class-based social movements" (2001, 94).

In the 1970s the government started to sell off the various companies it owned, and this proceeded in later decades at a growing rate and with an amplified ideological conviction. The justification is that privatization guarantees "an increased efficiency of the economy and the channelling of it to a path of growth suitable for the global market of the 21st century" (Eckstein, Rozevich, and Zilberfab 1998, 229). In the period from 1986 to 2000, eighty-three government-owned companies were sold for a total of US$8.7 billion (Government Companies Authority 2002, 21). In 2003 the governor of the Bank of Israel projected the next targets for privatization—the major public businesses and eventually the public service:

> The structural changes needed in the public services require a new approach to the employment agreements reached in a different era. When the private sector becomes more efficient at unprecedented rates and the back to growth policy demands the reduction of the tax burden and the government's expenditure, two conclusions can be drawn about public services: a. public businesses (airports and seaports, utilities, transport, communications and urban services) need to operate within the markets to a maximal degree. Practically this would depend on the current situation of each business: from government division to Government Company, government units to compete with each other, privatization of government owned businesses and Public Private Partnerships or PFIs. Public services ought to have greater flexibility in managing human resources in restructuring units and in budgetary planning—under regulation suited to the public sector. (Klein 2003)

A decisive, if unofficially declared, motive for selling of public corporations has been the power of their unionized employees. During the 1970s and 1980s, a lot of rhetorical fire was delivered by the business sector and the government at the direction of the "13 Big Committees"—the workers committees of the big public corporations. Their concerted power emerged not only as a competition to the Federation of Labour but also as its own last resort armament. Curbing the power of unionized labor is a major staple of the bourgeois revolution in Israel. Nehemia Strassler, a senior *Haaretz* economic journalist, flagrantly explains the problem of monopolies from the neoliberal viewpoint: "In the government monopolies the workers are the undisputed owners. Extra profits that would have lined the pockets of the owners had the monopoly been privately owned, in this case are handed to the workers in the form of exaggerated wages and pensions and inflated staff numbers" (Strassler 2003, 1–2; see also Bassok 2003). A senior public figure explained, in an unusual moment of outspokenness, this hidden agenda of privatization: "Our most dramatic revolution succeeded: crushing unionized labour in Israel, which was one of the heaviest burdens on the Israeli economy ... this is why the share of unionized labour in the economy dropped in the last decades from 70 percent to a mere 20 percent" (Arlozorov 2004, C1).

Because of its special historical role as the "state on the way" of the entire Jewish community in Palestine, the Histadrut in Israel had always functioned more like a labor department of the government than like an autonomous labor union. Nevertheless the sheer magnitude of organized work in Israel was a thorn in the side of the advocates of the bourgeois revolution. Successive neoliberal governments marshaled a public vendetta against the strength and independence of the Histadrut and succeeded in downsizing its scale and downgrading its status. The hiatus between the government and the Histadrut became finally unbridgeable when Mapai lost the government in 1977 to the Likud. Though Likud came to represent the working masses much more than the Labour Party does, it has been traditionally antiunion. In part this was caused by its nationalistic position, which defies the supposed divisiveness of the nation by class interests, and in part it was caused by its petite bourgeoisie constituency, which comprised urban merchants, contractors, and entrepreneurs that abhorred the ostensible socialism of the ruling party. Yet above all Likud was antiunion for the pragmatic reason that the union was considered as the bulwark of Mapai's bureaucratic power. In the 1960s and 1970s the Likud mobilized the protest of the new proletariat—new Jewish immigrants from Muslim countries, who did not have leftist persuasions to begin with and in whose view Mapai and the Histadrut were the ruling establishment. Together, the petite bourgeoisie Ashkenazi class and the new Mizrachi proletariat toppled Labour from government in 1977 and marked the Histadrut as their next target. As a first step the new government ostracized the special credit and financial privileges that the Histadrut enjoyed, among else with the assistance of one of the leading banks in Israel that the Histadrut owned (Bank Hapoalim—literally, the workers' bank). From then onward, instead of the state and the Histadrut operating as two arms of one political elite, the state started conspiring against the Histadrut and in the service of the interests of capital (Grinberg 2001).

Meanwhile the new Labour elite also did not bode well for the Histadrut. In fact, in the same way that Likud represented the small bourgeoisie and the workers, Labour came now to represent the interests and worldview of the big corporations and of the new managerial class and professional elites. And so when Labour returned to power, or to a shared power with Likud, nothing was more far removed from its agenda than the organized power of wage laborers. And so it fell to the neoliberal circles within the Labour Party, under the leadership of Haim Ramon in that case (who in late 2005 deserted Labour for Kadima), to press the final nail in the Histadrut's coffin. Ramon's election as secretary general of the Histadrut in 1994 and his short term there (until 1995) marked the end of the old Histadrut and the rise of a New Histadrut (Amir Peretz, later a chairman of the Labour Party, was then his copartner). The difference is essential—the old Histadrut was established in 1920 as a holistic collective organ of the Hebrew workers, and it functioned not only as a trade union but also as a cooperative owner of financial and industrial institutions, as an umbrella organization of collective agricultural settlements, and as a provider of a wide net of social and cultural services. The New Histadrut signifies a "thin" concept, focused solely on trade unionism, and hence the Histadrut was gradually stripped of all its other functions (a process that was in motion, to be fair, ever since the state was established in 1948) and all the while came to be a smaller and weaker trade union.

In 1995 the two pillars of the Histadrut's economy were sold off to American investors: Koor, Israel's leading manufacturing conglomerate, and Bank Hapoalim, Israel's second-largest financial institution at the time. This sell of Histadrut's major assets "marked an end of a chapter in the economic history of Israel," as was aptly (and gleefully) put in *Haaretz* (March 7, 1995; cited in Nitzan and Bichler 2002, 304). One cannot miss the symbolic meaning of the transmutation of Koor from being the Histadrut's flagship corporation to being a division of Disney Inc. Koor board meetings these days are conducted in English (Nachshon 1995). Public economic assets that were amassed collectively by several generations for the purpose of nation building and social construction were thus extracted from the public domain by a whim of elite and became owned by few proprietors. In his second function as minister of health, Ramon promoted the 1994 National Health Bill that severed one of the essential social services that Histadrut provided to its members: health insurance. The health fund had been a major incentive to enrollment in the Histadrut, as well as a major source of its funding, and the termination of this function dealt the final blow to the Histadrut.

Until the 1970s Israel was leading the industrialized nations in terms of union membership, which reached some 80 percent of the workforce. In 1996, after the connection between the health fund and the Histadrut was severed, membership in the Federation dropped to 49 percent (Cohen et al. 2003) and in fact dropped even lower when non-Israeli workers were counted as part of the workforce. Other figures for 2002 show less than 30 percent of employees were unionized in the Histadrut and less than 40 percent had membership in any workers' organization (Raday and Noam 2004, 59). This low level of unionized labor is still perceived as high and problematic by the business sector (for instance, Bior 2004c).

In the new millennium, capital and the government persisted with their attack on what was left of the labor unions, workers' organizations, and the right to strike, mobilizing the media and creating public opinion hostile to workers' rights, demands, and activities. A historical analysis of the changes in the attitudes of the government, the legal system, and the law to unionized labor in general and the Histadrut in particular shows a shift from an attitude supportive of labor power to a hostile attitude, which only at a recent point became more mixed, in an attempt to stave off the final collapse of the unions (Raday and Noam 2004; see also Ben Israel 2000). Yet despite such presumed moderation, following pressure from employers, in 2004 the Justice Ministry established a committee to review the status of the special Labour Court, which has a reputation of criticizing exploitative employment practices and the breach of employees' rights. On top of a slump in union membership and the decline in their legal status, a further process that emasculates organized labor, is the decentralization of collective bargaining. Nationwide or economic branch agreements, which had been previously negotiated by the Histadrut and the employers' representatives, are presently eroded. This is done with full governmental consent (Kristal and Cohen 2005). An indicator of the success of the onslaught against unionized labor is the fact that in the new millennium just a fraction of strike actions—1 percent—takes place in the private sector (Bior 2002).

Selling off public companies and curbing organized labor are just two items in an overall and enthusiastic adoption by the Israeli bourgeois class and the administrative elite of the vision known as the "Washington Consensus" (Steger 2003, 52–53). Other staples include the exposure of the local market to imports, the liberalization of currency, the deregulation of business practices, the cutting of taxation, the reducing of public expenditure, the decreasing of government debt, the plummeting of welfare allowances, and more. Taken together, these policies mark the government's withdrawal from involvement in the market, whether as business owner, policy maker, or regulator—a sure sign of the shrinking or dwindling of the state's role in the economy and certainly of its abandonment of its ameliorative social functions. Although Israel's social democratic governments up to the 1980s adhered to the principles of "mixed economy" (the public–private mix, etc.) and state intervention to balance and direct the market (the theoretical justification for this approach was famously proposed by the economist J. M. Keynes), in 1977 (the year Likud came to power) the government of Israel endorsed the neoliberal economic theory (as was promulgated by, for instance, economist Milton Friedman, who was indeed invited to give his blessing to the liberalization of Israeli economy). In 1985, after the economy suffered a three-digit inflationary spiral as a direct result of this policy, a joint "national unity" government of the Likud and Labour implemented a restructuring policy known as the "Stabilization Plan." With the explicit blessing of American and international financial institutions, this plan formally initiated the new agenda of the Israeli elite, turning Israel into a free-market, small-state society.

* * *

The elite that orchestrated this process floats slickly between the global and the local business and financial quarters. No better illustrations for this kind of corporate glocality can be provided than the career patterns of two of the recent governors of the Bank of Israel. Professor Yaakov Frenkel played an assertive role in the globalization and privatization of the Israeli economy in his role as the Bank's governor throughout the 1990s (1991 to 2000).[15] Before holding this office he held the chairs of International Economics at the University of Chicago and of the Economics of Peace at Tel Aviv University, was an economic counselor and director of research at the International Monetary Fund, and was an advisor to the World Bank. He is a member of the G-7 Council, the Group of 30, and other American and international prestigious associations. After retiring from the Bank of Israel, he joined the management of the American-based financial group Merrill Lynch, in a capacity of chairman of the global financial institutions group. Professor Stanley Fischer—an American citizen—became the governor of the Bank of Israel in 2005. Prior to this Fischer was vice chairman of the American bank Citigroup. During the 1990s he was deputy managing director of the International Monetary Fund, and before that he was head of the department of economics at MIT. Prior to his university position he was chief economist at the World Bank. Like Frenkel, he too is a member of renowned global and American clubs such as the American Academy of Arts and Sciences, the Council on Foreign Relations, the G-30, the Trilateral Commission, and more.

It is not surprising that an official policy statement of the Bank of Israel, a leading agent in the globalization of the economy, declares that the "opening of the Israeli economy to the world" is of highest priority and concludes from this that "the adoption of international standards of management in the private sector and in macro-economics [is required]":

> Accords and decisions that were endorsed have in common an opening of the Israeli economy to the world. In time this process gained the name "globalization." The idea behind it is that the small Israeli economy can realize its growth potential only if it is open to the free flow of goods services and capital. This openness required the adoption of international standards of management in the private sector and in macro-economics. Among others, the government had to lower taxation … reduced government spending … make the structure of certain economic sectors more competitive through structural reforms. (Klein 2003)

Thus by the 1990s the once omnipotent state of Israel came to be considered by its own elite not as part of the solution but rather as part of the problem—at least as far as economic and social issues are concerned. Almost all Israeli top governmental officials, Israeli senior economists in academia, and Israeli leading economic journalists subscribe to a simplistic version of free market, competitive economic, and "economics 101" wisdom, which leaves both political and social consideration outside their purview (Swirski 2006). Treasury policy papers, Bank of Israel reviews, recommendations of governmental committees, speeches of the Ministers of Finance, and research papers by economists in universities and other institutions read like manuals of the Washington Consensus. The policy guidelines of the governments of Israel typically include a declaration of purpose such as the following:

> [The government is committed] to increase exposure and the liberalization of financial and capital markets and the labour market … implement privatization and pass the ownership of businesses as well as authorities and banks to the public (by shares) and to private hands. (Government of Israel 2003)

Overall the state has weakened or at the least has assumed a new role, that of creating an environment convenient to global capital. Such is the way the government defines its role in the context of globalization:

> The Israeli economy is small and dependent on foreign trade. Successful development depends on specialization in areas of competitive advantage, so that it can manufacture and export

high quality goods at competitive prices. This trend requires
exposure to world markets and deregulation of administrative
and customs regulations. ... [The] government will work to inte-
grate Israel in the global economy. (Government of Israel 2003)

This message is unanimous. Professor Reuven Grunau, for
instance—academic director of the prestigious Tenth Caesarea
Conference of the Israeli Democracy Institute—clearly repeats it:

The role of government in the age of globalization may be
likened to a management of a manufacturing facility, the task of
which is to make it attractive for investors. (Grunau 2003, 42)

This doctrine, or rather set of mind, has a quintessential impact
on economic behavior in Israel, on all levels, as summarized by
an observer:

On the macro-economic level the most noticeable conceptual
changes are the recognition of the value of competition for economic advancement and the persistent effort to reduce inflation.
In so doing the Israeli economy had to comply with world
standards: deregulation and monetary restraint are mantras the
world over ... on the micro-economic level globalization coerces
changes in management: persistent drive for efficiency, consoli-
dation instead of diversification, perennial demands for growth
and profitability, cautious use and distribution of capital, and
more than all adding value to share holders. (Rolnik 1998a, C2)

Since the 1990s globalization has been the top priority for
Israel's economic–political elite. The managerial–economic

discourse of Israel is saturated with globalizing messages that call for increased competitiveness by the acceleration of liberalization, privatization, flexibilization, and the other economic principles of the Washington Consensus doctrine. Evidence to this is abundant in Israeli business press and magazines. One example, from many possible, is an article by an economics professor at the Technion published in the magazine *Executive*, the title of which describes its target audience. The article tells of Israel's twenty-sixth ranking on the global competitiveness scale in 1997 (meanwhile the rank went higher; see following text), analyzes Israel's advantages and weaknesses, and reaches the conclusion that to be more competitive globally Israel must reduce its public sector, reduce regulatory bureaucracy, improve financial services, increase privatization, and penetrate world markets (Meital 1997; for a later instance, see Gabai 2003).

The turn toward capitalist globalization bore its fruits. Israel gains today prominent ranking by international monitoring agencies that quantify the compliance of world states with the neoliberal prescriptions of marketization and that weigh other aspects of their international economic performance.

On the *Globalization Index* produced by A.T. Kearney and *Foreign Policy* magazine, Israel was ranked in 2004 in the twenty-second position. The ten highest locations in this globalization scale were, in order, Ireland, Singapore, Switzerland, the Netherlands, Finland, Canada, the United States, New Zealand, Austria, and Denmark. In places eleven to twenty-one were, in order, Sweden, the United Kingdom, Australia, the Czech Republic, France, Portugal, Norway, Germany, Slovenia, Malaysia, and the Slovak Republic. Behind Israel's twenty-second position were, in order, Croatia, Spain, Italy, Hungary, Panama, Greece, Japan, Botswana, and Poland. Turkey ranked fifty-fifth, China

Table 1.3 The A.T. Kearney Foreign Policy Magazine Globalization Index: Israel 2004 (Overall Ranking 22)

Economic Ranking 31	Personal Ranking 7	Technological Ranking 19	Political Ranking 44
Trade 23	Telephone 8	Internet users 21	International organizations 61
Portfolio 34	Travel 27	Internet hosts 18	UN peacekeeping 24
Foreign direct investment 30	Remittance and personal transfers 5	Secure Internet servers 17	Treaties 61
Investment income 26			Governments transfers 3

Source: A.T. Kearney, *Foreign Policy* magazine (2004).

ranked fifty-seventh, Egypt ranked sixtieth, and India ranked sixty-first (Kearney/*Foreign Policy* magazine 2004).

As shown in Table 1.3, this ranking combines economic, personal, technological, and political indexes. It is interesting that the index in which Israel gets the highest score (seven) is the personal criteria, next in line is the technological index (nineteen) (more on both aspects in Chapter 2), and lagging behind are the economic index (thirty-one) and the political index (forty-four). This goes well with the complaint of Israeli neoliberal ideologues, according to which Israel is blessed with human capital and technical know-how that are being curtailed by bureaucratic intricacy and political arbitrariness.

In a likewise manner Israel scores very high in the World Economic Forum's *Global Competitiveness Index*. In the 2006–2007 index it ranked fifteenth—up from the twenty-third position in the previous year. Israel scored exceptionally high in the areas of "technological readiness," in which it moved up twenty places to rank third in the world. Israel was praised by the World Economic Forum for "the development of a culture of innovation, supported by first-class institutions of higher education and scientific research," and it was noted, "Israel has become a world technology powerhouse" (World Economic Forum 2006). Incidentally in the competitiveness ranking for 2006–2007, Switzerland, Finland, and Sweden were the world's most competitive economies; Denmark, Singapore, the United States, Japan, Germany, the Netherlands, and the United Kingdom completed the top ten list; and the United States showed the most pronounced drop, falling from first to sixth.

* * *

As already noted, privatization, beyond being an economic policy, is also a social program and a political vision. The social program involves, as we saw, the impairment of unionized labor and of the bargaining position of employees in the labor market. Another major staple of it is the retrenching of the welfare state. This retrenchment is not always clear from the official statistical data. Thus, for instance, between 1985 and 2004 the welfare expenses of the government and other public authorities rose from about 23 percent of the GDP to almost 28 percent (BIAR 2004a, 183, Table D-1). Yet the realty behind these numbers is peculiar. The welfare expenditure is an expansive category, and in the case of Israel it incorporates two special weighty political items: the absorption of a large wave of Jewish immigrants (especially from the Russian Federation) and a huge project of buildup and upkeep of Jewish settlements in the occupied Palestinian territories (Swirski 2005). It is beyond doubt that the basis of the welfare state proper is being eroded. A team of Israel's most senior welfare analysts recently calculated the net benefit of the combined overall changes in the state policies of welfare and taxation between 2001 and 2006, as it pertains to the decimal brackets of income. In other words, they calculated how much an average family from each income bracket gains or loses as a result of, first, changes in the structure and amount of welfare allowances that the government dispenses to the population and, second, changes in the structure and amount of taxes that the government levies on the population. The results are striking: a family in the upper income bracket (the 10 percent richest families) has gained in 2006 compared to 2001 a monthly sum of NIS 1,246, whereas a family in the lower income bracket (the 10 percent poorest families) has lost a monthly sum of NIS 643.[16] Put simply, the policies of the government of Israel play a role the redistribution of income, only from the poor to the rich.

Moreover, the assault on the welfare state is carried out not only on the tactical level of cuts in budgets, in taxes for the rich, and in allowances to the poor[17] but also on a more fundamental strategic level, that is, a long-term structural undermining of the two main supports of the welfare state: its economic resources, which are composed of the taxes raised by the state to finance the welfare net, and the political resources, which are composed of the organized interests that maintain the welfare state, primarily the labor unions. As Abraham Doron, a prominent scholar of Israel's welfare state, puts it, the welfare state in Israel has undergone a process of marginalization; that is, it has been reshaped from the model of the universal welfare state (which in fact took hold relatively late, in the 1970s; see Rosenhak 2002) into the model of the residual welfare state or, in other words, from a model committed to an overall collective social responsibility to one that is committed merely to the treatment of the most needy:

> Marginalization is the gradual erosion and shrinking of welfare service systems that had a central role in serving all the population as a social right of the citizenry and turning them into residual systems based on hardship serving only the poorest and weakest. (Doron 1999, 438)

This implies a departure from the west and north European model of the welfare state, which aims at society in large by a wide spread of services, to the American model, which aims at a narrower target—the subsistence of poorest individuals in society.[18] Another way to put it is that Israel's social policy shifts from the concept of welfare to the concept of charity (if not in fact to that of negligence).

The history of the Israeli health service, which was mentioned previously, is an instructive example of this shift, albeit a seemingly exceptional case of "late nationalization." As mentioned, the National Health Service Bill of 1995 effectively nationalized health care and supposedly made it universally available (Shuval and Anson 2000, 139–51). The primary health care provider until that time was the Histadrut's Seek Fund (Kupat Cholim). But from a historical perspective this move produced two important side effects: one is the devastating blow to the main representative body of organized laborers, on which we dwelled previously, and the second is the slippery slope of national health service, which gradually turns into "basic cover" only (Filc 2004, 2005).

* * *

Furthermore beyond economy and society, privatization represents a whole new political vision. Privatization in the narrow economic sense is but the spearhead of a wholesale privatization process that entails the demise of the centralist state system, which grew out of the historical national-collectivist foundations of Israeli nationalism. The house built by "Zionist socialism," its institutions and beliefs, was thrown in the 1990s into the dustbin of history.

One arena where political privatization becomes visible is the judicial sphere. In the 1990s the Supreme Court under the presidency of Judge Aharon Barak initiated a "Constitutional Revolution," the overt side of which was the institutionalization of human and civil individual rights in Israel. This general intent, and the autonomy of the judicial branch that was the tool to weld it, has obviously been a significant dimension of the destatization of Israeli society. In this regard the court and its active judicial policy certainly took part in the spirit of the age of the expansion of individual rights and civil society.

Yet, on a more covert level, the court's fostering of the development of individual rights and a civil society in Israel was of a peculiar stance. It regarded a capitalist market economy as an exclusive key to the retreat of the state from the domineering of the private sphere (Hirschl 1998). Whether the capitalist market economy may infringe on some individual rights (or the rights of some individuals) and whether thus some social judicial remedy was in place was not seriously contemplated. Thus in fact the court has supported the development of only certain types of rights, those associated with liberal freedoms. It therefore has tended to prioritize rights associated with private property and individual choice over rights associated with the protection of labor or with collective or group rights. The Supreme Court has proved very cautious and reluctant when it comes to issues of social rights, as became evident when it rejected an intervention in the stipulation of "basic human needs" by the state or when it decided to disperse a certain social protest because it was obstructing public order and capturing privately owned space. In addition to this the court has contributed actively to the development of a novel legal framework that may serve as a foundation for the emerging corporate capitalism in Israel and the business ethic required for it (Hirschl 1998).

A different prime example of political privatization relates to the nature of the kibbutz as a communal and egalitarian form of settlement. Once the national-collectivist vanguard, and until the 1990s virtually the last institutional relic of Israel's socialist past, the kibbutz has started recently to undergo sweeping privatization. Whereas in the past the kibbutz economy was cooperatively owned and overseen by the kibbutz general assembly, recently the economy has been severed from communal oversight and footed on a professional basis. According to the pace of privatization of their property and services, kibbutzim are now classified into two models: a collective type, which retains more of the communal patterns, and a regenerated type, which moves fast into being just a regular suburb (Rosner and Getz 1996). Today about half of the 270 kibbutzim are in various stages of a privatization process that includes differential payment, private ownership of residence, and privatized means of production (in up to a 49 percent limit of the common property). Even the regenerated kibbutzim still retain a minimal type of social mutual aid, though more in the form of charity than of welfare. In the regenerated kibbutzim the wage differential between the managerial class and the menial laborers exceeds a tenfold difference.[19]

Privatization, then, is the new operating code of Israeli society since the 1990s. This code replaces the waning code of the welfare state, that itself had replaced in the 1950s and 1960s the collectivist–socialist code of the prestate in its day. The new code is expressed across the economic, social, political, and cultural board. Privatization is evident in politics in the decline of political parties and the rise of televised politics (Peri 2004; Koren 1998; Galili-Zucker 2004), in the commercialization of the publishing industry and of mass communication channels (Caspi and Limor 1999; Leibes 1999; Levi-Faur 2000), in the decollectivization of land entitlements (Yiftachel and Kedar 2000), in the denationalization of transportation and roads policies (Fletcher 1999), in privatization in all levels of education (Ministry of Education, Government of Israel. 2005; Brodet 2004), in general cultural values and imagery (Urieli 1989; Almog 1999; Roniger 1999; Lemish 2000), in fashions of popular music (Regev and Seroussi 2004), in sport management (Almog 1998; Ben-Porat 1998; Ben-Porat and Ben-Porat 2004; Galil 2003; Ram 2003), in the Hebrew slang (Almog 1993), in the state services, including soon the privatization of prisons, and so on and so forth.

Even the most statist of institutions, the army, is not exempt from the spirit of privatization, commercialization, and commodification. In this vein the army has decided to "launch a media campaign to re-brand the IDF's image both in Israel and abroad." A public relations person hired for this purpose relates that the army "is the most powerful brand in Israel ... it's a brand whose values are, warmth, security, home, and family." He even goes on to suggest that the "IDF brand" directly affects the "state of Israel brand" (Zoref 2003).

A fully detailed presentation of the privatization of all walks of life in Israeli society would require a whole book in itself (and see the encyclopedic account by Almog 2004). The *Haaretz* daily newspaper—a champion of the global, neoliberal, and civic stance—made a well-taken point when on the occasion of the state's year of Jubilee—1998—it published a special insert on the "End of Socialism" in Israel (Strassler 1998).

THE CONSUMERIST REVOLUTION

On top of the postindustrial and the bourgeois revolutions, a consumerist revolution has also taken place in Israel since the 1990s, and it has changed the lifestyle and material culture of individuals in Israel. Between 1950 and 1996 per capita private consumption rose by an average of 4 percent a year, and by 1996 it was 5.5 times higher than in 1950. Until the 1970s the rise in private consumption was usually lower than the rise in the GDP, but since then it has usually risen 1 to 2 percent above the rise in the GDP (CBS 1998a, 11–12). The composition of private consumption has changed as well: in 1950 basic needs (food, clothing, etc.) constituted 51 percent of the consumed basket; by 1996 the share of the elementary staples was reduced to 29 percent. The corresponding rise was in staples such as accommodation, electricity, fuel, services, and foreign travel (CBS 1998a, 11–12). In the year 2000, for instance,

4.8 million Israelis traveled outside the country—more than two-thirds of the entire population (CBS 2003b, Charts 2.1 and 29.4).[20] In 1970, in comparison, a mere half a million Israelis traveled abroad, which composed about a sixth of the population at the time. Thus the 1990s gave rise to a firsthand interaction of Israelis with foreign countries on an unprecedented scope, a significant change in a country where all the territorial borders are almost sealed. Judged by travel destinations, Israelis interacted overwhelmingly with Europeans (57.2 percent of all departures) and Americans (20.1 percent) (CBS 1997, 31, Chart 15), the same destinations to which the Israeli economy's umbilical cord is also tied.

Another indication of international interconnectivity is the volume of international phone calls. By the mid-1990s Israel had thirty-nine phone landlines for every one hundred people, ranking fourteenth in the world (Bezeq 1996, 117, Chart F1). More than a third of the population (35 percent) dials abroad more than once a month, and more than a quarter (28 percent) dials internationally at least four times a month. The total number of international calls, which indicates global integration, rises with education and income (Sigan 1998).

But even those who are not connected abroad through holidays, business trips, or even international calls get exposed to foreign lifestyles and consumer products in the living room. Since the 1990s Israelis are more exposed than ever to American television programs or Israeli versions thereof. Watching TV or VCRs is the most common leisure activity in Israel, practiced by 95 percent of the population. More time is devoted to it than to any other leisure activity. On average by the mid-1990s Israelis watched more than two hours of TV a day, with later data suggesting more than two and a half hours (CBS 1996a, 21; Gaoni 1999). Television broadcasting started in Israel only in 1967. For many years the channel of the Israeli Broadcasting Authority had a monopoly of the air. At the time television was set up in its nation-state context. One of its first broadcasts was of a military march in Jerusalem after the victorious conquest of East Jerusalem in the Six Days War. As an exclusive single channel, it served as yet another unifying national medium. The 9 p.m. news had become a national pastime (Katz and Hess 1995). In 1993 a revolution in broadcasting took place with the first opening of a commercial channel, Channel 2, to which another commercial channel, numbered 10, was later added, and cable broadcasting began. Soon after, satellite broadcasting joined, and Israelis enjoyed a commercial "open skies" policy (for a discussion of changes in Israeli media, see Limor 2003).

A similar process of diversification and commercialization took place with radio broadcasting. It started in 1948 with an official and authoritative "Voice of Israel" (Kol Israel), a state-operated radio station, and with the Army Waves (Galei Zahal), but since the 1960s additional channels were added, at the beginning as subsidiaries of the state and military stations, but since the 1990s on a commercial and communal basis. Today radio stations cater to distinct niches or compete over the same niche. In the 1990s the number of radio stations in the country, including the pirate ones, numbered around 150. In written media the process was similar: a shift from party papers and private press, albeit highly nationalistic, to commercial press that caters to different locales and tastes. By the 1990s political party papers were almost extinct (with the exception of the Orthodox sector). The Histadrut's paper— *Davar*, which was established in 1925 by Berl Katznelson, the spiritual head figure of Mapai—was finally closed in 1996. Book publishing also changed hands and changed orientation, from being organized along ideological lines into being a commercial enterprise. It is odd that some major publishers continue to carry their old ideological brand names, such as Working People (Am Oved) and the United Kibbutz (HaKibbutz HaMeuchad), whose meaning was extinguished long ago. The important exception for this trend is some public publishers with nationalist orientations (Yad Ben Zvi, Merkaz Zalman Shazr, Bar Ilan University, etc.). These developments in mass media changed their social role. Whereas in the past the media were strictly identified with party or state ideology, they now transmit a schizophrenic message: nationalistic in regard to state security and Jewish identity, and commercial postnational in regard to private lifestyles and mores.[21]

Whereas in the past the mass media were subsidized by state and parties, the media now mostly passed privatization and thus their feasibility became dependent on advertisement and hence on the scope of audience exposure, or what came to be called "the rating" (Weimann 1999; Bernheimer and Golan 1998). Per capita expenditure on advertising is on the rise in Israel, as is the total advertising expenditure that by the late 1990s reached around 1 percent of the GDP (about $963 million). As elsewhere, the advertising sector in Israel is one of the driving forces behind both commercial globalization and cultural globalization. Fifteen of the world's leading advertising companies are represented by local branches (*Haaretz* 1998, December 14). The following is a credo of a top Israeli advertiser, which sheds light on the meaning of commercial and cultural globalization from the perspective of an active participant:

Human society advanced from poverty to plenty. In the past demand outstripped supply. This was in Europe. In the U.S. the problem was reversed: for the first time in history, supply outstrips demand. Economic plenty is not produced by "taking" but through selling, tempting and distributing. The empires of today are categories of consumer goods, "Huggies" v "Pampers" for instance are the troops in today's battles. In the battle over the backside in Israel rages between "Tafnu-kim" and "Titulim." But Israeli companies are being taken over by multi-national empires. Our lives start to reflect the global corporate battles: our bread, toothpaste, razor, coffee, cereal…; milk might still be local (perhaps temporarily). Corporations are "tradable," not "American." Anyone can buy shares. We in Israel might live on the eastern seaboard of the Mediterranean, but our actions are determined further and further by multi-national corporations. Five years ago I would have defined my identity as of an Israeli fighting Israel's enemies. Today I am an Israeli fighting for a corporation operating in 163 countries. The Israeli advertising firm I work for joined forces with this corporation for a sizeable amount of money. Our company's Hebrew name will cease to exist too. The company will become a division of the corporation. Who is the enemy today? My corporate rivals. So this is not Americanization. Each one of us may find themselves a consumer or worker under some global framework. … It is sad but inevitable … are we so devoted to America? Are we losing our Jewish identity? Where are our pride and independence? We tried to postpone the end. It was a tough decision but an inevitable one. If we are not integrated we will not survive. Maintaining independence spells suicide. We are devoted to the empire but in a long term process. So by the time we lose our identity completely, it will be of little concern. It is a tough process but an inevitable one. (Advertiser 1998)

The final conclusion of the advertiser relates to the firm in which he is a partner, but the national analogy (empire, independence) is apparent. The talk of "survival," that in the past was preserved to national conditions, is now applied to conditions of business soundness.

A major aspect, economically and culturally, of the revolution in consumption is in fact a flip side of the coin of the postindustrial high-tech revolution in production; that is, the consumption and application of communication and information technologies. The informational and communicational connectivity of Israelis is among the highest in the world, and since the mid-1980s the government pushes to privatization and competition in this market.[22] More than 91 percent of Israeli households have television, and 70 percent have cable TV or satellite TV; close to 87 percent have at least one phone line, and close to 84 percent have at least one cellular phone; 53 percent have two cellular phones or more; more than 59 percent have at least one home computer (35 percent in the bottom income bracket, close to 55 percent in the fourth income bracket, 67 percent in the seventh income bracket, and more than 80 percent in the upper income bracket); and more than 35 percent have an Internet account (9.5 percent in the bottom income bracket, more than 26 percent in the fourth income bracket, close to 50 percent in the sixth income bracket, and more than 59 percent in the top income bracket) (CBS 2006a, Chart 8). A study in 2004 found that the number of Web surfers reached 2.7 million—40 percent of the population, with 82 percent surfing on a daily basis (Horesh 2004a, 2004b). In comparison it is found that more households own computers in Israel than in most European countries (with the exception of Iceland and Denmark) and that the rate of

Internet surfers older than the age of sixteen is close to the rate in Germany, Britain, and Austria and higher than in other European countries (with the exceptions, again, of the Scandinavian countries) (Mizrachi et al. 2005).

Thus all in all, from the austerity of the 1950s and modesty of 1960s, Israel developed to an affluent, hedonistic, and globalized consumer's society in the 1990s and 2000s. Consumerism has been symbolized by what was called the "Subaru syndrome," named after the Japanese vehicle that flooded Israel in the 1970s (Melman 1992). During the three decades between 1966 and 1996, the number of cars moving on roads in Israel grew almost fourfold, from 68 to 268 per 1,000 persons. The increase is mostly attributable to private vehicles, the number of which rose sixfold, from 33 to 204 per 1,000 persons (CBS 1996a 23, Chart 5). The private car is but the spearhead of an entire consumer revolution. In 2005 1.6 million private cars serve Israel's population of 7 million (CBS 2005, Table 24:14). Close to 58 percent of households own at least one private car, and more than 15 percent of households own two cars or more (CBS 2006b, Table 8).

Buying so much more also means more shopping. In the 1960s retail markets shifted from the local grocery store to the supermarket chains and in the 1980s to shopping malls and so-called power centers in the outskirts of cities and high roads. Sixty-three percent of household utilities, 53 percent of food stuff, and almost 40 percent of kitchen utensils, cosmetics, and personal items are bought now in chain stores (CBS 2006b, Table 5); 75 percent of clothing shopping is done in malls (about 48 percent in in-city ones and 27 percent in malls out of the city) (Kleingbail 2005). The first American-style shopping mall opened in Israel in 1985 (in the city of

Ramat Gan, which is adjacent to Tel Aviv), and since then dozens were added and many more are planned. Estimates are that seventy-nine shopping malls are currently operating in Israel, totaling around one million square meters of retailing space (Reily 2003). Twenty-seven percent of all commerce in Israel is conducted in shopping malls (still lower than the corresponding 50 percent rate for the United States and 40 percent rate for Britain and Spain), which offer the goods of most chains and franchises, Israeli and multinational, in most fields: fast food (McDonald's, Burger King), high fashion (Zara, Hamashbir), kids' toys (Toys "R" Us), home supplies (Home Centre), office supplies (Office Depot), and more. Store names are displayed many times in Latin letters or Hebrew transcription, and only few have Hebrew names.

One of the largest shopping malls to open in Tel Aviv was declared "a city within a mall," a luminous analogy for the social order of global capitalism. The malls have left city streets deserted, and the ones open on Saturday have become the recreational focus of the secular Israelis of lower and middle classes (in 2003 during election day, the seven malls owned by the Azrieli group alone attracted three hundred thousand people who were looking for a "nice protected place to spend election day") (Zoref 2003). The mall offers a new type of space in Israel: a privately owned public space with images of city streets and squares. This space is like a sterilized bubble enabling people to disengage from the space outside—the sweaty, weary, Mediterranean urban space. Though often having been the target of Palestinian suicidal bombers, the malls are well guarded and supervised at their entrance, so the presence inside them also offers people a measure of heightened security, in a society prone to insecurity. The mall offers Israelis the illusion of being "here," in the Middle East, yet feeling "there," in the opulent West. A visit to high-class malls, such as in Ramat Aviv, can feel like a substitute for traveling abroad.

The postindustrialization of Israel is a structural trend. Its concrete dynamics involve periodic fluctuations along the major upward curve, but these fluctuations are of no special concern for us here. It is enough to mention that around the very end of the 1990s, the sectors of communication and information technologies suffered a setback. This occurred in association with the outburst of what was labeled the exploding of the "high-tech bubble" worldwide. In conjunction with this, in the beginning of the 2000s, the economy suffered a recession. In the years 2001 and 2002, for instance, the GDP fell by 2 percent and GDP per capita fell by 6 percent, and for the first time in years real wages fell considerably and public spending fell with them (BIAR 2002, chap. 3). Among the causes of the economic recess was the outbreak of the second Palestinian intifada in September 2000 and a slug in world production and trade that can be partly (and certainly symbolically) attributed to the events of September 11, 2001. However, the structural change in the Israeli economy persists, and in the following years the curve moved upward again. Binyamin Netanyahu (then finance minister) said in his graphic rhetoric in 2003, "The traffic light has changed, the cars start moving, and the first to move are those ahead in the line: the high-tech industries" (cited in Strassler 2003). The year 2005 turned out to be the all-time peak in the profitability of the high-tech industry, 20 percent higher than the previous peak year of 2000. High-tech companies compose 40 percent of the 150 largest companies in Israel, and their combined revenues reach some $20 milliard, which equals 37 percent of the revenues of the 150 biggest companies (Dan and Bradstreet 2006).

Two

Polarization

What are the social, cultural, and political implications of the mostly economic transformations that were discussed in the previous chapter—the postindustrial, the bourgeois, and the consumerist revolutions? This chapter continues where the previous one left off and investigates the implications of globalization on Israeli social structure and political culture. These implications are tackled by focusing on three social class categories: the middle classes, the business elite, and the laboring classes. As in the previous chapter, the aim here is not to provide an overall account of the scene but rather to offer a symptomatic reading of those novel developments that reshape Israeli social structure and political consciousness since the 1990s.

On the whole, the argument made in this chapter is that the global capitalism that emerged vigorously in Israel in the 1990s bears a direct influence on the social trajectory and as a consequence also on the political priorities of the affected sectors and actors in Israeli society.

The overall outcome of the process of economic globalization is a new socioeconomic polarization; that is, the exacerbation of income disparities and social gaps. The different classes also concomitantly reshape their political positions in national matters, especially the Israeli–Arab conflict. Significant sections of the upper classes tend to prioritize global cosmopolitanism over expansionary nationalism, whereas significant sections of the lower classes tend to prioritize expansionary nationalism over global cosmopolitanism. Of course this claim should be carefully qualified. It does not entail that the population is divided neatly between "globals" and "locals" or that political positions are divided neatly between the classes. There are large gray zones, contingencies, and a dialectical pendulum, all in a changing international context, that undermine any precise theorizations. Yet some tendencies are discernable and do make a difference, as we hope to clarify in the balance of this chapter.

THE PREDICAMENT OF THE MIDDLE CLASSES

The "middle classes" is a wide category that is demarcated by a measure of ownership of some kind of capital. In the postindustrial capitalist society, such as Israel came to be in the 1990s, capital has to do not only with material or financial possessions but also with some educational and professional resources, or what Pierre Bourdieu termed "cultural capital" (Bourdieu 1984). As in other postindustrial societies (Bell 1976, 1994), in Israel, too, a "new middle class" develops around the core of the design, processing, programming, and elaborating information and data. This class not only grows wider but also becomes the axis of a whole new socioeconomic dynamic—as we saw in the previous chapter. In quite a restricted definition that includes academics, associate professions, and technicians and managers, this class included in 2005 more than 35 percent of the workforce. If one adds to this category clerical employees, it reaches close to 52 percent of the workforce (Central Bureau of Statistics [CBS] 2006c, Table 12:18).

Sociologist Ronen Shamir associates this class not with material capital or with spiritual authority but rather with rational specialization offering tools to navigate society "rationally," liberated ostensibly from any "ideologies." Shamir argues,

> The crisis of the state and the shift to a market society result in new class practices, based on a pact between liberal ideology aiming to privatize the economy and professional specialization supplying the scientific basis for such a shift (theoretical models of efficiency, profit, management etc.). (Shamir 1996, 251)

The new class of specialists craves to shift society from the path of (old) nationalism and (neo-) tribalism to the path of Western globalization. This class supplies the professional cadre and ideological framework to the liberal and neoliberal culture (and, in part or by implication, also to the post-Zionist culture), in regard to both national concerns and socioeconomic concerns (Keren 1995). So in the time of globalization, the middle classes, and especially their upper echelons, have come to be identified with economic liberalization and national decolonization. This was amply demonstrated in the 2006 election, when these classes landed their vote en masse to Labour and to the new Center party Kadima and thus broke the back of the ruling party since 1977, the Likud.

Shamir's depiction indeed captures the core of the new and upcoming middle class, but the category of course encompasses a larger variety of employees, stretching from middle-ranking civil servants to well-off corporate executives. It seems that this category stands with one foot in the realm of the state and another in the realm of the market. This seems to be the case both in terms of its sources of livelihood and in terms of the horizons of its consciousness. The process of globalization tends to sharpen the rift between the two feet, so to speak. The most obvious sign of this is the insatiable mobility that these classes experience—both upward and downward.

The contraction of state budgets and services hurts middle-class interests and positions no less (some would argue it hurts even more) than those of the lower classes. The middle classes are major beneficiaries of the state, both in the state's role as an employer and in its role as services provider. Although the middle classes were being lured to the seductions of the employment opportunities and consumption options offered to them by the new economy, their exposure to the hazards of the competitive market was also amplifying. The overall result of recent changes in the economy is that from 1988 to 2002, the middle-income segment in the population had in fact diminished substantially. What takes place is a process of polarization that steers the top sections of the middle classes into the higher rungs of income and its bottom sections into the lower rungs of income.

Sociologists Shlomo Swirski and Eti Konnor-Atias, Adva Centre's researchers, offer two optional statistical counts of this shrinkage of the middle classes. By one count, middle-class position is defined by the median income of households, which in 2002 included households in income brackets 4 to 7, with monthly income between NIS 8,000 and 13,350. Defined so, the middle class shrank by 15 percent, from around 33 percent of households to 28 percent, with its correlating share of income dropping by 25 percent, from 28 percent of the total to 21 percent. The second count is based on a definition of a middle-class position by the average income. It includes households in income brackets 5 to 8, with monthly income between NIS 10,550 and 17,500. Defined so, the middle classes shrank by 19 percent, and their share in income shrank by 20 percent (Swirski and Konnor-Atias 2004).

Whether pressed upward or downward, the general political attitude of the middle classes is changing, and in both cases the result is a distancing from the state. In case they climb up, they tend to discard their strong attachment to the state and develop an individualistic ethos, whether more in a neoliberal form (if they belong to the more technical side of the market) or more in a postmodern form (if they belong to the more artistic side of the market). In case they fall down, they tend, once more, to discard the state that disappointed them and look for substitutes in the form of communities of solidarity or identity politics.

On the cultural level, globalism tends to generate what is known as postmodern culture and hence to fragment cohesive identities, disrupt the sense of historical continuity, and discredit beliefs in foundational meanings. The middle classes, and especially the parts of them rich in "artistic capital" (as opposed to "technical capital"), are the prime carriers of such cultural effects. They tend to discard the old collectivist or republican ethos, with its emphasis on social commitment, and to supplant it with an individualist or liberal ethos, with an emphasis on individual rights and the attainment of personal achievements (Shafir and Peled 2002). Research into different aspects of Israeli culture corroborates this general observation: starting already in the 1970s, a culture developed in Israel that can be defined as "hedonist individualism." A lucid barometer of this can be found in the messages of commercial advertisement, which since the late 1970s onward have been found to "associate the products to qualities connected with the individual's life ... and to appeal to individuals as people who realize their personal aspirations, quite dissociated from national interests or the needs of the collective" (Urieli 1989, 61).

A similar tendency is also revealed in more highbrow cultural spheres, most eloquently in literature. In the 1980s and 1990s, a different wave developed in Israeli literature, giving expression to postmodernist and post-Zionist political culture (Balaban 1995; Gurevitch 1997). The reality betrayed by this literature is "frayed, arbitrary, random, lacking order, meaning or purpose" (Balaban 1995, 43), and it is distressed by an anxiety, which results from "an unravelling of meaning" (Taub 1997, 10).

A sentence from a book by filmmaker Avraham Hafner sums up the worldview typical of the characters in the literature that is written for and about the urbanized middle classes of the 1990s, a worldview that is adamantly post-utopian and therefore also postnational: "I believe there is no god. First. I believe history has no meaning. Any meaning. Second. I believe there is no sublime cause for humanity—not the victory of light over darkness, not any form of utopia" (cited in Balaban 1995, 43). In line with this, literary analyst Avraham

Balaban depicts the postfoundational consciousness of these same social classes and their endemic incredulity toward any "big narrative" and aptly relates these cultural traits to their postindustrial and neoliberal material base: "Writers of the 1980s grew up ... in a world ... with no consensus and no certainties, a world of mirrors and screens (cinema, TV, computer) reflecting each other. Their heroes are not seeking the lost totality for the simple reason that they do not believe in it from the first place" (Balaban 1995, 71).

Other illustrations to these post-utopian and postfoundational sensibilities can be found in the visual arts. Photographer Tiranit Barzilay is one of the artists typical of the zeitgeist of the postnational era in Israel. She stages groups of youngsters in whites or underwear in clogged, vacant spaces, resembling bomb shelters. Although these are familiar visual signs of Israeli national culture, the figures are staged in a very non-Israeli manner in frozen movements, and their eyes never cross (à la Hopper's drawings). Art critics have rightly found in these works an expression of post-Zionist anticollectivism and antiheroism: "Israeli 'togetherness' collapsed here with the grand narrative of Zionism, deconstructed to a vacuous framework for a fabricated ritual" (Katz-Freiman 1996, 100; see also Breitberg-Semel 1993; Castel-Bloom 1996).

Still another illustration can be found in everyday Israeli habitus. Sociologists Luis Roniger and Michael Feige pointed out the centrality in recent decades of the rife expression "freier," with the common pronouncement that one "is not a freier," which means that one does not lose out because of weakness or trepidation; one knows how to get one's due share, not letting others take advantage of one. They view the "nonfreier" as the negative of the old Zionist pioneer (halutz), and as such an expression of the post-Zionist zeitgeist, wherein the individual refuses to assimilate in the collective or be at its service (Roniger and Feige 1992). The "nonfreier" expression was later applied also in the film *James' Journey to Jerusalem* to illustrate how a foreign worker develops the characteristics of his Israeli employers, thus literally making the "nonfreier" into a postnational trait (Alexandrowicz 2003).

The impact of the new class positions is felt far beyond everyday affairs and spills over into the national domain. During the 1990s observers of military affairs in Israel estimated that even the ultimate public institution of state and nation—the army—can no longer function in the pattern of a republican "people's army" or "nation in uniforms," as the military had been conceived in Israel. There is an estimation that the military is destined to turn into a professional army of salaried recruits, as in other rich democratic societies (Cohen 1995; Ben-Eliezer 2004). In Israel there is a universal (though Jewish only) compulsory conscription of eighteen years old. Yet already by the late 1990s, only about 55 percent of each year's cohort have been recruited, and a fifth to a quarter of those recruited did not complete the mandatory three years of military service (for men), and only about a third took part in reserve duty.[1]

A related index of the fading of nationalism was what was dubbed the "motivation crisis" of the 1990s. This refers to a declining motivation of recruits to volunteer to serve in combat units. Even though this trend was balanced out over time, it is a stark indicator of a deep change in military–civil relations. Although in the past military service had been considered as the most prestigious way of contributing to the common good, especially in the circles of the veteran elite (who by and large constitute the middle classes), in the 1990s it became common in these circles to renounce the military service and to prefer more attractive and more gratifying routes of mobility and achievement (Levy 1997, 2003a).

One of the driving forces behind Yitzhak Rabin's peace initiative of 1993 was a sense of a certain demur in the militaristic atmosphere among the veteran elites, especially among the global, postindustrial, and postmodern generation of it, who grew up in the 1970s. After Rabin was assassinated in 1995 and the so-called "peace process" started to decompose, the estrangement of these circles from militarism was even accentuated. Many of them felt that in the past they were ready to sacrifice a lot to secure Israel's survival but that they were not sure that their effort would now be abused in the service of the Jewish settlers in the occupied territories and their messianic Jewish ideology, about which the secular middle classes are fundamentally appalled. Raison d'être under the banner of "security" is still sacrilege for these classes, but what they perceive as "ideological" rather than as "security" considerations in the national conflict is unacceptable to them. As the Likud and its populist electorate advanced politically during the 1970s and 1980s, the middle classes, the veteran electorate of Labour, receded to their private—indeed privatized—realms.

This feeling received yet another manifestation in the migration discourse that became spread among them or in the notion of "internal migration" that was coined. A *Ma'ariv* daily insert discussed a new phenomenon where "secular, educated, young couples with secure futures stop whining and leave the country. Reasons are many: Rabin's murder, the orthodox, the settlers, Binyamin Netanyahu, the occupation, the rule of law; and mostly a hard, anxious feeling of not belonging" (Kapra and Shelach 1998). Another symptom of the renunciation of the collectivity had been the melancholy atmosphere in this group after Rabin's murder. The Tel Aviv local paper *Ha'ir* named this group "the depressive sector" who "live in the shadow of the shattered Oslo dream." Journalist Einat Fishbein described succinctly the concerns of this group: "The depressive leftist sector, who were used to their positions on the high rungs of the social ladder, lost its way between the new elites and the impoverished city neighborhoods and development towns" ("new elites" is a reference to the Likud, Shas, and the rest of what was labeled "Netnyahu's Coalition"). Political psychologist Daniel Bar-Tal noted the symptoms of this group ailment: "grumbling complaints, immigration, abstaining from voting, introspection, apathy, passivity, escapism" (all citations are from Fishbein 1998).

In the beginning of the 2000s, a concern arose in Israel about a "brain drain" of the new middle classes—engineers, scientists, physicians, and other academicians. According to the findings of researchers Eric Gould and Omer Moav, among the population with a higher education the tendency to emigrate is greater than among those with a lesser education. More than 2.6 percent of all married Jews in the twenty-five to forty age group with a bachelor's degree and higher in 1995 were defined by the CBS in 2002 as emigrants, in comparison with only 1.1 percent among those with a lower education. The phenomenon is most noticeable among new immigrants, mostly from Russia. Among them in the same age group, approximately 4.6 percent of those with a higher education left the country during that period, compared to about 2 percent of those with a lower education. During the early 2000s each year nineteen thousand Israelis emigrated outside Israel, and in

2005 the number rose to twenty-five thousand. Altogether the official Israeli estimation is that seven hundred fifty thousand Israelis live abroad on a permanent basis, predominantly in the United States and Canada, which constitutes a bit more than 10 percent of the population of Israel. It is arguable that the proportion of well-educated individuals in this population is greater than in the overall population. Being associated with the neoliberal Shalem Center in Jerusalem, these researchers attribute the brain drain to an excessively "socialist approach to economic policy" that is responsible for high taxation and labor market inflexibility and that "encourage[s] the brightest stars in academia to leave the country by giving inordinate power to unions, which fight to equalize wages among workers rather than letting salaries reflect achievement and alternatives in the global labor market" (Gould and Moav 2006, 5).

The middle-class malaise is easily traced in many cultural manifestations, especially when the right wing is in government. A prime example of the emotional stress involved in the transition of the middle classes from militaristic collectivism to democratic individualism can be found in a newspaper interview with a combat pilot. After detailing his contribution to Israel's security and lamenting the evasion from peace by right-wing parties, he went on to describe the pains of the disengagement of his social group from the state, when it becomes identified with the national-religious (neo-Zionists) orientation:

We shall serve the country, but we will not excel like we used to. And I say so in pain …

Interviewer: Then who shall do the fighting?

Those who have the motivation. My kids will fight, but differently. The point is this: we got killed enough, I say "we" carefully, because this is the problem—this "we" shall raise outcry. I say that me, my friends and children have suffered enough death, whereas [instead] we could have been studying Torah, as others do. I maintain that motivation should be selective. I maintain that excellence should be selective … this is the fault-line, at least for me and my friends—so that if a kid asks me if they should return home for the war [many elite kids are studying and staying abroad, but they used to return to Israel in times of national emergency, such as in 1967 and 1973] I would answer, I don't know, you ought to weight it. If you were my own kid I would think twice about it, for there are no longer inevitable wars or just wars. What is just is to have no wars and that is a possibility today.

Interviewer: Coming from a colonel in the air force these are harsh words.

Indeed they are, nothing is taken for granted any longer. Once I would automatically tell my child: you must return to defend the country. Today I no longer know what it means to defend. If we have to go to war to open some tunnel by the Wailing Wall, I say I will not have this, I do not want it and it is not in the interest of the state of Israel.

Interviewer: You will be accused of the decline in motivation to serve in the army.

The decline in motivation is a clear process that has been taking place for years. I say this with a broken heart. … We must not be outside the camp; we must not become service "refusniks." I hope that quite soon there will be a sobering up here. What I say resembles the notion of "in praise of normalcy" coined by author A.B. Yehoshua. I want us to be like everybody else. I do not want us to be a light unto the gentiles. I don't want to live by the sword. I want us to be capable to speak to everyone, Arabs, gentiles. That there will be communication with everybody and that no peace communication shall be barred by messianic ideas or archaic ideologies. I tell my children there is nothing taken for granted left. That one has to be very selective. The quality of life is the most important parameter in this business. … The elite draws fire. Perhaps we should be like everyone, not to antagonize the majority, not to excel, not to run to the frontline bare-chested. We will not become fighter pilots, we will not become special commandoes, and then we shall be a part of the people. You live and you stay alive. (Rabin 1996b, B3)

These words do not represent a lone voice and are not exceptional. In 1999 reserve fighter pilots called a strike with the support of the commanding officers' forum, demanding increased monetary compensation for relatives in the event of death. This was a clear sign of replacing ultimate nationalism with instrumental individualism.

The problem of declining motivation, and its many reasons and consequences, was registered by the defense minister and chief of staff. A commission to assess the motivation of prospective conscripts, staffed by security chiefs and headed by a reserve general who was chief of army personnel, clearly stated,

"In the last ten years [1986–96] there was persistent decline in the motivation to serve in the army." The commission added that the three cornerstones of youth education—settlement, *Aliyah* (immigration to Israel), and security—have become meaningless to the youth. The void has been filling with individualistic values of achievement, personal aspirations, and a drive for self-fulfillment over public values and social commitment (Rabin 1996a).

The commission noticed a drop in the motivation of kibbutz youth, which was traditionally a main resource for elite combat units and the officer corps. The rate of kibbutz conscripts choosing combat units remained a constant 80 percent, but their willingness to continue reserve duty declined. In the past, kibbutz recruits made up some 50 percent of pilot training courses in the air force, but in 1997 only two graduates were of kibbutz origin. In later years there was not a single wing commander from a kibbutz. The clear reason provided by the united kibbutz movement resembles the reasons raised in the interview with the pilot quoted earlier: "After the Likud won the elections [1977] our youth said 'let them have a go, we did our bit' " (Barzilai 1997). Moreover it is not just personal motivation but also public willingness to invest in security that is on the decline. The army budgetary department reached the conclusion that "Israeli society changed from a mobilized ideological society to an a-ideological society, where service in the army is no longer deemed essential" (Barzilai 1997).

It is important to underpin the material background of this subtle but definite change of orientation of the middle classes. Communication scholar Dan Caspi made the following comment in the context of the 2006 military strike of Israel in Lebanon:

As the war proceeds and lengthens the sense emerges that
something does not tick there this time. ... Years of worship
of Americanization, bourgoisification and hedonization,
compromising of the spirit of achievement and the preference
of connections over capabilities, all have projected on the
human stock, and on the quality gap and the motivation gap
between Israel and its neighbours. The acquisition of advanced
technologies and its skilful manipulation might nurture delusions
of powers and superiority. (Caspi 2006)

What is the typical social profile of those who are economically liberal and politically moderate and roughly globalist and
somewhat postmodern in their worldview? The answer to this
question is linked to the three revolutions discussed in the
previous chapter. Research by sociologists Efraim Yochtman-
Yaar and Yochanan Peres shows that two social characteristics
have the highest correlation with such a worldview—being of
middle to high socioeconomic status and being secular:

The data unequivocally show that secularism is most influential
... its impact is consistent: the tendency to prefer democracy and
tolerance to nationalism rises hand in hand with secularism.
A dovish approach rises, too, and the sense of national threat
declines. The educated, secular middle classes are the most
democratic. (Yochtman-Yaar and Peres 1998/2000, 77)

This conclusion is supported by further analyses of the
data, showing that the group most committed to democracy
is what the authors dub "capitalist left"—roughly defined as
the educated, business, and professional middle classes, who

identify with the center and left of the political spectrum. The least committed to democracy are those they call "right-wing socialists"—roughly speaking, populist-nationalists who identify with the Likud, Shas, and other right-wing parties.

These globalist sectors of the middle classes consist of the offspring of the national "founding fathers" and army leaders, the farmers of yesteryear and fighters of yesterday. This social group was formed through its participation in state building and army service (Shapiro 1984; Ben-Eliezer 1998; Rosenfeld and Carmi 1976). This stratum now wishes to disengage itself from the smothering collectivist hug of the state and to realize its personal and professional potential in capitalist and civic society (Swirski 1993).

The "new Zionism" rhetoric of industrialist Steph Wertheimer is a fine example of these deep transformations in the culture of the middle classes (even though he belongs of course to the business elite that we discuss next): "The essence of Zionism used to be realization in a *kibbutz*. Today Zionism it is a Tefen-like *kibbutz* and development of export industries" (cf. Frenkel, Shenhav, and Herzog 2000). The term "Tefen-like *kibbutz*" is most telling. Tefen is a high-tech industrial park built around Iscar Metalworking Company, which is owned by Wertheimer. In 2006, 80 percent of Iscar was sold to the American firm Berkshire Hathaway, based in Omaha, Nebraska, and owned by the multibillionaire investor Warren Buffett, who paid $4 billion for his share. Wertheimer had meanwhile opened an industrial park in Turkey, near Istanbul. Iscar's global reach now includes production facilities in sixty countries and sales in nearly one hundred countries. "Today's Zionism" is thus turned into global "material" post-Zionism (Myre 2006).

THE ASCENT OF THE BUSINESS ELITE

While the up-climbing middle classes are vigorously changing their course from collectivism to individualism, the business elite celebrates Israel's change of course from etatism to neoliberalism. Globalization changes both the nature and the policies of the capitalist class in Israel. Whereas in the nation-state era private owners of big businesses had been a secondary elite, appended to the political elite, since the 1980s much power has shifted from the political to the economic elite.

As was suggested in Chapter 1, the new hegemony of capital is represented and advanced by the code of *privatization*. The word is easily associated with terms such as *decentralization* and *competitiveness*, but this is not necessarily so. Privatization in Israel simply shifted centralized control in the economy from public ownership to privately owned corporations. By one estimation about a hundred and fifty large business corporations account for more than half of all economic activity in Israel, in terms of both product and employment, and for about two-thirds of all export. Concentration of wealth is even higher, because many of these corporations are owned by an even smaller number of holding companies that are the power base of the economy in globalized Israel (Maman 1999). In the Israeli financial sector, concentration is even more extreme, with the top five institutions holding 78 percent of the assets and the top two institutions accounting for 49 percent of assets (Bank of Israel 2004b). In the Tel Aviv Stock Exchange, five capital groups account for more than 40 percent of the total value of traded shares (the five are IDB, Ofer Bros., Koor, Dankner, and Arison) (Koren 1999a).

Wealth in fact is largely concentrated in the hands of a small number of families, who reap the rewards of privatization. In the late 1990s Sever Plocker, the senior economic commentator of the country's most circulated daily *Yediot Ahronot*, observed,

> After fifty years of public and governmental involvement and ownership, the Israel economy, with the support of the government is entering a new stage. The control is passed to twenty families, local and foreign, who control over two thirds of the private sector directly or through cross ownership or subsidiaries. (Plocker 1998, 20–21)

Out of a traded share value of $50 billion, the government owns $5 billion worth of shares, and "interested parties"— mostly corporations—own shares worth $30 billion. Only about $15 billion are owned by individual investors, and those private investors are about 8 percent of the public (Plocker 1998). More precise data emerged from a Business Data Israel report about the concentration of ownership in the "big economy" by the rich families. According to the report, five hundred corporations employ 560,000 employees, who compose 40 percent of employees in the private sector. These companies earn a yearly average of NIS 570 milliard, which compose 59 percent of all the yearly income in the private sector (in comparison, the big five hundred companies in the United States take 38 percent of the earning of the private sector). Twenty percent of this earning—NIS 114 milliard—accrue to the fifteen rich families. About 9 percent—NIS 51.3 milliard—accrue to foreign investors. The state share in the big five hundred is about 3 percent only (Goldstein 2005).[2]

And so, as in the former communist countries and the liberalized Latin American countries, the transition from collectivism to liberalism implies not a decentralization of economic power but rather a transition from public centralization to a private one, with the old state and public economy oligarchies sharing the loot and becoming new capitalist oligarchies overnight.

One rung on the ladder of wealth just below the "fifteen families" are few thousands of millionaires and multi-millionaires. According to the world wealth reports of Capgemini and Merrill Lynch, in 2005 there were 7,400 millionaires living in Israel, who have liquid assets worth more than US$1 million each. Among them, 84 have liquid assets worth more than US$30 million and are classified as multi-millionaires. The number of Israeli millionaires per capita is twice the world average, and the increase in the number of multimillionaires—compared to 20 percent in 2004—is significantly higher than the world growth rate of this category, which is 8.5 percent (Capgemini and Merrill Lynch 2004).[3] *The Marker*, the business journal of *Haaretz*, started to publish in 2002 a yearly list of the five hundred richest people. In each successive year the threshold becomes higher. In the beginning a fortune of US$10 to 20 million would ensure entry to the list; in 2006 the threshold was about US$50 million. In that year the combined wealth of the five hundred jumped 16 percent compared to a year before, from US$54 to 63 million. The top sixteen members on the list accounted for about 40 percent of the combined sum (Lipson 2006).

Just below the top fifteen families and the top 7,400 millionaires comes the "top percentile" of wage earners. It consists of about twenty-four thousand persons. The gross average monthly intake for this percentile is NIS 74,000 (women's income for the percentile is NIS 31,000), and more than two-thirds of the percentile (68.5 percent) are independent business people with an average monthly intake of NIS 191,000, with the corresponding figure for wage earners at NIS 42,500. Top percentile earnings are flying high above the rest, including the "top decile" bracket of earners. The average monthly intake for the tenth bracket is NIS 26,000, and for the ninth bracket it drops to NIS 11,400 (this data is from late 1990s [Government of Israel 1999, Charts G4, G6, G5]).

In the 1980s and 1990s, social prestige moved, together with the material resources, from the state and its elites, such as military officers, to the private sector and its rising stars: successful businessmen and executives. On bookstore shelves, the "victory albums" of the various battalions and their generals, which used to be on display in the 1960s, especially after the victory of the 1967 war and before the shambles of the 1973 war, have been replaced with formulaic books about corporate success stories and their executives, both translated and made in Israel. Newspapers that used to run special inserts on historic wars and heroic battles now have inserts on managerial success stories, such as "Israel's best managers" (Perel 1997; *Yedioth Ahronoth* 2004). Another fine example from the *Haaretz* daily is a special insert on "Israel's growth decade—1988–1997," which ran the following caption on the cover: "They set up companies and business empires and within a decade accumulated a personal fortune of tens or even hundreds of millions of shekels. 16 Israeli business people bring you the story of the decade of economic revolution." The decade is narrated in terms of growth and prosperity (as if this narration of the decade represents all who passed through it). All sixteen chronicles have a color frame presenting the year of departure of the business hero (1988) and year of his arrival to riches (1996). The person's "worth" at each point in time is boldly emblazoned under each year tag, and between the two dates is the chronicle of his entrepreneurial voyage. Eliezer Fishman's story, for one, reads like this: "1988. 20 million shekels. Age 44, five years after the collapse of 'Ronit Investment Fund' and the fall of the stock exchange's star duo who ran it, Rieger-Fishman, Eliezer Fishman ploughed his way back into the Israeli business world. ... 1997. 1.0 billion NIS. Age 54, Eliezer Fishman is one of Israel's ten wealthiest people and its biggest property tycoon" (Rolnik and Lipson 1997). The lifestyle of the new rich and famous—luxury cars, exotic holidays abroad, penthouse apartments, lavish villas, and other extravagances—provide the fantasy for the rest of the population (who usually have to settle for much less).[4]

We have mentioned the peak of the wealth pyramid—the fifteen families, the few thousand millionaires, the top income percentile. Let us now move down in the scale and register the tenth bracket of income distribution. In the 1980s and 1990s, a new class of senior civil servants and corporate executives developed, with earnings well above other wage earners in the country. Nearly two thousand functionaries in the public sector and a further five hundred senior state officials form a "wage elite," with an average monthly salary of between NIS 30,000 and 108,000 (for 2002), not including social benefits estimated at a further 35 percent (Wage and Labour Agreements Comptroller 2004).

The trend of widening income disparities did not spare the public sector. During the 1990s (1992–99), gross pay in the public sector rose by 18 percent for the bottom quintile (junior workers) and by 33 percent for the top quintile (seniors). By the end of the period, seniors were earning 4.02 times as much as juniors, compared with 3.57 times as much in the beginning (Sussman and Zakai 2004, 6), and this without counting the outsourced manpower in the public sector. It is worth noting at this point that some 11 percent of teachers and kindergarten workers earn less than minimum wage and thus must rely on social security welfare and that nearly 20 percent of the fifty-five thousand public sector employees earn less than minimum wage and also have to rely on welfare benefits (Bior 2004b).

The managerial strata in the state service are just one component of the Israeli wage elite. In the private sector any public pay is considered low. The average monthly wage of managers in the 490 publicly traded companies in Israel was, in 2002, NIS 119,000. Senior management in the hundred largest corporations averaged NIS 243,000. On top of the wage, these managers usually received various extras, most commonly in the form of stock options. The important factor is the escalating inequality trend. In 2002 managerial earnings (in cost-to-employer terms) were seventeen times higher than average pay and thirty-six times higher than minimum wage, compared to thirteen times and thirty times higher in 1994, respectively (Swirski and Konnor-Atias 2003, 10).

The twenty-five highest paid wage earners in publicly traded companies in 2003 earned on the average NIS 445,000 (roughly US$100,000) per month. This is more than 130 times the minimum wage in Israel. The fifteen top managers on this list added a further NIS 1.1 billion in stock options realized during the year. The top two hundred managers had an aggregate salary of NIS 500 million, on average NIS 2.5 million per annum or NIS 208,000 per month (Starkman and Alon 2004).

THE PLIGHT OF THE WORKING CLASSES

Whereas in globalizing Israel the middle classes are in a predicament and the upper classes are in ascendance, the lower classes are suffering a devastating plight. One of the results of the new structure of the labor market that emerges out of the globalization and postindustrialization of Israel is the high and escalating disparities in income distribution.

In 1986 the share of income of the top decile bracket was 8.6 times higher than that of the bottom decile bracket; by 1996 the ratio had increased to 10.7. The share of income of the top three brackets of the population increased from 52 percent to 55.3 percent. The share of the bottom three brackets dropped from 13 percent to 11.7 percent during the same period (Swirski, Yaron, and Konnor-Atias 1998, 6).

Bank of Israel analysts describe the inequality trend of the 1990s as follows: "On the one hand the pay of skilled employees is on the rise, due to increased demand (especially in the high-tech sector); on the other hand, the pay of unskilled employees is declining because of exposure to foreign labour and goods based on cheaper labour" (*Bank of Israel Annual Report* [BIAR] 1998, 150). It is true that the average hourly pay in the electronics and metal industries (NIS 42 in 1997) is nearly double that in textile, clothing, and leather (NIS 22) (Dori 1998, 51). Yet this explanation is partial, relating only to salaried workers of middle and lower incomes. The trend of growing disparities in income distribution is structural and consistent (with occasional fluctuations) and independent of the gaps between welders and seamstresses; it has more to do with the gaps between labor and capital.

The category of individuals who are defined officially as "poor," that is, whose income is lower than the poverty line, is growing, and this becomes more so as the Israeli economy becomes more sturdy. Two standard poverty indexes are "poverty rates," which measures the ratio of the poor in society, and "poverty gap," which measures the depth of poverty. Since the 1990s both these indexes have been high and rising. Between 1979 and 2002 the percentage of families whose market income did not reach the poverty line rose from 27.9 percent to 33.5 percent (612,800 families). The rise in percentage for individuals is even sharper, up from 23.8 percent to 32.3 percent (1,954,100 individuals). However, the sharpest increase is among children, from 23.1 percent to 38.3 percent (760,100 children) (data for 1979: Swirski and Konnor-Atias 2001, 15; data for 2002: Achdut, Cohen, and Endwald 2003, 117, Chart 4). The poverty gap is defined as the gap between the "average poor" income and the poverty line. This index is on the rise (for instance, between 1999 and 2002 it rose from 25.1 percent to 26.1 percent) (Achdut, Cohen, and Endbald 2003, 118). We have to stress that poverty is not confined to those not working: 38 percent of poor families have one working income earner (Achdut and Cohen 2001, 45).

One of the reasons for the rise in inequality is the same process of privatization that we discussed earlier; privatization concentrates wealth at the top and simultaneously drains it at the bottom. The curbing of the public sector means, among other things, the pull down of the level of wages. The cost of labor in the private sector is only one-third to two-thirds of its cost in the public sector: in 1992 the yearly average cost per employee in the private sector was NIS 44,000 per year; among employees of Histadrut corporations, it was NIS 65,000; and in the governmental sector it was NIS 115 (BIAR 1995, 117, Chart B 41). Globalization depresses both pay and work conditions and in some sectors almost eliminates local employment opportunities altogether.

The labor-intensive sectors of traditional industries such as textiles, food, construction, and agriculture were never a source of high pay or adequate social benefits, but they at least offered some employment and modest income to the population in the peripheral areas. Yet in the past two decades, capital has been liberated from its dependence on local labor and has found ever-cheaper substitutes for it.

One method is outsourcing work to sites where labor is cheaper. This trend has been led by the textiles industry. More than twenty-five Israeli textiles manufacturers, including market leaders such as Delta, Polgat, Kitan, Argaman, Lodzia-Rotex, and Gibor-Sabrina (some founded with generous public subsidies in the first wave of industrialization in the 1950s and 1960s), have relocated their assembly lines to neighboring countries (Egypt, Jordan, Turkey, and the Palestinian Authority Areas, when security allowed). Some estimates put the exports from these relocated facilities at 10 percent of all textiles manufacturing in Israel by the mid-1990s (in the worth of around US$100 million) (Meiri 1998).

The Confederation of Industry actively supported the Oslo initiatives of the Rabin–Peres government. The support was led by then-president Dov Lautman, owner of the large Delta Galil textile firm. The fate of this firm points to the future of textile workers in a globalized Israeli economy. Delta Galil prospered in the 1990s despite the sector being considered traditional and on the decline. The year 1998, for instance, saw the company's record net profit, with share value rising by 214 percent during that year (Rolnik 1999). An economic analyst described the sources of Delta's success as follows:

"Labour intensive processes were relocated to Arab countries, while capital and technology intensive ones remained in Israel." In the latter part of the 1990s, some 50 percent of the firm's total manufacturing output came from Egypt and Jordan (Rolnik 1998b).

Yair Rotlevy, head of the textiles and fashion division at the Confederation of Industry, put the blame for relocation on Israel's minimum wage law, so unpopular with employers, and brazenly described why globalization means unemployment (or else draconic wage contractions) to the employees in the traditional industries in Israel:

> On the one hand, I do understand the difficulty of living out
> of the minimum wage ... on the other hand, when the labour
> cost of an Israeli seamstress is a $1000 a month, one can not
> compete with countries where monthly pay is $200, $70 or
> even $20. Countries in Southeast Asia, where slavery still
> subsists, manage to export $40 million worth of goods to Israel
> every year, exempt from taxation as the final goods get delivered
> here from Europe as duty free European goods. (Peri 1998, 39)

In 2004 the minimum wage was set at NIS 3,350 a month, 47.5 percent of the average wage. In response to the Histadrut's demand to raise minimum wage to NIS 4,500, or 65 percent of the average wage, Oded Tira, president of the Confederation of Industry, explained, threateningly, that such a move would result in the closure of three hundred factories paying workers minimum wage and the relocation of another eight hundred to one thousand manufacturing facilities to Southeast Asia, where pay is lowest (Bior 2004a). It should be marked that nearly 32 percent of salaried employees in Israel earn less than minimum wage (Sinai 2004; Bendlak 2004).

As a matter of fact, Delta—considered an Israeli firm—had become an intermediary link between first-world consumers and third-world production workers, dutifully fulfilling the intermediary role of semiperiphery in Immanuel Wallerstein's world system. The global architecture of the Israeli industry was described by Labour MK Dalia Itzik, then minister for trade and industry, as follows:

> Ultimately, because of competition from cheap labour, only a few "islands" of production lines will remain [in Israel], with skilled labour concentrating on added value—that is management, sales and marketing, design, export services, accounting and supervision. (quoted in Ben David 2003, 80)

In the late 1990s Delta was dependent on one major purchaser, British retailer Marks and Spencer, which accounted for 51 percent of all purchases. Marks and Spencer's profitability was hit, and a drop in share value of Delta followed. Despite that, or possibly because of that, Delta's CEO Arnon Tiberg expected improved performance "because Delta's competitors for sales to M&S have not started relocation to countries where manufacturing is cheaper" (Gavison 1998, C9) Delta had already started this move. Tiberg mentioned relocating Scottish manufacturing to Romania and Bulgaria. Delta employs 5,800 workers and estimates that "relocating 100 workers from a country with high labour cost such as Israel or Scotland, to a country with low labour costs, increases operating profit by a million dollars" (Gavison 1998, C9; Simanovsky 1999).

To round up the Delta story, in 1998 *Haaretz* daily's business section selected Dov Lautman its "man of the year" for wisely maneuvering his firm's competitive advantage on the world markets: "with cheap labour in Egyptian facilities, high product quality [developed and designed in Israel] and physical proximity to its main export market—Europe" (Rolnik 1999, C7). Delta's CEO Arnon Tiberg was nicely remunerated for his business success: the annual cost of his salary in 1998 was NIS 2.4 million, or 200,000 shekels a month (Koren 1999b), some seventy times higher than the average pay of an employee in the textile sector, which was NIS 2,837 (CBS 1998b, Chart 12:27). According to Oded Tira, president of the Confederation of Industry, in the years from 1999 to 2004, one hundred fifty Israeli companies relocated some of their manufacturing out of Israel. These are companies of all sectors, traditional and advanced, that relocated to Southeast Asia, west Europe, Turkey, Egypt, Jordan, and elsewhere, employing a total of around fifty thousand workers. The corresponding loss to the Israeli GDP is estimated to be between NIS 8 and 10 billion, or 2.5 to 3 percent of the total national product (Zarhia 2004).

In addition to the export of production sites to places out of the country where labor is cheap, another route of the capital owners to depreciate their expenses on labor is the import of cheap labor—not unionized and unprotected foreign workers or work migrants. The phenomenon of non-Israeli workers became essential in the Israeli labor market and economic structure during the 1990s, although employment of Palestinian workers played a similar role since the 1970s (Semyonov and Lewin-Epstein 1987). About 100,000 Palestinians from the occupied territories were employed in Israel in the 1980s, constituting some 9 percent of all wage earners at that time

(Kondor 1997, 47, Chart 1). But in construction and agriculture their share was closer to half the labor force (Kondor 1997, 48–51). In the early 1990s, following security restrictions on Palestinian entrance to Israel, a massive importation of foreign workers began (mainly from Asia, Africa, and eastern Europe). In the year 2000, 312,000 non-Israeli workers (214,000 were foreigners and 98,000 were Palestinians) were employed in Israel, making up 14 percent of the workforce with fewer than twelve years' education (Gottlieb 2002, 699).

About half of the foreign workers (48 percent) are employed in construction; of the rest, 15 percent are in agriculture, 14 percent are in food services, 8 percent are in industry, 7 percent are in businesses, 6 percent are in domestic services, and 2 percent are in finance and insurance (BI 18.12.2000). In globalized Israel, foreign workers compose the lowest underclass, which concentrates in the three "D" jobs: dirty, dangerous, and difficult (Kemp and Reichman 2003, 3). The reason for employing non-Israeli workers is obvious. Bank of Israel economists state, "The ratio of foreign workers is particularly high in labour-intensive sectors, so their employment reduces the cost of production and the final price for the consumer, increasing the industrialists' profits" (Sussman and Romanov 2003, 3).

Migrant workers affect the Israeli labor market both directly, by replacing Israeli employees, and indirectly, by depressing wages in labor-intensive sectors, especially on the lower rungs of the pay ladder. In construction, for example, in 2001 the cost of foreign labor was 40 percent lower than Israeli labor and 20 percent lower than Palestinian labor (Gottlieb 2002, 10). Employing foreign labor (through importation or relocation) is one of the elements that squashes the level of payment of local employees. The gross pay of workers from the occupied territories, for example, was two-fifths of average pay for an Israeli worker (and that is a conservative estimate, not calculating the unreported workers). As a direct result of cheap labor importation, there has been a considerable drop in the (already low) pay of Israeli workers in agriculture and construction: on a basis of 100 points being industry average pay, agricultural pay dropped from 62 to 50 points and construction pay dropped from 104 to 77 points (Kondor 1997, 51). The scope of importation of cheap foreign labor with no rights correlates with the scope of unemployment that became rife in Israel, rising to more than 10 percent of the workforce in the 1990s (BIAR 2002, chap. 1). As the importation of labor is relevant in particular to unskilled menial work, so the levels of unemployment for unskilled menial work rose even higher.

Yet another method of worsening work conditions, reducing wages, and limiting social benefits in globalized Israel since the 1990s is the subcontraction of work through manpower companies. Employment through subcontracting shifts the responsibility for the employees' welfare to an agent who is but a middleman, extracting commission for connecting employer to employee. Most often the manpower companies (especially the small and medium ones, accounting for 70 percent of this market) serve as "a conduit for organizations wishing to reduce the cost of manpower" (Nadiv 2003, 38). The state comptroller mentions in an official report that employment by subcontracting over the long term is "taken up to avoid the responsibilities of direct employment or collective employment agreements, unpopular with employers" (State Comptroller 2001, 563). In the 1990s some 120,000 workers were employed through more than three hundred manpower companies, accounting for more than 5 percent of the workforce, 70,000 of whom were employed in the public sector (State Comptroller 2001, 562). This is a tenfold increase compared to the rates in the 1980s. It is also probably the highest rate in the world. In most developed countries the number of people employed by manpower companies is less than 1.5 percent (Nadiv 2003, 24–25). The state comptroller found that the state regulation of the commitments of manpower companies was insufficient, and he describes the situation of subcontact employees as follows:

> The low socio-economic status of many of the workers … the temporary nature of their work, their split among the employers, and the ability of the manpower company to move workers from one employer to another, create a dependence of the workers in the manpower company, discourage them from organizing and damage their negotiating power. Moreover, the unions have difficulty representing the interests of manpower employees. Their low ability to organize and the fact that they pay their union fees through the company to the union that signs deals with that company, limit their options of union representation. (State Comptroller 2001, 562)

Yet another characteristic of the new labor market in globalized Israel is the expansion of part-time employment (defined officially as working fewer than thirty-five hours a week). In the year 2000 permanent part-time employment accounted for 14.5 percent of the workforce, or three hundred fifty thousand employees. Only a quarter of these employees declared that they chose to work part-time.

Exportation of production sites, importation of labor, sub-contraction of employment, and part-time employment are not all of the characteristics of the new labor market. On the very lowest rung of the ladder of exploitation and humiliation of manpower in globalized Israel, lower even than Palestinians and migrant laborers, are the women, mostly from Russia and eastern Europe, traded and enslaved for prostitution. Although sex services are not new, they acquired in the 1990s an appalling magnitude and a hideous nature. In this period an unprecedented massive trade in women developed in Israel, comprising between a few hundred and three thousand women enslaved and smuggled into the country each year. Estimates put client figures for this industry at one million—about one-seventh of Israel's population and in fact almost one-third of Israel's male population—and a larger proportion of the male population older than eighteen years of age. Cross-border trafficking of women became a prospering economic activity demonstrating *ad absurdum* the exploitative logic of globalization—operating production lines in peripheral economies, in this instance in the form of sex tourism, or importing indentured cheap sex labor to the clients in the core economies.

The Ministry of Labor and Welfare Affairs coined the term "second-class workers" for the employees contracted through manpower agencies. But this is an understatement when applied to some categories of workers in globalized Israel. Reports by the U.S. State Department in 2003 and 2004 found that persons in search of work in Israel are trafficked into situations of coerced labor, where they suffer physical abuse, fail to receive their wages, have their passports withheld, and more. The reports mention migrant workers in Israel under conditions equivalent to servitude (Kav La'Oved 2004, 1; also see

Ellman and Laacher 2003). The Israeli government, its various ministries and agencies included, is complicit in supporting such practices, denying not just workers' rights but basic human rights. When it does act, it is to filter out or deport the victims of such offenses, but rarely does it indict employers or change the conditions that support such infringements of human rights.

We cannot expand here on the history of work policies in the Zionist movement and the state of Israel, but these have certainly come a long way, from the days of the national ethic of reclaiming work by the Jewish national worker to the age of the postnational import and export of labor as a means for post-Fordist, private capital gain. Researcher Ella Koren makes a well-taken point in calling migrant work "a social pilot scheme" where "what succeeds can be gradually incorporated from the margins to more mainstream sectors"—Palestinians from the occupied territories, Israeli Arabs, new immigrants whose Jewish status is not certain, Mizrachim, women, and even individuals of the declining middle classes. Moreover, the very existence of an excluded class, that is, a class of employees who are noncitizens (and rightless), "leads the state to reformulate its relations with the citizenry in two ways: to fuse together ethnicity, nationality and citizenship on the one hand, and unravel the connection between political rights and social rights on the other hand" (Koren 1998, 28–29).

* * *

In the previous discussion of the predicament of the middle classes, we dwelled on the implications of the socioeconomic changes on political attitudes. Let us now return to this question and ask more specifically about the possible connection between the globalization-induced class polarization, which we described in this chapter, and the changes in the political attitudes in Israel, in particular with regard to the Israeli–Palestinian conflict. In other words, what is the connection between the globalization of the Israeli economy and the Israeli policy toward the colonization of the Palestinian territories?

At the beginning of the 1990s, it seemed that globalized capitalism functioned in favor of a reconciliatory orientation in the Israeli–Palestinian conflict on the part of the Israeli business and political elites, as well as a large part of the middle classes. As the winners of globalized capitalism became more materialist and more individualist in their ideological outlook and daily practice, they turned their aspirations toward integration into the global economy and assimilation into the cosmopolitan culture. They started to relinquish Zionist expansionary ends, and they started to move toward concluding the national conflict and the tolls it exacts on life, property, and future prospects. There was in this regard a "Fukuyama effect" in the air; that is, a sense that liberal capitalism was about to supersede national chauvinism.

Yet as the 1990s—and furthermore as the 2000s—progressed, it came to be realized that globalized capitalism functions also as a facilitator of a resurgence of national chauvinism, this time in the cloak of ethnoreligious nationalism. Therefore a sense of a "Huntington effect" also spread in the air; that is, a sense of an insurmountable clash of cultures. The social categories that provided mass support for the reescalation of the Israeli–Palestinian conflict and the continuation of the occupation of the Palestinian territories were the losers of globalization—the laboring classes. They were of course mobilized politically by the ideologically nationalistic elites, both religious and secular. In the political system the main conduits of mobilizing this support were the Likud Party, the National Religious Party (Mafdal), the Shas Party, and the other satellite parties of the right-wing and religious block. In cultural terms, the idiom of mobilization against the upper classes' secular, global cosmopolitanism was the cultivation of a quasi-religious, lower-class, local return to Judaism. What was labeled in 1996 as the "Netanyahu Coalition" epitomized this combination of populist antielitism and popular Jewish traditionalism. It included minorities such as Mizrachim, Orthodox Jews, settlers, and secular national extremists and excluded (rhetorically) the secular, urban, upper-middle classes (Ashkenazim) and practically all Israeli Arab Palestinians.

This class and culture juncture came to be the central fault line of the bifurcation we discuss throughout this book: the dialectical struggle between an emerging Israeli McWorld and a backlash of a Jewish Jihad. One cannot escape here Marx's dictum about the bourgeoisie who spawn its future grave diggers in the form of the proletariat, only this time a proletariat with a vengeance—not so much anticapitalist as antisocialist and antiliberal and yet supportive of neoliberalism.

And so in Israel, since the 1990s, the stronger socioeconomic classes tend to support the center-left-wing block, that is, the Labour-led coalition with its globalization and "peace process" agenda, whereas the lower socioeconomic classes tend to support the right-wing and religious block, that is, the Likud-led coalition and its localization and conflict agenda.

This class and culture split finds ample manifestations in the political culture widely speaking and direct expressions in political behavior, as indicated in voting patterns. Electoral research in Israel, as well as a host of opinion polls, find repeatedly that political preferences are strongly correlated with class position and class structure. Table 2.1 demonstrates this trend (without a claim to statistically establish it). It shows the distribution of votes to the Knesset between the center-left block and the right block, in two separate elections to the Knesset, in 1999 and in 2006, divided by the socioeconomic status of the city. In the upper part of the table is shown the split of the vote between the two blocks in the ten wealthiest (Jewish) cities in Israel—the overwhelming vote for the center-left block is noticeable. The bottom part of the table shows the split of the vote between the two blocks in the ten poorest (Jewish) cities. In this case there is an overwhelming vote for the Right. Obviously the "ten most" are relatively small and relatively homogeneous places, socially and cultur-ally, and therefore no quantitative conclusion can be inferred directly from this data to the rest of the population, in inter-mediate social positions and in larger and mixed places. Yet the extremes are certainly an acid test to the broad political trends. Incidentally, overall the table indicates a basic stabil-ity in voting over time. The only notable exception is some rise in the vote for the center-left block in the ten poorest cities in 2006 compared to 1999; for instance, from 12 percent to 37 percent in Sderot. This change is entirely circumstan-tial—the head of Labour in 2006 was Amir Peretz, a citizen of Sderot (and therefore a neighbor of most of the other poor cities, which are in the same southern region of Israel).

The McWorld versus Jihad bifurcation finds a clear expres-sion in the different political preferences of the populations of secular and relatively wealthy Tel Aviv and orthodox and relatively impoverished Jerusalem. In the elections of 2003, for instance, the right-wing parties in Israel (which include

Table 2.1 Voting for the Center-Left-Wing Block and for the Right-Wing Block in the Elections to the Knesset in 1999 and in 2006, by Social Status of City: The Ten Wealthiest Cities and the Ten Poorest Cities (Jewish)

	Vote for Center-Left-Wing Block		Vote for Right-Wing Block	
	Elections of 1999 (%)	Elections of 2006 (%)	Elections of 1999 (%)	Elections of 2006 (%)
Ten Wealthiest Cities				
Makabim Re-ut	67.5	NA	11.0	NA
Ramot HaShavim	83.5	79.0	4.0	4.0
Shoham	45.0	59.0	19.0	26.0
Kfar Vradim	71.0	72.0	11.5	10.5
Kochav Yair	57.0	57.0	23.5	24.0
Kineret	52.0	63.0	15.5	21.5
Kfar Shmaryahu	72.0	74.0	8.0	10.0
Omer	69.0	71.0	12.5	15.0
Har Adar	65.0	70.5	12.0	15.5
Savyon	64.5	72.5	17.0	14.0
Ten Poorest Cities				
Ofakim	11.0	27.5	64.5	55.0
Beitar Ilit	—	—	76.0	94.0
Kiryat Malachi	12.0	28.5	62.0	53.5
Netivot	4.0	13.5	71.0	82.0
Yerucham	13.0	15.0	66.0	40.0
Emanuel	—	—	88.0	81.5
Sderot	12.0	37.0	58.5	56.0
Mizpe Ramon	20.0	42.0	49.0	48.0
Or Akiva	12.0	30.0	62.5	62.5
Dimona	15.0	35.0	58.5	56.5

Source: For the 1999 elections, see the Knesset site http://www.knesset. gov.il/elections/index.html; for the 2006 elections, see Ynet News, http://go.ynet.co.il/pic/news/elections_2006/all/all.htm.

111 Polarization

continued

Table 2.1 (continued)   Voting for the Center-Left-Wing Block and for the Right-Wing Block in the Elections to the Knesset in 1999 and in 2006, by Social Status of City: The Ten Wealthiest Cities and the Ten Poorest Cities (Jewish)

Note: Figures rounded to 0.5. Vote of less than 1 percent for any party was not included. The center-left block includes the following parties: 1999: Labor, Meretz, Shinui; 2006: Kadima, Labour, Meretz. The right-wing block includes the following parties: 1999: Likud, Israel Betienu, Shas, Mafdal, Yahadut HaTora; 2006: Likud, Israel Betienu, Mafdal, Shas, Yahadut HaTora.

the center-right Likud, small extreme nationalistic parties, and religious and orthodox parties) won 53.8 percent of the votes in Israel. Yet in Jerusalem the right-wing coalition won 72.9 percent of the vote, compared to only 43 percent in Tel Aviv. The center-left parties won 37.8 percent of the national vote, yet in Tel Aviv they received 51.6 percent of the vote, whereas in Jerusalem they received only 22.2 percent of the vote. Thus the contention that Jerusalem is a hothouse of Jewish chauvinism and that Tel Aviv is, on the contrary, a hothouse of Israeli liberalism is not just a matter of images. It is because of such differences that Tel Aviv and Jerusalem are referred to in this book in an "ideal type" manner, as both actual sites and symbolic icons that stand for the two contrasting political cultures in Israel—an Israeli McWorld and a Jewish Jihad.[5] Historian Shlomo Ben Ami, former minister in the Labour government, described the relations between Tel Aviv and Jerusalem in the following way:

> This schism [between the cities] today converges inside it all the schisms in Israel. "Tel Aviv" is the manifestation of an updated "Israeliness," one that does not hold the Uzi [shotgun] anymore, and does not follow the plough, but believes in the state of

Israel as a judicial entity and central axis of secular national identity. This is no more a mobilized society. It substituted the pioneering ethos with an urge to "[economic] growth," a belief in all sorts of "information highways" and the fascination of the "global village," in which there is a room for Madonna and McDonald's. This is Israel who is eager for peace and ready to pay high price for it. ... This yearning of "Tel Avivian" Israeliness for "normalcy" at all cost is regarded by the other Israel, the "Jerusalemite" Israel, as a shallow yearning, devoid of historical depth and liberated from the burden of Jewish memory and history. ... The "Jerusalemite" Israeliness is the yearning for Jewish roots, is the manifestation of almost perennial fear from the Arab and a deeply rooted distrust in non-Jews. The peace that the labor party reached for held within it the threat of returning of the [Palestinian] territories, but also the threat of the "returning" of history itself, the forgetfulness of Jewish memory and the decline of Jewish identity. The "Tel Avivian" peace was considered as an attack on the Jewish tradition and roots, and in fact on the Jewishness of the state. (Ben Ami 1998, 336–37)

In the 2006 Knesset elections, pollsters estimated that the typical voter of Kadima tends to be older than age fifty, secular, well-to-do, well educated, and veteran Israeli or Ashkenazi by descent. What propels the decisive tendency of the climbing middle classes and upper classes to vote for the parties that project moderate national policies?

Let us reiterate. In the past two decades a change in the social and economic orientation of the upper and middle classes in Israel took place. Although in the past these classes were at the spearhead of Israel's national and military mobilization—and incidentally the social and economic capital of these classes was in the main based on rewards accruing from the cooperative economy and later from the military–industrial complex—they have recently changed their order of preferences and turned their orientation—as well as their sources of wealth and power—from the national-military arena to the global capitalist arena.

Now this orientation toward globalization is shackled by the endurance of colonization. The Israeli elites and middle classes cannot simultaneously have national colonization and economic globalization. Colonization generates resistance and violence, which deter investment, growth, and international trade; globalization requires a hospitable safeguarded environment and smooth exchange with the developed world. For more and more Israelis who are on the winning side of globalization, the specter of being left behind it because of the colonization of the impoverished Palestinian territories seems unreasonable. The Labour in the early 1990s and Kadima in the early 2000s gave expression to this combined sentiment of neoliberalism and noncolonialism. That they have not actually delivered on their promises is a result of various factors (and a matter for a different study). The point we make here is only that in conjunction with the socioeconomic polarization the different classes are also polarized politically, wherein among some parts of the middle-class and upper-class winners of globalization there is a tendency to develop an interest in peace or at least in a "nonwar," whereas among some parts of the lower-class losers of globalization there is a tendency to develop in response an antielite and anti-Arab populism.[6]

In a distinctive analysis of the Jewish sector in the 1999 electoral campaign, sociologist Michael Shalev and his associates reached similar conclusions: socioeconomic status is a good gauge for political vote, even though this variable intermixes with other variables such as ethnicity and religion (Shalev and Kis 2002; see also Shalev and Levi 2005). Shalev analyzed the individual level and the ecological level (voting districts). Among his most elementary findings are the following: there was high correlation between indicators such as housing density, level of education, and monthly income and support for Netanyahu (right wing) or Barak ("left wing");[7] the lower the socioeconomic level, the higher the support for Netanyahu, and vice versa. When localities were classified by the class composition, in the top quintile (wealthy towns) support for Netanyahu was 25 percent, whereas in the lower quintile the support was 68 percent (Shalev and Levi 2005 100, Chart 3). Shalev's data confirm the thesis about substantial correlation between the socioeconomic status of (Jewish) Israelis and political preferences. His conclusion is highly relevant here:

In the spirit of Pierre Bourdieu, one can argue that in Israel the struggle over identity and borders is never disconnected from class interests. Peace, liberalization and privatization together are a coherent formula for the success of the dominant Ashkenazi middle and upper classes in today's world, a world of globalization, high-tech and the end of the cold war. ... This is the context for *Shas* party's talk of the material interests of its underprivileged class Oriental supporters, who are the losers in liberalization, facing independent subsidized social services or a less generous welfare state. Another explanation [different but not contradictory], stems from the high correlation in Israeli society between socio-ethnic differentiation and the division of social statues and political power. According to this approach the main political rifts between the socio-ethnic classes are a reflection of the politics of status. This approach claims that the success of *Shas* party derives from its traditional religious perception of Israeli identity, that in the context of Israel's tri-layered status system (Palestinians, Orientals, Ashkenazim) ensures the Orientals a place above the Palestinians and a platform to challenge Ashkenazi hegemony. (Shalev and Levi 2005, 124)

We have to stress that the electoral trends we enlist do not entail that the Right has a socioeconomic policy that benefits the lower classes or that voting correlates with social and economic policies; quite the contrary. Rather, the socioeconomic situation translates into political attitudes through mechanisms that were variously called "politics of status" (Shapiro 1991) or "neo-populism" (Filc 2006); that is, a politics of identity or a politics of communities, which empowers symbolically the lower classes and offers them a sense of belonging, together with targets of superiority mixed with contempt in the form of an "other," be it Arabs, the Left, or the elites. It is a historical irony that substantial parts of the lower classes channel their protest against Labour's elitism to a support of the right-wing block, which boasts "social sensitivity" although it is in fact fully—and enthusiastically—compliant in the dismantling of the state's social commitments and in channeling to the settlers in the occupied territories resources that could have assisted the Israeli periphery.

The change of priorities of the climbing middle classes and of the business elite from nationalism to capitalism found its foremost expression in the historic initiative of the Rabin–Peres government in 1993, which signed the Oslo Accords and recognized the Palestine Liberation Organization (Nitzan and Bichler 2002; Ben-Porat 2006; Shafir 1998).

The link between peace and prosperity (or peace and privatization, as phrased by Peled and Shafir [1996], the first scholars who offered a systematic analysis of this intermix) was expressed well in a "Peace Now" flyer published after the signature of the Oslo Accords, reading, "The seed of peace shall yield economic growth ... for you." The image on the flyer is of a flower cut from U.S. dollar bills. The flower represents locality and growth, whereas the dollar represents the world and wealth. The flyer goes on to explain, "Peace means no war which is a good enough reason to pursue it. But peace is also the first step on the way to economic growth."

The change in priorities of the Rabin–Peres government in 1993 can be interpreted, then, as a policy shift from national colonization to economic globalization. The conceptualization of the new agenda of decolonization in the sake of hyperglobalization was summed up by Shimon Peres's term "the New Middle-East." Peres charted a path of a free market regional cooperation combining neoliberalism and political constitutionalism. From this perspective national conflicts were a thing of the past, and the order of the future is a transborders economic dynamic, fueled by international investment and high-tech development (Peres 1995). Peres's rhetoric seems as if it were cut out of a common globalization textbook:

> National relations used to correlate to the physical dimensions of the world: land area, natural wealth, population size, and geographic location. The competition over these dimensions bred conflicts that often escalated to military ones. ... In the

late twentieth century national relations correlate mostly to life's qualitative dimensions: scientific development, knowledge base, level of education, applied technologies, stability attracting capital and good will. These make up power today putting the economy high above the military as a factor of national strength. (Peres 1995, 38)

The expectation of the Israeli political and economic elite was, then, that the peace process would promote a chain of structural changes in the Israeli economy and would bolster its growth. The assumptions were that diminishing the insecurity, instability, and risk would lead to the reduction of the defense burden and release resources for civil utilities, to the attraction of foreign investment, to the expansion of foreign commerce (with the lifting of the Arab boycott), to a cooperation among the countries in the region based on the relative advantages of each (which meant for Israel new markets for its products and access to cheap labor), to a significant increase in tourism, and to the turning of Israel into a regional center of business, finance, and technology. As summarized in a document published by the Ministry of Foreign Affairs, "The implementation of the political arrangement [the Oslo Accords] will bolster the trend of the strengthening of the trade and business services sectors in the Israeli economy, while possibly turning Israel into a regional strategic center for international companies in many fields, such as finance, communications and logistics. In addition, the Israeli economy's relative advantages in industry will be based on high-tech technology and human capital" (Ben-Tzruya 1993).

Despite this recognition of the economic advantages of the peace process, the factors failing it proved stronger than those promoting it. While the Oslo Accords were decomposing as the 1990s and later the 2000s progressed, successive governments aimed—in the face of surmounting difficulties—to "square the circle" and salvage at least the capitalist side of the Rabin–Peres breakthrough, without being committed to the decolonial flip side of it. As mentioned, Netanyahu is the personification of this contradictory trend. Despite recurrent setbacks and utmost failures in achieving decolonization, it is clear that in the view of the globalized middle classes and the elites of contemporary Israel, the continuation of the occupation of the Palestinian territories is perceived now as a liability.

Finally, the total collapse of the peace process, following the resurgence of the Right to government in Israel, in the wake of Rabin's assassination and the Second Palestinian Intifada, led the elite to reformulate its "profits and peace" project, only with the twist of aiming to preserve profits and bypassing peace. What started in the early 1990s under the Yitzhak Rabin (Labour) government as a peace process was ultimately continued in the early 2000s by the Ariel Sharon (Likud, later Kadima) government as the unilateral withdrawal program. The beginning of the implantation of this policy was the withdrawal of Israeli troops from the Gaza Strip (and portion of the north West Bank) in 2004. The aim in the beginning of the 2000s was the same as in the beginning of 1990s—the perfection of neoliberalism through a depletion of neocolonialism.

Three

Post-Fordization

In the economic sense, globalization is the drive of the capitalist system toward becoming a well-integrated, though internally diversified and unequal, planetary system. A new division of labor and a new allocation of goods take place, across and within nation-states, with a decreasing intervention and diminishing effect on the part of nation-state governments—with the exception of a few governments and a few policies that aim to facilitate this specific "free market" outcome. A new political economy thus emerges, in which the multiple nation-state political units correspond no more (or less than hitherto) to the single global economic unit. In this new global capitalism, the old liberal objective of separating politics and market obtains more than ever before. Whereas the public remains to a great extent a matter of the distinct national arenas, the market turns out to be thoroughly transnational. The economic is thus effectively secluded from the political, at least insofar as the political means a democratic, or publicly driven, intervention.

As Seyla Benhabib puts it, the result of neo-liberal globalization is "the formation of a world proletariat, participating in global markets but lacking a *demos*" (Benhabib 2004, 23). This new structure of relationships between market, state, and society sets the stage for one of the more conspicuous results of globalization—the rise in inequality and economic gaps between rich and poor, included and excluded, and winners and losers of globalization.

The globalization of capitalism is thus a matter not only of the spatial expansion of the market but also of the political contraction of states, or at the least of the social functions of states (in distinction from some functions of economic and security management). Because societies are still confined to national settings, the transnationalization of the market means that the market eludes society. That capitalism is in a position to venture a transition to a postnational mode of operation is due above all to the new information, communication, and transportation technologies, which are the carriers that transmit the flows of capital, labor, commodities, and information along the global networks (Castells 1996). Marx's famous dictum to the effect that "the windmill gives you society with the feudal lord; the steam mill, society with the industrial capitalist" (Marx 1847/1963) is pertinent here, where the computerized mill, so to speak, gives you post-Fordist global capitalism (Dyer-Witheford 1999). Advanced technology is indeed the medium that extracts human practices from their bounded national locations and relocates them in a virtual— but simultaneously real—global space. As technological speed shrinks territorial distance, time compresses space. David Harvey dubbed this process "time–space compression," and Anthony Giddens called it the "disembededness" of social interaction (Harvey 1989; Giddens 1990). In this new global high-tech capitalism, the vectors of social interaction seem to be transmuting from the quasi-Newtonian mechanical postulates of structure, hierarchy, and command, which are the conceptual counterparts of the territorial nation-state and Fordist capitalism, to the postulates of flexibility, complexity, and networking, which came to be the conceptual counterparts of transnational globalism and post-Fordist capitalism (Barney 2004; Jessop 2002; Urry 2003).

To the extent that capitalist economy becomes indeed transnational, a whole trail of social, political, and cultural consequences follows. This chapter analyzes the contours of the epochal transition of capitalism from its national to its global form, or from Fordism to post-Fordism, with a focus on one major outcome of this transition—the new pattern of wealth distribution, namely, the rise in inequality. A short presentation of this trend worldwide antecedes the analysis of the case of Israel, and both sections are followed by a theoretical account of the transition from the national-Fordist model of capitalism to the transnational post-Fordist one.

The claims made in this chapter are as follows: first, that globalization exacerbates economic inequality; second, that this is generated by the passage of capitalism from a state-centered and state-restricted (and socially moderated) mode of operation to a transnational mode of operation in which state (and largely politics) is circumvented; third, that neoliberalism is the doctrine that provides the intellectual justification and ideological legitimization to the transition from state capitalism to global capitalism; fourth, that this overall transition threatens to reverse the achievements of decades of equality struggles and the conditions that in the past enabled such struggles to take place within the nation-state framework; and fifth, that in fact it is not globalization as such that generates social disruption but rather the social complexion of it, namely, its being ruled "from above" by the megacorporations and their neoliberal political counterparts, whereas the checks and balances situated "from below"—by trade unions and social-democratic parties, for instance—are being severely hampered.

* * *

In the modern era, struggles for equality were encased in the tension between capitalism and democracy within the nation-state framework. Capitalist society is based on the principle of private ownership of property and, as a consequence, on economic and social inequality. Democratic society is based on the principle of common decision making and, therefore, on civil and political equality. As a result a society that is both capitalist and democratic functions on the basis of two divergent assumptions: inequality in the socioeconomic sphere and equality in the judicial–political sphere. In the concept of social citizenship as articulated by T.H. Marshall (1963), these principles are seen as historically consecutive and accumulative, but it seems that the contemporary tendency is for the decoupling of them. One clear result of this is, as mentioned, the growth of inequality, but yet another is the attempt of the victims of this process to rearray struggles for equality as struggles for identity or to prefer the politics of recognition over the politics of (re-) distribution.[1] This, because the politics of collective cultural rights is left as a last resource, after the politics of collective social rights (i.e., class rights) has been undermined because of the renewed distance and decreasing effect between states (and the democratic public sphere) and markets (on the question of the relationship between cultural and social rights, see Fraser and Honneth 2003; Banting and Kymlicka 2003).

Modern social history has been in no small part the history of the tensions between these principles and the attempts to reconcile them—the inequality of property and the equality of citizenship. The main means of struggle for those without property lay in the civil and political levels, through social movements, trade unions, and political parties. These struggles usually addressed the state, which was called on to exercise the authority invested in it, on behalf of its nation, by offsetting inequalities created in the market.

If we read, then, modern history through this political-equality–social-inequality prism, we can delineate the major regime types of the twentieth century in the following way. In the case of communist states, the former Soviet Union and its satellites, the state resolved the tension between capitalism and democracy by abolishing both. Property was nationalized, and under the pretext of social and economic equality, civil and political equality was demolished. The United States of America presents almost the total adverse, wherein both capitalism and democracy are accentuated, but under the pretext of civil and political equality (or rather freedom) only a modicum of commitment to redistribution is honored. In western and northern Europe, a model of a welfare state developed, which in Marshall's spirit retains some sort of functional and normative balance between the assumptions of civil and political equality and of economic and social inequality.

Hence, three major types of regimes have crystallized by the middle of the twentieth century in the economically developed world: a socialist totalitarian regime, which legitimizes itself by the promise of material equality; a democratic capitalist regime, which legitimizes itself by the promise of political equality; and a social-democratic regime, which attempts to deliver a great measure of both political equality and social equality. A fourth type of regime of right-wing totalitarianism emerged in Europe in between the world wars but was defeated in war. More moderate versions of right-wing authoritarianism appeared later in large parts of the third world (which were not under communist tutelage). All of these regime types were characterized by the centrality of the state in the regularization of national social relations and certainly in the administration of international affairs.

Whether one considers the state as a transmitter of social relations, as an arena of social relations, or as an actor in its own right, in all the twentieth-century regimes the state served as an axis of society. Yet globalization cracks this axis. It threatens to diminish the state's axial role in the social regime as a kind of judicial mediator between the economic market and civil society and thus the political and social arrangements that have been established between classes under the state's imperative (Held et al. 1999). The doctrine that serves as an intellectual gloss and policy guide to economic globalization is free market neoliberalism (Harvey 2005).

As a consequence, in contrast with the trend of socioeconomic equalization that evolved in the course of the twentieth century, mainly following World War II up until the 1970s, the trend prevailing since then is one of increasing social and economic inequality. Communist Party rule still exists in China, but it is combined with a swift turn toward competitive market economy. In Russia and eastern Europe this type of regime totally collapsed, and versions of parliamentarism combined with free marketism reign. The relatively equal and democratic regime in west and north Europe is severely challenged by the globalization of the labor markets and the markets of consumer goods. In the former third-world countries, it sometimes looks as if the choice is between an authoritarian state and a failed state, if not both. Thus two main forms of regime are predominant in the beginning of the twenty-first century: in economically developed societies exists the unequal and democratic regime type, which is embodied mainly by the United States, and in economically underdeveloped societies exists the unequal and nondemocratic regime type.

As for the U.S. type of regime, of political democracy combined with intensifying social inequality, a recent report titled *American Democracy in an Age of Rising Inequality* expresses concern about the future of democracy in the United States, stating, "Progress towards realizing American ideals of democracy may have stalled, and in some arenas reversed" because of the recent rise of income and wealth disparities (American Political Science Association 2004, 1). This should be regarded as an alarming note worldwide.

THE NEW INEQUALITY WORLDWIDE AND IN ISRAEL

In what follows we relate to inequality on the intranational level and on the international level. We present here the most basic quantitative indicator of inequality—inequality in the distribution of income.

A pertinent starting point for the deciphering of today's social trends is the United States. As it turns out, in 1968 the level of equality in the United States reached its twentieth-century peak. From then on the trend has been of a rising inequality with a steep rise in the past decades. In the period

Table 3.1 Division of Income between Households in the United States in 1964 through 1994 according to Quintiles, the Top 5 Percent, and the Gini Index

Year		Bottom	Second	Quintile Third	Fourth	Upper	Top 5 Percent	Gini Index
1964 (%)		5.1	12.0	17.7	24.0	41.2	15.9	0.361
	$	NA						
1974 (%)		5.5	12.0	17.5	24.0	41.0	15.5	0.355
	$	8,312	19,751	31,830	45,971	81,447	123,800	
1984 (%)		4.7	11.0	17.0	24.4	42.9	16.0	0.383
	$	7,996	19,313	32,005	48,189	88,608	133,757	
1994 (%)		4.2	10.0	15.7	23.3	46.9	20.1	0.426
	$	7,762	19,224	32,385	50,395	105,945	183,044	

Source: U.S. Census Bureau (2000).

Note: The Gini coefficient ranges from 0.0, which indicates total equality in income (when each household has the same income), to 1.0, which indicates total inequality (when one household has all the income). The second row shows each year's average yearly income in dollars (adapted to 1994).

from 1964 to 1994, the level of inequality in market income rose substantially, as shown in Table 3.1 ("market income" is the income gained in economic activity, as distinct from "disposable income," which is the income after state redistribution by means of taxation on one hand and allowances on the other hand).[2]

As shown in the table, the growing gap in the distribution of income is made up of a real decrease in the share of income incurring to the bottom quintiles (the two lowest), a relative decrease in share of income incurring to the middle quintiles (third and fourth), and an increase in the income incurring to the higher quintiles, and especially to the top 5 percent of income earners. Hence the Gini coefficient increases in this period from 0.361 to 0.426.[3]

The United States is the most outlier case of inequality and of inequality rise among the economically developed countries, yet it represents the general drift in the world at large. One more aspect of income inequality that ought to be highlighted is that it does not spread evenly in the populace as a whole. Categories of origins, gender, age, education, and others are represented differentially in the income slots. In the United States, for instance, some 42 percent of the white households are situated in the two top quintiles in contrast with 24 percent of the Hispanic and some 22 percent of the black ones; around 59 percent of the Hispanic households and more than 60 percent of the black households are situated in the lower two quintiles (U.S. Census Bureau 2000). In other words, the trend of inequality strikes harder in those categories of population that are not of European or of "white" origins. Needless to say, such a distribution "ladder of color" exists elsewhere in various variations.

However, these fundamental indexes of income distribution by quintiles and demographic categories do not reveal the full extent of the inequalization trend. For example, the income indexes do not compute the household's investment in labor for the given income. In the United States, although the income share of the middle and lower quintiles decreased, the number of annual work hours for which this income was received increased from 3,020 in 1979 to 3,335 in 1997—an increase of 10 percent (Faux and Mishel 2001, 102). In addition the conventional indexes of income do not take into consideration the laborer's level of production per work hour for which income is received. In the United States in the two decades between 1979 and 1998, the median wages per hour for a male employee decreased by 13 percent and the production per work hour increased by 22 percent (Faux and Mishel 2001, 102).

The American case demonstrates, even if excessively, the trend that characterizes the era as a whole: a rise in the inequality of distribution of income between individuals and households, when considered in strict statistical categories, and between labor and capital, when considered in broader relational sociological terms. This trend is taking place, with few exceptions, in the wealthy countries, in the poor ones, and in those in between. Of course the intensity of the trend is not identical all over the world. The rate of the increase in inequality differs in accordance with local social–historical circumstances and welfare policies, and those depend, in our view, on the balance of power among the classes (more on this later in the chapter). During the 1980s and the beginning of the 1990s, two broad patterns of inequality arose in the industrialized world: an Anglo-American and Australian pattern, with an early start (in the 1970s) and relatively intense slope, and a west European and Canadian pattern, with a relatively late start (in the 1980s) and a moderate slope. There is also a noticeable distinction between those countries that evince a state-initiated reduction in market-generated inequality (Canada, Israel, New Zealand, Finland) and those countries in which the market dictates more directly the final pattern of distribution (United States, Sweden, Australia, and others).[4] These data are displayed in Table 3.2.

Most evidence suggests that inequality is on the rise. A *Human Development Report* 2005 by the United Nations, concluded from data from seventy-three countries for which data are available that fifty-three countries, with more than 80 percent of the world's population, have seen inequality rise, whereas only

Table 3.2 Changes in Inequality (Based on the Gini Index) in Nineteen Industrialized Countries in the 1980s

Country	Economic Income	Disposable Income (after Benefits and Taxes)
Britain	++	+++
United States, Sweden	++	++
Australia, Denmark, New Zealand, Japan, Holland, Norway, Belgium	+	+
Canada, Israel, Germany	+	=
Finland	++	=
France, Portugal, Ireland	=	=
Spain	None	=
Italy	—	—

Source: United Nations (1999, 39).

Note: For an explanation of the Gini Index, see Table 3.1. The following is a key to the changes in the Gini coefficient: +++ indicates an increase of 30 percent or more; ++ indicates an increase of 16 percent to 29 percent; + indicates an increase of 5 percent to 10 percent; = indicates a change of −4 percent to +4 percent; and — indicates a decrease of 5 percent or more.

nine countries, with 4 percent of the world's populations), have seen it narrow (United Nations 2005, 55). The pattern of rising inequality is especially noticeable in the postcommunist countries and especially in China (Kaplinsky 2005, 41–43).[5]

So far we have surveyed the trend of inequality that obtains within states; let us now examine the trend of inequality on an international level. The simplest and most conventional index of comparison of the distribution of wealth internationally is that of gross domestic product per capita (the value of total economic production divided by the number of the populace). Table 3.3 presents the worldwide data for the last quarter of

Table 3.3 Gross Domestic Product per Capita in 1975 through 1997 (in 1987 US$)

Location	1975	1980	1985	1990	1997
The whole world	2,888	3,136	3,174	3,407	3,610
The industrialized countries	12,589	14,206	15,465	17,618	19,283
Eastern Europe and the Soviet Union	—	—	—	2,913	1,989
Developing countries	600	686	693	745	908
Less developed countries	287	282	276	277	245
Subequatorial Africa	671	661	550	542	518
Arab countries	2,327	2,914	2,252	1,842	—
East Asia	176	233	336	470	828
West Asia (without China)	1,729	2,397	3,210	4,809	7,018
Southeast Asia and the Pacific	481	616	673	849	1,183
Southern Asia	404	365	427	463	432
Southern Asia (without India)	857	662	768	709	327
Latin America and the Caribbean Islands	1,694	1,941	1,795	1,788	2,049

Source: United Nations (1999, 154, Table 6).

the twentieth century by categories of economic development of world regions.

The table shows clearly that in the period under discussion, the differences between the wealthy countries and the rest of the countries in the world increased (except for the new industrialized countries in Southeast Asia). Thus, for example, the ratio in gross production per capita between the industrialized countries and the developing countries remained around 1:21, the ratio between the industrialized countries and the less developed countries sprung from 1:44 to 1:79, and the ratio between the industrialized countries and the Latin American countries rose from 1:7.4 to 1:9.4. The exceptional case that stands out in this set of data is eastern Asia (without China). When compared to the industrialized countries, the ratio decreased from 1:7.3 to 1:2.7. At the end of the 1990s, the gross domestic product per capita was lower than in the previous decade in eighty countries; in other words, they were poorer in absolute terms, and not only relatively (United Nations 1999, 2). In addition, the gap in wealth between the top quintile and the bottom quintile in the world grew from thirty times more in 1960, to sixty times more in 1990, to seventy-four times more in 1997 (United Nations 1999, 3). The fortune of capital owned by the three wealthiest persons in the world is larger than the total national gross product of forty-eight underdeveloped countries, and the fortune owned by the two hundred wealthiest persons in the world amounts to more than the total income of 41 percent of the world's inhabitants (United Nations 1999, 36, 38).

And we have not yet accounted for the humane price of this data: some 840 million persons suffer from malnutrition, around 1.3 billion people live on less than $1 a day, and about 1.1 billion people have a life expectancy of fewer than 40 years (United Nations 1999, 36, 38, 28). This is only the tip of the iceberg of the suffering that poverty and inequality generate. As for the trend over time, according to the World Bank estimate shown in Table 3.4, between 1990 and 2001 the number of people living below the $1 per day level rose sharply in most parts of the world other than Asia. This trend is even more starkly evident when considering the number of people living below the $2 per day line (Kaplinsky 2005, 32–33).

Table 3.4 Poverty Rates and Number of Poor in 1990 and 2001 (World Bank Estimates)

	Poverty Rate: Percentage below $1.08/day and Number of Poor (1,000,000)		Poverty Rate: Percentage below $2.15/day and Number of Poor (1,000,000)	
	1990	2001	1990	2001
East Asia	29.6	15.6	69.9	47.7
(including China)	472	284	1,116	4868
China	33.0	16.6	72.6	46.7
	377	212	830	596
East Europe and	0.5	3.7	12.3	19.7
Central Asia	2	18	58	94
Latin America	11.3	9.5	28.4	24.5
	49	50	125	128
Middle East and	1.6	2.4	21.4	23.2
North Africa	6	7	51	70
South Asia	40.1	31.1	85.4	76.9
	462	428	958	1,059
Sub-Saharan Africa	44.6	46.5	75.0	76.3
	227	314	382	514
Total	27.9	21.3	61.6	52.8
	1,219	1,101	2,689	2,733

Source: Kaplinsky (2005, 32). Based on World Bank, http://www.developmentgoals.org/Poverty.htm#povertylevel.

Having established the trend of rising inequality worldwide in the last two decades of the twentieth century, let us now turn to the case of Israel, add some data to that provided in the previous chapters, and afterward present a structural account of this phenomenon.

Since the 1990s the Israeli economy has undergone an accelerated process of globalization (see Chapter 1). In Israel, as in

Table 3.5 The Distribution of Income among Households in Israel in 1990 and 2004 (in Percentages), and the Average Income for Household in Each Decile in 2004 (in NIS Current Prices)

Decile	1990	2004	Change 1990 to 2004	Average Household Income, 2004 (NIS Current Prices)
10th (top)	24.4	27.8	+3.4	37,864
9th	15.9	16.4	+0.4	22,280
8th	12.7	12.7	0	17,283
7th	10.7	10.4	−0.3	14,193
6th	9.2	8.7	−0.5	11,785
5th	7.8	7.3	−0.6	9,873
4th	6.6	6.0	−0.6	8,153
3rd	5.5	4.8	−0.7	6,549
2nd	4.4	3.7	−0.7	5,055
1st (bottom)	2.7	2.3	−0.4	3,127

Source: Swirski and Konnor-Atias (2005).

Note: Figures are based on average gross monthly income of household of waged employees. A tenth of percent deviations are the result of calculation methods.

other places, economic globalization has unequivocal social results: it widens the social gaps and it induces on one hand the formation of a business elite and wealthy professional strata and on the other hand the downfall of the lower social strata to a position of "underclass," steady underemployment, and sub-income (see Chapter 2). As shown in Table 3.5, between 1990 and 2004 the share of the two high-income deciles (deciles nine and ten) increased from 40.3 percent to 44.2 percent of the national income and the share of the eighth income decile remained stable, 12.7 percent, so altogether the share of the upper three deciles in the national income increased from 53 percent to 56.9 percent and the share of the rest of the seven deciles decreased in proportion.

Between 1979 and 2004 the Gini coefficient—the common statistical measure of income inequality—rose from 0.4318 to 0.5193 when measured before transfer payments and direct taxes, or from 0.3181 to 0.3752 when measured after transfer payments and direct taxes (Achdut 2006, 448, Table 23).

It must be emphasized that the conventional statistical data, such as the table we present here, do not tap into the whole measure of inequality. A significant part of the gap in income is not conveyed by the data. First, the data relate only to wage earnings and do not tap into the distribution of other types of income. In particular, the data do not include ownership of assets and various capital profits. Second, a significant portion of the income of the upper echelons of the wage earners is not tapped into because it accrues in the form of side benefits that do not appear directly in the paycheck.

Third, the data do not tap into a significant part of the low-income earners, those who are not official Israeli citizens, such as Palestinians and immigrant laborers (see Chapter 2). If all these omissions were compensated for, the measure of inequality would have been higher.

In Israel, as anywhere else, income gaps are not color-blind, and different categories of the populace sliced by nationality, ethnicity, or gender are represented nonproportionally in the deciles of income. According to the Adva Center's annual *Social Report*, in the 1990s (the data are for the years 1990 to 1999) the income from wages rose only among the Jews; among the Arabs and "others" it decreased. Along these lines the gap between these groups grew significantly. Among the Jews there was an increase in the income of both Mizrachim and Ashkenazim, so that the gap remained constant. In 1999 an Ashkenazi wage earner earned one and a half times more than a Mizrachi wage earner and twice as much as an Arab one (Swirski and Konnor-Atias 2001, 10). The gap between men's and women's incomes remained almost constant as well: in 1990 a woman's wages per hour stood at 79 percent of that of a man's, and in 1999 it stood at 81 percent (Swirski and Konnor-Atias 2001, 81).

The incidence of poverty in Israel, as calculated by the National Insurance Institute, is high and on a continuous increase. In 1989 the threshold of a third of the population below the poverty line was passed. Between 1979 and 2004 the incidence of poverty in all families (before transfer payments and direct taxes) increased from 27.9 percent to 33.4 percent (2,184,100 persons). The incidence is reduced by transfer payments (welfare allowances, etc.) and direct taxes to 17.2 percent and 20.5 percent (1,534,300 persons), respectively (Achdut 2006, 425, Table 1, and 447, Table 22). Poverty is not merely a result of unemployment: in 38 percent of the poor families there is one active wage earner (Achdut and Cohen 2001, 45).

Like the incidence of poverty, the incidence of wealth is also on the increase, but whereas the former tends to stretch at the bottom, the latter tends to cluster at the top. In 1994 the salary of directors of the one hundred largest companies on the Tel Aviv stock market was thirty times higher than the minimum salary and thirteen times higher than the average salary; in the year 2000 it was twenty times higher than the minimum salary and seventeen times higher than the average salary. This is without taking into account the option of shares in the value of NIS 10.5 million, on average, that constituted a part of these directors' remuneration packages (Swirski and Konnor-Atias 2001, 12).

The inequality that is created in the labor market in Israel— and measured by market income, that is, before the intervention of redistributive taxation and allowances—is comparable to the inequality in Latin America. Yet governmental redistributive mechanisms somewhat offset this tendency, so the gaps in the disposable income, that is, the income families or individuals have at their disposal, become somewhat more moderate and approach west European standards (Dahan 2001, 20–24).[6]

In consideration of this, the state is presented in its role of offsetting the inequalities that the market produces. Yet states designate markets, and in this role they often contribute to the growth of inequality rather than to its decline. They might contribute to it in a passive way by avoiding redistributive policies but also in an active way by implementing policies that either decrease the benefits of wage earners or increase the profits of businesses. The governments in Israel have in the recent two decades reduced consistently and substantially the taxes levied on corporations and employers.[7]

NATIONAL CAPITALISM AND FORDISM

We have established, thus, that the end of the twentieth century and the beginning of the twenty-first century is an era characterized by extreme inequality and exacerbating inequality both within and between states. This tendency contravenes the wisdom of the neoliberal economic doctrine, according to which in the free market a gradual leveling of prices (including the price of labor) is expected, and the wisdom of the sociological modernization doctrine, according to which nonmodern societies are expected to follow the stages of development of the modernized societies up to the leveling of social conditions. So why is it that the common phenomenon among classes and between countries is, in fact, divergence rather than convergence, as the previously mentioned theories assume? Why is it that the tendency for income equalization that characterized the twentieth century, and certainly its third quarter, has reversed since the last quarter of the twentieth century? And most of all, how does the phenomenon of rising inequality relate to globalization?

There are two main approaches to these questions: one, pushed by the World Bank and other global institutions, regards poverty and rising inequality in the globalizing economy as *residual*. By this view these phenomena result from the lack of sufficient integration into the global market and its rules. A contrasting view considers poverty and rising inequality in the globalizing economy as *relational*. By this view, pressed by activists and academics critical of globalization, these phenomena result from an excessive integration to the global market and its rules (Kaplinsky 2005, 47–48). In what follows we wish to offer a structural and class-based account of the relational perspective of poverty and inequality.

We maintain that the rise in income inequality heeds the growth of power inequality. What is changing fundamentally in the era of globalization is the balance of power within the triangular relationships made by capitalists, wage earners, and the state, which has evolved throughout the twentieth century (with notable ups and downs) and which was consolidated in the post–World War II era (albeit with distinct variability). This change in the balance of power is a major dimension of the transition of capitalism from the national and Fordist framework to the global, transnational, and post-Fordist framework. In this passage the power of one vertex of the triangle—capital—increases on account of the other two, labor and the state. The new inequality results, then, from the renewed power of capital vis-à-vis labor, with the state receding to the background.

The trend of relative equalization in the distribution of wealth that established itself by the mid-1970s reflected the balance of power among the social forces that developed in the course of the century and reached a peak after World War II. In the developed countries a triangle of relations was formed, the vertices of which were capital, labor, and state. By and large, organized labor compelled capital to reach a social pact, with the state acting as initiator, mediator, and supervisor. Two threats that became imminent during the second and third decades of the twentieth century historically played a role in the softening of capital: the threat of communist attraction (as manifested by the 1917 revolution) and the threat of economic crisis (as manifested by the 1929 economic crash). World War II (1939–45) played a great facilitating role in the development of class compromise and welfare societies. This triangular deal proved convenient to all parties, promising the "steering of capitalism" in a manner more stable and enduring (on this, see Offe 1984). It provided employers with industrial peace, employees with improved work and benefit packages, and the state with an expanded fountain of financial means and popular support. All this enhanced its role as the guarantor of economic infrastructures and the provider of social welfare, as well as the holder of the supreme monopoly over the means of coercion and violence (Tilly 1993).

Just as the state constituted the primary framework for the workings of society during the twentieth century, so the industrial corporation constituted the primary framework of economic production. In its essence it was a hierarchical bureaucratic organization, producing standard products by way of repetitive work tasks in an assembly line. It enabled its employees to lead a middle-class, familial-consumerist mode of life, or at least to aspire to it. This overall social-productive system was termed *Fordism*, taken after the system designated by the famous American car manufacturer Henry Ford, on the eve of World War I (Jessop 1994a, 1994b, 2002).

The term *Fordism* is closely linked to several other terms, which highlight various aspects of this regime. *Corporatism* (mainly in northwestern Europe and Japan) was the aspect of the triangular bargain of production–employment–welfare that was maintained among employer federations, trade unions, and the state (Schmitter and Lehmburch 1979). *Keynesianism* (named after the economist John Maynard Keynes) was the aspect of the state's macroeconomic, anticyclical interventionism, namely, the initiation of employment in times of depression by means of deficient budgetary transfer (Keynes 1936/1997). The *welfare state* appellation denotes the aspect of general social commitment undertaken by the state in the form of a welfare net, as well as universal services such as subsidized housing, health, and education (Pierson 2006; Esping-Andersen 1990, 1996). Part of the secret of economic growth under Fordism was the *military–industrial complex* at its core (Kurt 1999). An additional side of Fordism was *social democracy* as the dominant ideology of social responsibility and of the state's interventionism in the economy, an ideology that was supported by the important political parties of that period (Allen 1996). Finally, on the international level Fordism was sustained by a stable trade and currency framework based on the Bretton-Wood agreement and supported by the United States.

In many postcolonial countries a nondemocratic version of quasi-Fordism developed simultaneously, in the framework of which bureaucratic–authoritarian governments or, in other cases, socialist–nationalist governments—as in Israel's case—undertook the guidance of industrial and social development by means of import-substitution industrialization and social reforms (O'Donnell 1979). In the Eastern Bloc, of course, communist regimes reigned, implementing their own centralist-bureaucratic version of social-economic developmentalism (which, beginning in the 1970s, atrophied at an accelerated rate). The Fordism that prevailed from the 1950s until the 1970s had two major pillars: economic growth and social (re-) distribution. When economic growth somewhat halted in the 1970s, capitalism began to get somewhat disorganized (Offe 1985) but also reorganized along new lines, a process that would lead to a change in the balance of social powers and to the deterioration of the social distribution (Lash and Urry 1987).

We already mentioned the triangular shape of Fordism; that is, its being founded on a pact among the three vertices of labor, capital, and the state. This model is portrayed graphically in Figure 3.1. Between each two vertices exist reciprocal relations; namely, each factor (vertex in the triangle) gains something and in return each one contributes something (in the figure these transactions are marked by the arrows). The Fordist formation is based, as said, on a compromise and a balance among the three major social components. For instance, capital provides labor with paid employment, labor

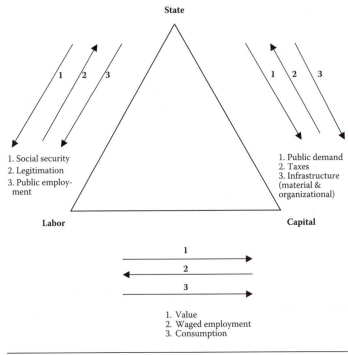

State

1. Social security
2. Legitimation
3. Public employ-
   ment

Labor

1. Public demand
2. Taxes
3. Infrastructure
   (material &
   organizational)

Capital

1
2
3

1. Value
2. Waged employment
3. Consumption

Figure 3.1 This figure shows the triangular model of Fordism.

produces added value (which is the source of capital's profit),
and some of the wages return to capital through the consum-
ing of products. The state provides labor with a social safety
net, and it is also a large source of employment; in return it
receives from the population the legitimacy that allows it to
act as a superior arbiter in capital–labor relations. The state
also provides capital with demand and infrastructures, and in
return it collects taxes from capital, taxes that in return constitute the source of its independent maintenance and the social
support that it provides. The core of Fordism is, therefore,

the reciprocity that exists in the relations between labor and capital, with the mediation of the state. This social regime has a double benefit: it allows the capitalist mechanisms of economic development to thrive, while at the same time it moderates the tribulations associated with capitalist unequal social distribution. This mutuality and balance is what is being lost nowadays under post-Fordist global capitalism.

GLOBAL CAPITALISM AND POST-FORDISM

In the post-Fordist social regime, which evolved in the course of the past two to three decades, the power of one of the vertices of the earlier Fordist triangle—that of capital—has been amplified substantially compared to the other two. This is what made possible the trend of renewed inequality that characterizes the period. The reinforced power of capital, the weakened power of organized labor, and the withdrawal of the state in post-Fordism were facilitated by two related factors: first, the development of information, communication, and transportation technologies, which contributed simultaneously to a more concerted and potent management control and to a more fragmented and dislocated labor force; and second, on the basis of the same material infrastructure, the development of transnational networks of material and symbolic transactions, the major component of globalization. These two conditions granted capital an accelerated mobility and enhanced versatility so that business activity can be monitored and manipulated from a distance and in instant time (Dicken 2003). With this enormously enhanced competence, capital spreads through a space of transnational flows and undermines the reach and efficacy of states and unions that are adapted to the space of places (Castells 1996; Riain 2000). Globalization thus pulls the rug of location, so to speak, out from under the feet of social states and organized labor (on the post-Fordization of Israel, see Filc and Ram 2004).

Just like the Fordist social model that preceded it, the post-Fordist social model is a multifaceted social regime (Lash and Urry 1987). A central aspect of this new regime of the accumulation of capital is the flexibility of the process of production and of labor relations. However, as against a common, mistaken perception, the significant implication of this flexibility is not the decentralization of economic control but rather its hypercentralization. Capital now acts in the form of network hubs instead of the vertical hierarchical solid firm, whereas labor is involved in a worldly expanse as a temporary, part-time, low-cost, and underorganized resource that may be hired and fired arbitrarily through subcontracting arrangements. In other words, corporate foci of control are discharged of their former territorial-cum-national long-term and binding relations with the waged employees and the social environment and adopt a "lean and mean" way of engagement (Harrison 1994; Panitch et al. 2000).

In terms of macroeconomics, post-Fordism is characterized by neoliberalism; that is, it fosters financial and commercial liberalization and deregulation of the economy and implementation of a restrained budgetary policy, whether under the banner of "neoconservatism" (Thatcher in the United Kingdom, Reagan in the United States, Kohl in Germany, Netanyahu in Israel) or under the banner of "new Labourism" (Blair in the United Kingdom, Clinton version in the United States, Barak in Israel). In terms of ideology, post-Fordism is characterized by the passage from modernist politics of redistribution and relative equalization to a postmodernist politics of identity and recognition; that is, from a universal politics of classes to a sectarian politics of ascriptive communities (which are legitimized by multiculturalist and postcolonialist discourses). In terms of politics, post-Fordism is characterized by the passage from interest group and party parliamentarism, which operates in conjunction with class associations, to media-fed and plebiscite populism and individualized massification, which dismantles the parties and unions of the collective struggles era. Baudrillard referred to this with his term the "fatal masses" (Baudrillard 1988) (these aspects are dealt with in other chapters of this book).

Returning now to the triangular model by which we depicted Fordism, we may depict post-Fordism in turn in the shape of an inverted triangle, which is adjacent to the base of the Fordist triangle, or "hanging" upside down beneath the Fordist triangle. This inverted triangle model of post-Fordism is depicted in Figure 3.2.

The inverted triangle is formed in the chart by the addition of a new vertex to the structure of social relations, made of information, communications, and transportation technologies. These technologies facilitate the circumvention of the state by capital in its ties with labor. In other words, capital can interact with labor while neutralizing the political factor or bypassing the state's authority. The new technologies thus release capital from the political limitations that organized labor used to cast upon it and thus disrupt the set of relations that existed within the territorial nation-state and the Fordist regime of accumulation. Hence, a kind of new polygon is formed, in which the mediating factor between capital and labor is moved from the political arena to the technological arena. This in fact is at the root of the depolitization of the economy, in the sense

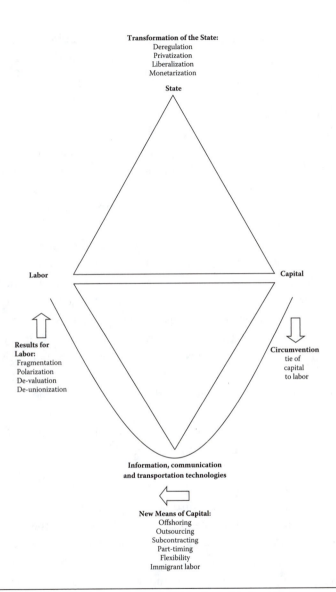

Figure 3.2 This figure shows the inverted triangular model of post-Fordism.

of adjoining capital and labor from distant locations, without their having a common binding political framework, while disjoining capital and labor, which persist within a common political framework (the nation-state). Labor is thus in fact disenfranchised. The old critical-sociology nightmare of the "management of things" taking the place of the communication among people—such as Marx's famous theory of fetishism of commodities or Habermas's concept of the colonization of lifeworlds by systems—acquires a compounded dimension when the "space of flows" bypasses the "space of places" (Castells 1996).

The state is also undergoing change. In the name of the doctrine of monetarization, it retreats from intervention in the economic cycle, which characterized the Keynesian policy. It opens its borders to free trade, a policy termed *liberalization;* it sells off public corporations and property, in a *privatization* scheme; and it reduces the direction and supervision of economic activity, a policy named *deregulation.* On the whole the state tends to withdraw from the wide social commitment of the welfare state. In the former third world as well, the developmental state project is being abandoned for the sake of integration into the global market under Washington Consensus terms of "restructuration" for competitiveness (Hoogvelt 2001; Sklair 2002).

This overall transition from the Fordist national welfare state to the post-Fordist global neoliberal state generated at the turn of the twenty-first century a kind of reversal to the social conditions present at the turn of the twentieth century. Capital is now able to dictate the new, truly flexible work and employment conditions instead of dealing with social pacts, economic regulation, social welfare, and collective bargaining. At the kernel of this new social state are transnational economic transactions, such as *divesting*, *outsourcing*, *offshoring*, *subcontracting*, and other transactions with the logic of cost cutting. The overall societal effect of the rush for cutthroat efficiency and competition has been termed a "race to the bottom," for which contemporary capitalism has gained the reputation of being "lean and mean" (Harrison 1994).

Finally, the following question emerges: why, despite this deterioration in its status and compensation, does labor not initiate a mass counteroffensive or even a counterdefensive? Labor docility is a result of the structural changes discussed previously. The transnationalization of the economy under post-Fordism generates an overall exhaustion of the conditions that constituted the basis for the workers' political and public organization in the Fordist era. First, the labor force undergoes horizontal *fragmentation* and *diversification* more than ever before, which is an upshot of the internationalization of the production process. Second, labor undergoes a vertical *polarization*, which distances its upper professional and technical sectors from its lower menial and disposable sections. Third, as a result of the inexhaustible labor-force supply on a world scale, manpower undergoes *devaluation*. Fourth, all of these conditions, along with the ideological and political power of capital, move to crush the workers' organizations and submerge the leftist parties in an overall *deunionization*. Fifth, and finally, with the hypertechnologization of production, management, and control, a *depolitization* of class relations takes place, as the state is circumvented and loses its centrality as an "addressee" for labor's grievances. The unequivocal result is the increase in gaps and in poverty. In the long run, this trend endangers the foundation of the democratic regime in the capitalist–industrialist society, the foundation of which is the balance of power between the classes (Fox-Piven 1991; Clark and Lipset 2001).

* * *

The process we just described of a transition from a national and Fordist model of capitalism to a transnational and post-Fordist model is orchestrated "from above" by a transnational capitalist class (TCC) of financiers, professionals, and managers. These actors implement the project of dismantling Fordism in the developed countries and its parallel developmental regimes in other parts of the world. This is worked out by international organizations such as the World Trade Organization, the World Bank, and the International Monetary Fund. The American government is obviously the prominent agent of globalization. These organizations compel various countries all over the world to follow plans for "structural adjustment" and "economic rationalization," which rake them into the open market, where they become prey for the transnational corporations (TNCs) (Ellwood 2001; Robinson and Harris 2000; Sklair 2000).

Thus the post-Fordist globalization that is dependent on information, communication, and transportation technologies and transnational corporations creates a new regime of division of labor and distribution of income, both within and between states, while it weakens the public sphere and crumbles the workers' active organizations (unions and parties) and leaves private capital as the sole potent social player. The unequivocal result is a new distribution of income that favors the power centers of the global system and their local agents. This, as we have demonstrated, takes place in Israel as in most other places.

Four

Americanization

One of the far-reaching consequences of globalization in Israel is the Americanization of its political culture. This means, first, that certain features of political life that not so long ago were identified as typically American are becoming the common way of doing politics or of thinking and talking about politics in Israel (like in many other countries). More substantially this means, second, that politics is in some sense depoliticized. By this is meant that public rational deliberation and selection among alternative programs are displaced by political practices that are less rational and that reduce alternative choices (if not, in some sense, utterly obviate them). By the Americanization of politics we thus mean, in Jürgen Habermas's terms, the decline of the (genuine) democratic public sphere—yet within the framework of (formally) democratic institutions (Habermas 1989).

Israeli political culture had been originally shaped, for better or worse, along the lines of its European legacy. It consisted of an amalgamation of east European authoritarian elements, such as strong and hierarchical political parties, as well as collectivist penchant, and west European liberal elements, such as individual rights and free universal elections. The Israeli political culture has been characterized by deep class and doctrine divisions and their explicit articulation and representation in party and parliamentary politics, as is common in European political culture. American political culture is substantially different. It has been usually characterized by more diffused ideological divisions and by its oscillation around the center of the ideological spectrum. The European pattern of politics may be identified as modern, whereas the American one, in its recent accentuation since the 1980s, may be identified as postmodern. This chapter thus offers an analysis and interpretation of the transformation of Israel's political culture from the modern European pattern to the postmodern American pattern.

In line with the overall thesis proposed in this book, in the sphere of political culture, as in other spheres, globalization is a two-pronged process, generating both McWorld commercial effects and Jihad communal effects. Two dimensions of the American postmodern political culture are thus of special interest to us: the communalization of politics, that is, its transformation from class-based divisions to community- and identity-based divisions, and the commercialization of politics, that is, its transformation from an orientation on ideology (as a comprehensive worldview) into an orientation on sporadic choices of "issues" (rendered into professionally packed messages). Both dimensions—the communal and the commercial—are intensely mediated by the mass media, especially the television. In Israel the transition from a modern, class-based, and ideology-party-based political culture into a postmodern, communal, and commercial-media-based political culture has been particularly swift, and we will illustrate it here along two points in time: the elections of 1996 and of 2006.

* * *

The 1990s signaled a third phase in the transformation of political culture in Israel. The first phase began in the 1930s and ended in 1977. This phase was characterized by the unilateral hegemony of one party in Israeli politics: the Labour movement, and in its core Mapai (*Mapai* is an acronym for "Party of the Workers of the Land of Israel"), a centralized bureaucratic socialist and nationalist party. The second phase began with the electoral upheaval (Mahapach) of 1977, which deposed Labour for the first time in the country's history from the governing role. The torch of national leadership was passed to the Likud Party, though not with the same hegemonic status (*Likud* is literally "integration"). Instead, a two-block contest between Left and Right was ushered, with regular advantage to the latter. In terms of political culture, the second phase signaled a transition not only from Left to Right, and from hegemony to contestation, but also from a politics led by a bureaucratic mass party to a politics led by a populist party headed by a charismatic leader (in this case, Menachem Begin; see Shapiro 1991). The third phase started in the 1990s, and in it the role of parties, as organizational and ideological political foci, has declined altogether. In their stead politics acquired the two-edged feature of postmodern Americanized politics: communalism and commercialism.

Several reforms in the political structure both represented the decline of parties and contributed to it. One such reform was the implementation of the method of primary elections of candidates in the major parties in the beginning of the 1990s. This method passes the nomination of party candidates from closed committees to rank-and-file members and thus eventually weakens the influence of the party apparatus. Yet the results of it are dubious. Although the intention was to decrease the clout of party oligarchies, at several instances authority was trusted to party centers (conventions), which consisted of a few hundred to a few thousand activists and became magnets for political as well as personal corruption. Attempts to overcome such fallout by passing primaries to the whole corpus of party members were also found questionable, since "membership" lost the loyalty and continuity that characterized it in the ideological parties era—members could now join just a short while before primaries and could be enrolled by "voter's contractors" to bias the results. Be that as it may—the standing and effectiveness of parties were far from enhanced by this system.[1]

Another consequential reform that was ushered in during the 1990s was the split of the vote to two separate ballots—one for the prime minister and one for the parliament. The reform of direct elections of prime minister represented a widespread sentiment in the public and elite circles that wished to curb the influence of parties and of party ideologies and to invest popular authority directly in the hands of the head of the executive branch. This has been a clear indicator of the drift of the political culture from parties to "personalities." The reform that was enacted in 1992 and implemented in the 1996, 1999, and 2001 elections created a dysfunctional "presi-parliamentary" system and was thus reversed in 2003. Yet the deep-seated changes in the political culture do prevail.

The decline of party politics reached full fruition in 2006, when the whole traditional party map was scrambled. Senior figures from the two historical rival parties Labour and Likud deserted their parties and joined hands in the establishment of the new party of Kadima, which won the elections and led the ruling coalition. The Kadima Party is the incarnation of the postparty politics in Israel. Its implicit, and sometimes explicit, message was as follows: enough with ideological divisions, enough with partisan divisions, enough with political parties—just choose for office the best political team.

The end of party ideology is vividly portrayed in the following journalistic descriptions of the election campaign of 1996. One article argues that it has become more and more difficult to discern a real difference between the two main parties:

The *Likud* will speak again on "The Peace" and Binyamin Netanyahu (*Likud*) will declare that "one must not despair of peace" and Shimon Peres (Labor) will continue with his repeated military excursions and will talk a lot on "the security" and on the "annihilation of terror." Both parties will proceed painting their posters with two colors—blue and white—and one might be confused between a party begging us not to loose hope on peace (the Labor party? no, the *Likud*) and the party which promises to annihilate the terror (the *Likud*? not at all, Labor). (Kim 1996a, B1)

Yet another article repeats the same impression:

We are in the midst of a drenched swamp in which the question is not who among the politicians tells the truth, but rather who among them cheats more competently. It is an awkward situation: precisely before "the most decisive elections," in which we are supposed to make a crucial choice between two antithetical alternatives—we are caught in a very intricate hide-and-seek game, in which the two political blocks, under the leadership of two tricksters, compete about which will camouflage itself better, will be swallowed in the background, or will be disguised as something else. ... [We approach the elections] like blind people who perceive something in the dark, something two pimps promise us is an elephant, while hinting that after the elections it will turn out to be a camel, who will be assembled by a committee with the participation of the religious-nationalist party. (Rosenblum 1996, B1)

Lest it be thought that we are discussing here a peculiar phenomena of a certain election campaign, another *Haaretz* columnist comes to our help with the following review:

All the election campaigns that have been conducted in Israel in the past decade [1995–2005] have been deceptive. Yitzhak Rabin misled the Israeli public (and himself) when he was elected in 1992 on the basis of "We're tired of corruption," without saying a word about Yasser Arafat, about the Palestine Liberation Organization, or about the Oslo plan. Benjamin Netanyahu knowingly misled the Israeli public when he was elected in 1996 on the basis of the promise to abide by the Oslo Accords, without saying a word about the fact that his real intention was to suffocate Oslo elegantly. Ehud Barak deliberately misled the Israeli public when he was elected in 1999 on behalf of the elderly woman lying in the hospital corridor (for lack of space), without saying a word about the partitioning of Jerusalem, about a withdrawal from the Jordan Valley, and about descending from the Golan Heights to the shores of Lake Kinneret. And Ariel Sharon misled the Israeli public in good faith when he was elected in 2003 after firmly opposing then Labor leader Amran Mitzna's plan (to evacuate Gush Katif and to take unilateral steps to separate from the Palestinians), and without saying a word about evacuating settlements, about a unilateral move and about a withdrawal from the Gaza Strip without receiving anything in return.

The deception was not a coincidence, nor was it localized. It was not the result of an accident or a mistake. To the contrary, the deception was systematic. It stemmed from the fact that while the worldview of Israel's elected leaders was right-wing or left-wing, the worldview of their electorate was and remains centrist. (Shavit 2005, B2)

Given such cumulative impressions, according to which democratic politics is definitely not about reasoned choice among clear alternative programs, we ponder in this chapter what it is about and how it is done.

MODERN AND POSTMODERN POLITICS

Political parties and social movements had been formulated and used to be functional in modern, industrial, national societies, where, with the decline of the medieval corporations and estates, they served to formulate new public interests (Duverger 1959; LaPalombara and Weiner 1966). In democratic societies parties and movements are major instruments of mediation between civil society and states. Since the second half of the nineteenth century and more so during the twentieth century, these were the frameworks that molded dispersed masses into consolidated publics, turned vague social interests into articulate programs, and enabled the wide, formerly disenfranchised population to actively participate in the shaping of its national life. Though the twentieth century witnessed how apparatuses of political parties became ruling oligarchies (Michels 1962) and instituted totalitarian regimes, one still does not have an example or a concept of modern democracy that can do without intermediary and structuring public associations such as political parties. The United States is exceptional among Western democracies in the marginality of parties to the political process (Wattenberg 1998; Rae 2006; Ware 2006). Yet nowadays that exception seems to have become a rule.

Although in Europe social movements and political parties have fulfilled an important role in the shaping of democratic regimes and policies, in the United States parties reached their zenith in the last third of the nineteenth century and later declined in importance, so much so that the twentieth century was labeled "the anti-party century" in the United States (Rae 2006). In the first half of the twentieth century, some party branches turned into corrupt patronage machines of local bosses, whereas in the second half of the century, special issue movements, think tanks, lobbies, and other cabals competed successfully with parties over the political space. As a student of American parties summarizes it, "By the last quarter of the 20th-century the American parties seemed to have become little more than the instruments of candidates or interest groups that captured the party label" (Rae 2006, 201). There are various reasons for the feeble state of political parties in the United States: the presidential regime form; the nonproportional system of representation; the federal system; regional, religious, and ethnic divisions; the Lockean liberal roots of American political culture; and the strong individual-istic ethos are the more salient of them (Ware 2006).[2] It is not in vain that the theory of the "end of ideology" was first pronounced in the United States and about the United States (Bell 1960).

There is agreement in the political science and political sociology literature that political parties do not perform a most vital role in American politics (McSweeney 1990; Rae 2006; Ware 2006). They do not command the loyalty of large publics, they do not enroll dues-paying membership, they are not supported by solid social bases, they do not operate exten-sive organizational or economic apparatuses, and they do not propagate holistic and distinctive ideologies. Even on more pragmatic grounds, U.S. parties are secondary to the political process: they do not train politicians or finance or run their electoral campaigns, and they do not affect in a systematic manner the policy formation of the ruling administration. It is assessed that by the 1960s the modern mass political parties practically disappeared in America and "candidates were able to develop an alternative to the party centered campaign—the candidate-centered campaign organization— that made the modern mass party collapse" (Aldrich 1995, 269). During campaign times American politics is conducted by teams of experts and professional advisors in the fields of public relations and communication, public opinion polling, marketing, and so forth, and in between campaigns politics is conducted by the executive branch and by the administra-tion, whereas party politicians play the role of commentators (Newman 1999).

Thus it is not a gross exaggeration to maintain that political parties are today marginal in U.S. politics. Political scientist William Crotty summarizes this succinctly:

> The new era has seen a weakening of party bonds, a seismic increase in the cost of politics, a polarization of the electorate, the growth of an independent vote, a rise in the importance of issue voting, and candidate-centered (as against party-centered campaigns … [the] actual influence [of the political party] over voters and office-holders has declined. (Crotty 2006, 30)

Certain factors enhanced the decline of political parties in the rest of the West, as well as in Israel, in the past two decades. One factor is the changed structure of stratification, and it mainly affects social-democratic parties, which are the exemplary mass parties (the Democratic Party in the United States). The transition from cohesive social cleavages, which are typical of industrial societies, to the fragmented cleavages, which are typical of postindustrial societies, erodes class solidarities that used to make up the backbone of Left-inclined political mass parties. A second factor, related to the first, exists in the cultural sphere. The transition from a materialist to a postmaterialist political culture abates the holistic world-views that parties used to convey and facilitates the transfer of politically minded activists to single-issue movements or even single-issue campaigns. A third, related factor contributing to the decline of political parties are the new technologies of mass communication and promotion, especially commercial television, which enable political candidates to approach vast numbers of potential voters directly and which thus make redundant the mediating functions of parties (branches, meetings, etc.). In addition, political parties tended to become bureaucratic and to alienate themselves from their own rank and file. To all these can be added the factor of the zeitgeist, the spirit of the current postcommunist age, in which the obsolescence of all ideologies, and the triumph of liberal capitalism, seems to make "old politics" pointless (Inglehart 1997; Fox-Piven 1991).

* * *

The new type of a McWorldist commercial politics and a Jihadist communal politics pervades today also Israeli politics. In Israel, as in the United States, political candidates tend not to present programs but rather to emit images, carefully packed and delivered by experts. Professional teams, public relation firms, and advertisement techniques are the main carriers of political campaigns. Candidates carefully monitor public opinion polls conducted by professional agencies (which compete on the accuracy of their predictions) and strategically tailor even their most minute wordings and gestures to directed market niches. Television has gained an almost total monopoly on election campaigns, to the degree that even actual public meetings are carefully staged by the detail so as to be transmittable by the media (entry of candidates at the beginning of national news broadcast time, short verbal messages, emphasis on colorful visuals—flags, balloons, doves, etc.).

Political analyst Orit Galili argues that in the 1990s a new brand of politicians emerged, the "new politicians," of whom Binyamin Netanyahu and Ehud Barak—respectively, Likud and Labour prime ministers in the 1990s—make conspicuous cases, together with Britain's Tony Blair, America's Bill Clinton, and a few others. These new politicians are geared more to the media messages and to opinion polls than to any fixed or comprehensive worldview (Galili-Zucker 2004). Communication analyst Yoram Peri maintains, likewise, that during the 1990s the mass media have acquired a new role in Israeli politics and turned it into what he labels "mediapolitics." In this era politicians zigzag continually to adjust their positions to oft-shifting whims of the media and the polls. In Peri's analysis Netanyahu is a major protagonist, and his politics is dubbed "Telepopulism." Netanyahu is compared in this regard to present-day populist politicians, such as Italy's Silvio Berlusconi and Argentina's Carlos Menem (Peri 2004).

Political analyst Dani Filc drew a distinction between two sorts of populisms in Israel. The first type is an "inclusive populism," one that ushers low social categories into the national political arena. This was the populism of Menachem Begin, the historical leader of the Likud during the 1970s and 1980s. The second type is an "exclusionary populism," one that mobilizes the same low social categories but without their genuine inclusion (politically and, moreover, economically). Furthermore, and as a compensatory mechanism, this inclusion is mainly propagated on the basis of the exclusion of other social categories—the Arabs, in the case of Israel. Netanyahu has promulgated such exclusionary populism since the 1990s. One slogan associated with him was "Netanyahu is good for the Jews," emphasizing the extreme ethno-nationalism of the Likud (Filc 2005). Netanyahu indeed stands out in the wider phenomenon that we analyze here as the Americanization of Israeli political culture. He in fact personifies the dialectical tension between McWorld and Jihad, as he is both an ardent promoter of free market in Israel and a zealot supporter of the nationalist-religious Jewish settlers in the occupied territories.

CONCEPTUALIZING THE AMERICANIZATION OF POLITICS

It is on the background of American exceptionalism of having a post-modern political culture *avant la lettre* that one should comprehend the evolution of that distinctively American theory of politics that identifies political election with commercial selection. In such a political market, providers and consumers attempt to maximize their political utility on the basis of straightforward cost-and-benefit considerations. Some fifty years ago, political scientist Anthony Downs turned this American political reality into a rational-choice theory of democracy. He defines a political party as "a loosely formed group of men who cooperate chiefly in an effort to get some of their number elected to office" (Downs 1957, 25). Needless to say, class and ideology are conspicuously absent from such a definition. In the American political-market model of Downs, in distinction from the European sociopolitical model, political parties have neither social class referents nor a programmatic worldview. They do not stand for, express, mobilize, or articulate any social group or social categories and do not represent a cohesive worldview. They are instead depicted as teams running for office by marketing themselves to a multitude of dispersed individuals. Democratic politics is bluntly rendered into market terms. The interest of the parties is ruling. Ruling is not done for something; something is done for ruling: "Political parties are not agents of specific social groups or classes; rather, they are autonomous teams seeking office *per se* and using group support to attain that end" (Downs 1957, 97). What is the meaning, in this model, of an electoral campaign? Downs determines that in cases such as the American two-party system (and this can be applied somewhat more vaguely to other "two-block" systems), electoral processes are nothing but regular marketing campaigns in which each party tries to persuade the voters (consumers) to cast (purchase) its own ballot (label).

Given that logic, the political campaign, like any commercial campaign, focuses on the potential voters located around the center of the ideological–political spectrum, the less decided ones, those who hesitate between the two alternatives, and even those moderates who prefer one of the parties but are not adamant about it. These voters are open to persuasion. The appropriate method of any one party to draw such potential "floating votes" to its own side is to blur as much as possible the distinctive positions of the party and to make it look like the other party as much as possible. In other words, Party A has to make an appeal neither to its "persuaded voters" nor to the "persuaded voters" of Party B. The same goes for Party B. What Party A ought to do is to convince the moderates of Party B that it is much like their own party, only Party A is a bit better, and to likewise convince the floaters that Party A is not far from Party B but is a bit better. Party B ought to do the same. The result of this protocol is that the parties start to look alike; they voluntarily lose their distinctiveness. In Downs's own words,

> Overlapping policies [are] a rational strategy in a two-party
> system. Therefore, in the middle of the scale where most voters
> are massed, each party scatters its policies on both sides of the
> mid point. It attempts to make each voter in this area feel that it

centered right at his position. Naturally, this causes an enormous overlapping of moderate policies. ... Clearly, both parties
are trying to be as ambiguous as possible about their actual
net position. ... Ambiguity thus increases the number of voters
to whom a party may appeal. This fact encourages parties in
a two-party system to be as equivocal as possible about their
stands on each controversial issue. (Downs 1957, 135–36)

"Political rationality," proceeds Downs, "leads parties in a
two-party system to becloud their policies in a fog of ambiguity" (Downs 1957, 136). In such a foggy situation, the voter's
decision is by and large affected by "foreign" considerations,
such as the personality of the candidate, family voting patterns,
historical or sentimental attachment to the party leaders, and so
forth. In Israel's elections one sees, for instance, the workings of
slogans and images as well as of talisman and oaths (especially
in cases of the populist religious parties such as Shas) as substitutes for party programs. It is at this point that modern rationality is turned into premodern and postmodern irrationality.
In a competitive, commercial, electoral framework, functional
rationality (utilitarian strategy) propels political parties to blur
their positions and lose their perspectives. For the voters such
mist thwarts rational choice, and elections become substantially
irrational. In the words of Downs, "We are forced to conclude
that rational behavior by political parties tends to discourage
rational behavior by voters" (Downs 1957, 136).

* * *

Otto Kirchheimer, a scholar associated with the Frankfurt
School, characterized a long time ago the Americanization of
European politics in terms closely resembling those of Downs's

theory, albeit from a different historical and normative perspective (Kirchheimer 1969). Kirchheimer drew a distinction among different types of political parties. What is relevant to our case is the transition from a "mass-integration party" to a "catch-all party." The supreme objective of the catch-all party, like the parties in Downs's theory, is to increase the number of its voters. For the sake of achieving this goal, the party has to engrave itself in the minds of a multitude of persons as a well-recognized object. The party's name, and perhaps its specific visual (and nowadays audiovisual) symbols, has the same function as a merchandise label offered in the standard commodities market. It has to be common enough to be liked by as many potential voters as possible yet be a bit distinctive to be identifiable and make a claim for distinction. In a consumptive-oriented society, parties appeal to the widest electoral denominators. Obviously parties tend to lose their social, ideological, and pragmatic identities, and they turn into standard commodities.

In such a state of affairs, there are many and various factors that intervene in the voters' choices, and in many cases the choice is quite random—the appearance and style of candidates, the impact of passing events, and even the timing of elections as related to holiday seasons or the weather on polling day. Kirchheimer maintains, just like Downs, that in such cases politics becomes basically irrational:

> The instrument, the catch-all party, cannot be much more rational than its nominal master, the individual voter. No longer subject to the discipline of the party of integration—or, as in the United States, never subject to this discipline—the voters may,

> by their shifting moods and their apathy, transform the sensi-
> tive instrument of the catch-all party into something too blunt
> to serve as a link with the functional power holders of society.
> (Kirchheimer 1969, 200)

When a party becomes a label or a logo, it loses its specificity and can no longer represent an idea or an interest but only market itself. It may well win office, but for what purpose? For Downs the office is the purpose. Kirchheimer is terribly worried about such politics. When there is no mediation between state and populace, when parties no longer perform this function, "we may yet come to regret the passing—even if it was inevitable—of the class-mass party and the denominational party, as we already regret the passing of other features in yesterday's stage of Western civilization," concludes Kirchheimer.

* * *

The perspective of Kirchheimer receives support and articulation in the work of another Frankfurt scholar, Jürgen Habermas. Habermas considers the democratic polity, and especially its public sphere, which is its core, a mediatory link between the private and governmental spheres, between individuals and states.

In principle the public sphere is the rostrum for the articulation of social and political opinions, which are considered an informed and rational dialogue or communication. Such a public sphere cannot subsist unless it is shielded as an autonomous sphere, unrestricted and undistorted by egoistic desire (such as private profit), coercive interest (such as state domination), or communal excitement (such as ethnic identity). It is entailed that when such desires, interests, or excitements intervene, the public sphere is colonized by considerations alien to its essence and distortional to its reasoned outcome. In such a situation parties cannot fulfill the democratic objectives, because commercial, administrative, and communalistic considerations are qualitatively different from civic, public ones. The former are dictated by instrumental rationality or, alternatively, by primordial irrationality, the latter by communicative rationality. So writes Habermas,

> In the manipulated public sphere an acclamation-prone mood comes to predominate, an opinion climate instead of a public opinion. Especially manipulative are the social psychologically calculated offers that appeal to unconscious inclinations and call forth predictable reactions without placing any obligation whatever on the very persons who in this fashion secure plebiscitary agreement. The appeals, controlled according to carefully investigated and experimentally tested "psychological parameters," must progressively lose their connection with political program statements, not to mention issue-related arguments, the more they are effective as symbols of identification. … Hence the presentation of the leader or the leader's team plays a central role; they too need to be packaged and displayed in a way that makes them marketable. (Habermas 1989, 217–18)

* * *

Having analyzed the new Americanized political culture from a modern-liberal perspective (Downs) and from a modern-critical perspective (Kirchheimer, Habermas), let us finally highlight the same kind of politics from a postmodern perspective. Especially relevant to our case is the point of view of Jean Baudrillard, whose key concept is simulacrum. The simulacrum is not an image of anything but rather a nothing in itself (see the analogous concept of George Ritzer [2003]). When one peels it layer by layer, one finds under this signifier not anything signified but rather another signifier. Postmodern cultural reality is nothing but a chain of simulations and simulations of simulations (Baudrillard 1988).

Baudrillard deals not with the ontological question of whether "reality really exists" (as many wrongly perceive) but rather with the sociological phenomenon that, in our Americanized society, the commercial audiovisual image is a major dimension of reality. Mass communication invents images and disseminates them. Consumers purchase symbolic products. A whole "political economy of signs" produces products, the value of which is their status distinction. America is the leading producer and exporter of what Benjamin Barber terms the "infotainment telesector": the "wedding of telecommunication technologies with information and entertainment software" (Barber 1995, 60). These technologies are directed to the soul and not only to the body: "Merchandising is as much about symbols as about goods and sells not life necessities but life's styles" (Barber 1995, 60). In Baudrillrad's view, "We live in the indefinite reproduction of ideals, of phantasms, of images, of dreams which are, from now on, behind us and that we must, nevertheless, reproduce in a sort of fatal indifference" (Baudrillard 1992, 21–22). Politics loses its meaning; there is only a simulation of politics—the commercialized political campaign. The Left-versus-Right struggle loses its meaning; there remains only one big Center.

The diagnosis of Baudrillard is congruous with that of Downs on one hand and Kirchheimer and Habermas on the other hand, with only a slight difference: for Downs the commodification of politics is rational; for Baudrillard it is fatal. Kirchheimer and Habermas propagate a return to critical rationality; Baudrillard sees not a solution but only a blurred doubling of an already simulated reality.

POSTPARTY POLITICS IN ISRAEL

The elections in Israel since the 1990s indeed have a Baudrillardian scent about them. The 1996 election campaign took place in special circumstances after one of the most traumatic events in Israel's political history: the assassination of Prime Minister Yitzhak Rabin of the Labour Party. The assassination had been the peak of an acrimonious wave of right-wing hate rhetoric and an almost street-war campaign waged by it against the government's rapprochement with the Palestinian Liberation Organization (PLO) and the signing of the Oslo Accord between Israel and the PLO in 1993. Rabin was accused of betrayal, and a death warrant was issued by settlement rabbis against him (*pulsa di-nura* is the Aramaic term used for it). Netanyahu, the Likud's candidate, personally participated in some of the most ferocious events that preceded the assassination: marching behind a black coffin representing the (desired) death of the peace process and speaking in demonstration up from a balcony in front of a picture of Rabin in a Nazi SS uniform, which was prominently displayed to the crowd. None of these brutish political realities were raised in the electoral campaign. The Labour under Shimon Peres opted for a reconciliation with the ultraright, the Jewish settlers, and the Likud rather than for a sharpening of the difference in politics, ideology, and political culture between it and the Right. In short time even the commemoration of Rabin had became a depoliticized national ritual, in which the person is memorized but the political causes of his violent death are obscured (Vinitzky-Seroussi 2002).

As said, the assassination of Rabin was connected directly to one of the crucial turning points in the country's history: the mutual recognition of Israel and the PLO, and the declared mutual commitment for a peace process, in which Israel would eventually relinquish most (if not all) Palestinian territories it holds from the 1967 war. Yet the sharp choice facing Israel was not presented clearly to the public by any of the (big) parties or candidates contending for the prime ministerial position. In a word, although expectation was for a very serious debate between two adversarial political and ideological positions—to continue or to discontinue the Oslo process (the withdrawal from the occupied territories, the recognition of the PLO, etc.)—the atmosphere of the 1996 elections was in fact most apolitical and placid—almost unrealistically so. The real issues and real differences of opinion were carefully swept under a commercial carpet made of images and jingles. The leading parties and candidates and their spokespeople all promised "peace and security"—a slogan any reasonable person would have opted for. The actual conditions and programs for attaining these desirable outcomes were of course absent from the political discourse.

The two big parties, Likud and Labour, have competed in blurring their plans. The Likud was the master of camouflage. Netanyahu had to close an initial gap of more than 15 percent between himself and the Labour candidate Shimon Peres. And close the gap he did. Finally he won the elections with a margin of 14,729 votes (out of 2,972,589 legible votes) (Weiss 1997). One method was to present an inverted mirror in front of Labour. Labour campaigned for "Peace and Security," and Likud campaigned for "Security and Peace." Labour posted banners with "Peace and Security," and Likud posted the same banners, only adding "Netanyahu," namely, "Netanyahu: Peace and Security." A newspaper report exposed the genealogy of this slogan: "This is how the election slogan of Bibi [Binyamin Netanyahu] was created: First, the words 'peace' and 'security' were selected. In the second stage, they tried to compose a succinct and poignant sentence. After difficult dilemmas, the publicists came up with the punch-line: 'Netanyahu; Making a Secure Peace.' After long deliberations, tough dilemmas, and exhaustive research, the Likud exposed the elections slogan" (Barzel 1996, 10). Another newspaper report exposed the methodological concept behind the repetitive screening of Likud's video clips: "Each scene in the Likud election clips includes implicit messages, direct or indirect. The fast pace intends to catch the eye of the beholder. The repetition of messages intends to internalize them. The Likud headquarters intends to broadcast parts of the clips even twenty times over. Not for lack of material. This is the language of commercial advertisement reproduced to the use of politicians" (Barzel 1996, 10). In an almost direct allusion to Downs's theory, Arthur Finkelstien, Netanyahu's American top campaign advisor, "dictated a negative, focused, repetitive campaign. He advised that all attention would be given to the target audience only. The hard core of the Likud would show up anyhow. Only a few clips should be produced, and transmitted repeatedly. The audience is dumb. If you hit it again and again, it gets the message" (Barnea 1996, 6).

Yet another insight from behind the scenes of the election campaign comes from Gari Dagon, a producer and photographer of Netanyahu's election portrait poster: "Bibi is a handsome man. He is very photogenic and looks much nicer in the photos than in real life. It has nothing to do with politics. The flag of Israel [in the background of Netanyahu] creates a strong reaction of sensuality, curiosity and empathy. Just like when one watches a good-looking woman on the beach. To me it is reminiscent of photos of James Dean or Marlon Brando. ... I believe that in such a tight electoral campaign it has an enormous weight" (cited in Azoulay 1996). On the role of ideology (i.e., "political principles") as guidelines for politicians, a political correspondent who followed Netanyahu closely commented, "The person [Netanyahu] is a smooth electoral machine. At least from the outside it looks as if there is no internal truth that guides him. He utilizes the ideological line toughly or softly, in response to public opinion polls, in order to create a public momentum which will advance him" (cited in Gvirtz 1996, 20).

The medium-sized parties were busy with rendering their political positions into campaign jingles: the religious-nationalist party (Mafdal) run a jingle about the Zionist "soul," and Meretz, a secular liberal party, purchased exclusive rights to a jingle based on a famous peace song (that was also sung at the end of the peace demonstration just before Rabin was shot). No party specifies its political program. One actor who was hired to appear in the campaign broadcastings of two main competing parties, Likud and Labour, expressed very well the (post-) political spirit of the age: "I don't care at all for whom I am recording. I relate to these two parties in the same manner I would have related to the jingles of Elite and Osem [two big commercial foodstuff providers]. I lease my voice net" (Adiram 1996, 7).

The across-the-board unity of minds over social and economic issues is yet another noticeable phenomenon of the Americanization of politics. A commentator spoke about "one big right" (where "right" meant neoliberalism) (Kim 1996b). Another commentator who scrutinized the economic orientations and policies of the two big parties mentioned, sarcastically, that the only difference was that of style: "An external reviewer who attempts to draw a line between the day on which the 'Shohat economy' [Labour minister of finance] ended and the 'Meridor economy' [Likud minister of finance] started will fail ... the same tune, the same performance. ... Well, there is one difference between the two. Shohat goes very well with bar-b-que meat ... Meridor goes very well with goose pate" (Plocker 1996).

So an evasion of the real issues, and the substitution of a political debate with audiovisual images and sound bites, became the order of the day.

The total blurring of party identities had been already exercised in the important elections for the Histadrut (Federation of Labour) in 1994, important because the old Labour establishment was deposed from power for the first time since the establishment of the Histadrut in 1920. The election was won by an alliance composed of the following factions, which form nothing but a postmodern hodgepodge: Mapam (historically a socialist-Zionist party), Ratz-Shinui (a liberal-Zionist party), and Shas (a party of Mizrachi religious fundamentalism), led by one of the conspicuous neoliberal leaders of Labour, Haim Ramon. The same kind of organized confusion was celebrated in the images that candidates projected in the general elections of 1996. One candidate for prime minister, Shimon Peres, was pictured in battle dress to resemble Rabin; the other candidate, Netanyahu, was pictured in a staged prime-minister's office (assembled in a television studio) to resemble a prime minister. Simulations of simulations; images of images; everybody was united in an official condemnation of Rabin's assassination, but everybody carefully evaded the question of the political causes and public responsibility for it or the political conclusions from it. Everyone demonstrated their deep willingness for a dialogue with the other side, for which the Left readily blurred its own identity, and the Right hid its own.

Only in some small, enclosed, and extreme enclaves was the campaign carried out in confrontational Jihadist manner rather than in reconciliatory McWorldist terms. One case in point are the ultra-Orthodox neighborhoods of Jerusalem, where the walls were covered with "plasters" describing the vote for Netanyahu as a religious injunction—"remember Amalek" the walls cried, memorizing an archaic nemesis. A picture of the pious Rabbi Kaduri and the candidate Netanyahu was presented. The blessing of Kaduri, previously promised to Shas voters, was now endowed to Netanyahu voters as well (Barnea 1996).

* * *

Benjamin Barber warns that the blend of McWorld and Jihad jeopardizes democratic culture, especially the institution of the public sphere where citizens can communicate and deliberate policies: "More than anything else, what has been lost in the clash of Jihad and McWorld has been the idea of the public as something more than a random collection of consumers or an aggregation of special political interests or product of identity politics" (Barber 1995, 286). And he proceeds to explain the distinction between the concept of the democratic public on one hand and the concepts of premodern faith politics and postmodern consumption politics on the other hand:

> The voice of civil society, of citizens in deliberative conversation, challenges the exclusivity and irrationality of Jihad clamor but is equally antithetical to the claims of McWorld's private markets to represent some aggregative public good. Neither Jihad nor McWorld grasps the meaning of "public," and the idea of the public realized offers a powerful remedy to the privatizing and de-democratizing effects of aggressive tribes and aggressive markets. (Barber 1995, 287)

It seems that in the new political culture that emerged in Israel in the 1990s, it becomes more and more difficult to refer to a public that can withstand the social devastation of post-Fordism and the cultural desolation of premodernity that is formed by the dialectical intersection of globalization and localization. It appears that in Israeli politics in the era of globalization, the democratic public sphere can barely survive under the twin pressure of McWorld and Jihad.

That this is so was cast into stark relief in the elections of 2006. These elections were carried out explicitly in the spirit of post-ideology. The common sense was that all past ideologies and distinctions—especially the Likud–Labour and the Right–Left ones—had been exhausted and expired, and what was called for was a nonideological pragmatic politics. The new party of Kadima carried the day. A senior politician of the new party expressed very succinctly its meaning when stating, "We cut ourselves off from all kinds of ideologies. This is the distinction of *Kadima*. Seated here are former members of the Labor Party, of the *Likud* Party and non-affiliated members. We do not carry on our backs anymore kitbags filled with the heritage of [Zeev] Jabotinsky [founder of the right-wing opposition to Labour in prestate Israel] or of Berl Katzanelson [founder of the Labour movement in prestate Israel]. We face only the future" (Rabad 2006).

Both Likud and Labour suffered blows from the new party of Kadima (literally, "forward"). Kadima was created by Prime Minister Ariel Sharon of the Likud and a little later listed also the most senior living politician of Labour, Shimon Peres. It enrolled leading figures from the Left and Right, who now swore to the Center—again with fuzzy promises of peace and security. Kadima swayed about one-third of the voters from each of the two big parties, as well as most of the voters from the former Shinui Center party (that disintegrated just before the elections because of internal power rivalries and corruption scandals). Kadima, headed by Ehud Olmert, a former deputy of Ariel Sharon who won his seat by default when Sharon was hospitalized a short while before the elections, emerged from the elections as the new axis of the government. Only weeks after the new peace coalition of Kadima and Labour took place, the peace and security chatter was shattered by the new Lebanon war of 2006. If this war was premeditated, it was not reported to the electorate; if it was not premeditated, it exposes the big void behind the barren "peace and security" post-ideological rhetoric of Israel's postpolitical politics. Either way, it seems that the postideological electoral politics of Israel since the 1990s fails to articulate the politics required for the actual attainment of peace and security. The Americanization of politics thus depoliticizes a polity badly in need of politics.

Five

McDonaldization

The previous chapter addressed the implications of globalization on Israeli political culture, and on its center stage was the concept of Americanization. This chapter addresses the implications of globalization on Israeli popular everyday culture, and on its center stage is the concept of McDonaldization. The enveloping question we inquire about here is whether globalization leads to universal cultural uniformity or whether it leaves room for particular habits and cultural diversity. Among social scientists, the global–local encounter has spawned a continuous polemic between "homogenizers," who believe that globalization generates a worldwide universalization of culture, and "heterogenizers," who believe that particular, local, or indigenous cultures survive or even thrive. Yet such dichotomous framing compels a flattened adjudication of what is in fact is a doubly layered outcome. Globalization has diverse effects: it homogenizes on the structural level (the McWorld effect), and it heterogenizes on the symbolic level (the Jihad effect). In this view global technological, organizational, and commercial flows do subsume and appropriate the local, or consume it, so to speak, yet this happens with no necessary abolition of local symbols, cultures, or habits. It is indeed the peculiarity of contemporary structural globalization that it not only enables but also can at points even encourage local symbolic idioms.

To establish this argument, at least as the case of Israel goes, this chapter analyzes the process of McDonaldization (Ritzer 1995) of Israeli culture. The McDonald's chain opened its first hamburger outlet in Israel in 1993. Since then it has been involved in a variety of symbolic encounters, two of which we will closely examine here: first, the encounter between McDonald's, as the epitome of global fast food, and the veteran local version of fast food, namely, the falafel, and second, the encounter between McDonald's, as a symbol of global-American consumer culture, and local national identity and ideology, as it evolved around the McDonald's branch located in the Golani Junction in northern Israel.[1] We argue that in both encounters local idioms have thrived but only on the symbolic level. On the structural level they have been subsumed, appropriated, or substituted by global social relationships.

The concept of McDonald's is considered here as a commodity in the Marxian sense; that is, a manufactured object embodying social and cultural relations (Marx 1967, 71–83). Like Rick Fantasia, a student of fast food in France, we argue here that fast food has "less to do with food than ... with the cultural representations of Americanism embodied within it" (Fantasia 1995, 229). Thus behind the McDonald's commodity one should look for the societal relations of production and consumption.

MCDONALD'S AND POPULAR CULTURE

The industrialized hamburger first arrived on Israel's shores back in the late 1960s, although at the time it did not see much success. In 1972 Burger Ranch opened a local hamburger joint that expanded into a chain only in the 1980s. It took the launching of a local McDonald's franchise, however, for the "great gluttony" of the fast hamburger to begin. McDonald's opened its first branch in Israel in October 1993. Burger King, at the time the world's second-largest hamburger chain, opened in 1994.[2] Between McDonald's arrival and the year 2000, sales in the hamburger industry soared by 600 percent. By the year 2000 annual revenues from fast-food chains in Israel reached NIS 1 billion (about $200 million according to the 2002 exchange rate) (Barabash 2000).[3] McDonald's is the leading chain in the industry, with 50 percent of the sales, followed by Burger Ranch with 32 percent, and Burger King with 18 percent. In 2002 the three chains had a total of 250 branches in place: McDonald's had 100, Burger Ranch had 94, and Burger King had 56 (Tzoreff 2003).[4]

McDonald's, like Coca-Cola (which reached Israel in 1967)—both flagship American brands—conquered frontline positions in the war over the Israeli consumer. The same is true of many other American styles and brands, such as jeans, T-shirts, and Nike and Reebok footwear, and megastores, such as Home Center, Office Depot, Super-Pharm, and so on.[5] Apart from the spread of fast-food chains, other Americanisms have found a growing niche in the Israeli kitchen: frozen TV dinners and fast-food deliveries (Barabash 2000). These developments stem from changes in the familial lifestyle: the increased employment of women outside the household (close to 50 percent of women), the growth of singles households (close to 6.5 percent of families), and the rise in families' income. All this, along with accelerated economic activity, has raised the demand for fast or easy-to-prepare foods. As has happened elsewhere, technological advancements and business interests have set the stage for changes in Israeli eating habits. Another typical development has been the mirror process that accompanies the expansion of standardized fast foods, namely, the proliferation of particular cuisines and ethnic foods as evinced by the sprouting of restaurants that cater to the culinary curiosity and open purses of a new yuppie class in the larger Tel Aviv area.

As in other countries, the arrival of McDonald's in Israel raised concerns about the survival of the local national culture. A common complaint against McDonald's is that it impinges on local cultures, as manifested primarily in the local eating habitus, both actual and symbolic.[6] If Israel ever had a distinct national equivalent to fast food, it was unquestionably the falafel—fried chickpea balls served in a pocket of pita bread with vegetable salad and tahini (sesame) sauce (Chen 1998a). The falafel, a Mediterranean delicacy of Egyptian origin, was adopted in Israel as its national food. Although in the 1930s and 1940s the falafel was primarily eaten by the young and impecunious, in the 1950s and 1960s a family visit to the falafel stand for a hot, fast bite became common practice, much like the visit paid nowadays to McDonald's. The falafel even became an Israeli tourist symbol and served as a national dish at formal receptions of the Ministry of Foreign Affairs (Zach 2000, D1). Indeed one kiosk in Tel Aviv advertises itself as a "mighty falafel for a mighty people."

Despite the falafel's fall from glory in the 1970s and 1980s vis-à-vis other fast foods, such as shawarma (lamb or turkey bits in pita bread), pizza, and hamburgers, and notwithstanding the unwholesome reputation it developed, an estimated 1,200 falafel eateries have continued to operate in Israel. Altogether they dish up about two hundred thousand portions a day to the 62 percent of Israelis who are self-confessed falafel eaters. The annual industry turnover is some NIS 600 million ($120 million)— not that far short of the hamburger industry (Kotan 2000; Zach 2000). Thus it is surprising enough that McDonald's presence, or rather the general McDonaldization of Israeli food habits, led to the falafel's renaissance rather than to its demise.

The falafel's comeback, vintage 2000, materialized in two forms: gourmet falafel and fast-food falafel. The clean, refined, gourmet Tel Avivian specimen targeted mainly yuppies and was launched in 1999 in a prestigious outlet located in the financial district, which is swiftly being gentrified. It was branded "the Falafel Queens"—a hip, ironic feminist version of the many "Falafel King" outlets, perhaps the most popular designation for Israeli falafel joints, which always take the masculine form. The new, "improved," gourmet model comes in a variety of flavors. The Queens offered, apart from the traditional brown variety, an original red falafel, based on roasted peppers, and a green falafel, based on olive paste. Unlike the usual offer of soft drinks, here beverages came in exotic mixes, including orange Campari and grapefruit-arrack ice. Owner Ella Shein rightly noted that the falafel's revival reflects a composite global–local trend:

> We have opened up to the world culinary speaking, we have been exposed to new raw materials, new techniques, a process that occurs simultaneously with a kind of return to one's origins, to one's roots. (Kotan 2000, 9-10)

Apart from its "gourmetization," the falafel has simultaneously undergone McDonaldized standardization. The Israeli franchise of Domino's Pizza inaugurated a new Falafels chain, setting itself a nationwide target of sixty branches. Its reported intention was to "take the tidings of Israeli fast food abroad" (Kotan 2000, 9–10) (by now this initiative has faltered). The falafel has thus been rescued from its historical parochialism and was upgraded to a world standard bearer of Israeli fast food, or, as one observer put it, it has been transformed from "grub" into "brand" (Zach 2000, D1). Another falafel chain, by the name of Maoz (Hebrew for "fortification"), which reportedly operates twelve falafel eateries in Amsterdam, Paris, and Barcelona, has also tried an Israel venture. The new chains have developed a concept of "clean, fresh, and healthy," with global outcomes in mind, because "if you are handed an inferior product at 'Maoz' in Amsterdam, you won't set foot in the Paris branch" either. In contrast to the traditional falafel stand, which faces the pavement and absorbs street fumes and filth, the new falafel was planned to be served indoors, at spruce, air-conditioned outlets, where portions are wrapped in designer bags and sauces flow out of stylized fountains (Kotan 2000). At Falafels the balls were not molded manually but dispensed by a mechanical implement at the rate of eighty balls per minute. There were two falafel varieties—the Syrian Zafur and the Turkish Baladi. And as befits an industrial commodity, the new falafel had been engineered by food technicians and subjected to taste studies in focus groups (Zach 2000, D1).

Like any other post-Fordist commodity, the falafel of the new chains was conceived not only as a matter of matter but, as stated previously, as a matter of concept or, to be more precise, of fantasy, rendering the falafel's own past as nostalgia or retro (cf. Jameson 1991). Branches were designed in a nostalgic style, to evoke yearning within the target population, and they carried old-fashioned retro-styled soda pops. Thus was the local Israeli habitus dusted off, branded, and designed so as to be marketed as a mass standardized commodity. Against its old reputation as a greasy fast food, the new falafel was also linked to the new environmental and nutrition trends. The proprietor of Maoz noted that "salads, tahini, and falafel are healthy foods, and we have taken the health issue further by offering also whole-wheat pita bread. The health issue is becoming so central that we are now considering establishing a falafel branch that would serve only organic vegetables" (Kotan 2000, 9–10). To sum up, the distinction between the old falafel and the new, post-McDonald's falafel was identified in a local newspaper report as follows:

If in the past every Falafel King took pride in the unique taste of his own product, the secret of which was sometimes passed down from father to son, and which acquired a reputation that attracted customers from far and wide, in the new chains, the taste would always be the same. Uniqueness and authenticity would be lost for the sake of quality and free market rules. (Zach 2000, D1)

One major change in Israel's culinary habitus as a result of its McDonaldization, therefore, is the demise of the old, presumably authentic, falafel and the appearance of the new, commodified "falafel 2000." As we see in the previous description, falafel survived McDonald's and even revived as a direct result, but this on an expressive-symbolic level. On the structural–institutional level, falafel was reshaped by its encounter with McDonald's into a competing fast food on one hand and gourmet food on the other hand.

McDonald's had yet to surmount another—no less challenging—culinary hurdle: the Israeli carnivorous palate. The rise in the country's meat consumption is an indicator of its economic growth. Between 1960 and 1970 there was an almost 100 percent jump in meat consumption, the portion on the Israeli plate taking up an ever-growing share. In 1999 Israelis consumed on average more than twice the meat downed three decades earlier, an increase unmatched by any other food staple.[7] Given this hankering for meat, especially of the grilled variety, the McDonald's hamburger appeared rather puny, and the Israeli consumer tended to favor the competing Burger King broiled product. In 1998 McDonald's bowed to the Israeli appetite, changing both the preparation and size of its hamburger serving. It shifted to a combined technique of fire and charcoal and increased portion size by 25 percent. The Israeli customer now has the distinction of being served the largest hamburger—120 grams—marketed by McDonald's worldwide. But the most striking fast-food modification to the Israeli habitus is the *combina*, a slang Hebrew word for a tricky combination, launched in 2001 by Burger Ranch—a packaged meal for four eaters that taps into the local custom of sharing and, to quote the marketing blurb, allows for "a group experience while retaining individual dining expression" (Walla News 2001).[8] To even better fit the Israeli taste, McDonald's added later to its menu a McShwarma dish. In addition, in response to attacks in the media worldwide, in books such as *Fast Food Nation* (Schlosser 2000), and in movies such as *Super Size Me* (Spurlock 2004), the hamburger chains in Israel, as abroad, started to understand the consumption power of the new dietary consciousness and to make some practical and rhetorical strides in the direction of lower-calorie food, such as offering low-calorie salads or a grilled chicken sandwich on a whole-wheat roll (Rosenblum 2004).

We may conclude that the heterogenizers who argue that local idioms survive or revive are not entirely mistaken. It may even be the case that the global brand contributed somewhat to the renaissance of the local product. And yet the homogenizers would be correct to argue that in the process, the global tainted the nature and meaning of the local. The new falafel is a component of both a mass standardized consumer market on one hand and a postmodern consumer market niche on the other. This sort of relationship between McDonald's and the falafel, in which the global does not eliminate the local symbolically but rather modifies or appropriates it structurally, is typical of the global–local interrelations epitomized by McDonald's. So much emerges also in yet another encounter between McDonald's and Israeli culture, to which we turn next.

MCDONALD'S AND THE NATIONAL CULTURE

Golani Junction, a major intersection in northern Israel, named after a renowned infantry brigade, was the arena of another encounter between McDonald's and Israeli culture, this time in a direct collision with Israel's most sacred of sites—a memorial for fallen soldiers. It was felt by many that when American consumerism invaded such sites, it overextended itself. To anticipate the end, the Golani Brigade's reputation for toughness notwithstanding, it lost this one battle.[9] The junction was named in the wake of the Israeli war of independence in 1948, Golani having been the military unit in charge of combat in the area. Its casualties were memorialized by a temporary monument, which in the late 1950s was replaced with a permanent one. During the next couple of decades, it became the commemoration site for all Golani soldiers lost in battle, and a museum of the brigade's legacy was erected there. In December 1994 a McDonald's outlet opened its doors at Golani Junction, instantly raising a public outcry that the restaurant was diminishing the site.

What is the legacy of the Golani memorial site and museum, and why was the mere presence of a McDonald's branch perceived as a threat to it? The venue is part of a dense network of hundreds of memorial sites on various scales, scattered all over the country, the aim of which, like elsewhere, is twofold: to consecrate soldiers who died in battle and thereby motivate soldiers going into battle and to inscribe in "blood" the affiliation of the two arches of the nation—the "people" and the "land" (Mosse 1990; Almog 1991). The Golani site hosts annual memorials, inauguration parades for conscripts, and educational activities for soldiers, youth groups, and visitors from abroad.

McDonald's large golden "M" pole towering above the junction was perceived by some as belittling the site and indeed as the desecration of a national shrine. A father of a fallen soldier, and one of the leaders of the campaign against McDonald's, put it eloquently:

> Golani devotees regard the site as a place to commemorate and commune with the dead, on both the personal and collective levels, as well as a place to perpetuate the glorious combat legacy of the Golani unit for generations to come. … McDonald's

restaurant brims with tacky, flashy and vulgar American trappings incongruent with the nature of the site and offensive to our sensibilities, the sensibilities of Golani's retired and current soldiers, and some of the Israeli public. (D.Y. 1998, B6)

After the request by the Friends of the Golani Site to relocate the restaurant was turned down, the group demanded that its appearance be modified, focusing on downplaying "showy, American hallmarks," according to the same letter. For example, they asked that the golden "M" atop the tall pole be removed. This specific demand was granted; not only was the "M" removed but it was replaced with the oak-tree insignia of the Golani Brigade.[10]

The basic dissonance between Golani and McDonald's is described further by the bereaved father:

The encroachment by private business interests on public-national sites, such as the memorial site at Golani Junction, should sound an alert, especially at a time of concern about waning motivation for military service. We deem the coarse intrusion [of such interests] into the memorial site an assault on the fundamental national and social values fostered in the past and still fostered by the Golani brigade. ...The generation of our sons internalized a heroic legacy founded on commitment to and self-sacrifice for lofty causes. And what will the next generation inherit? McDonald's and cheeseburgers? (D.Y. 1998, B6)

But is the contrast between the global commodity and local patriotism as clear-cut as the Friends of Golani would have it?

A closer look at Golani Junction indicates that the seam between the sacred military ethos and the profane consumptive ethos is far hazier. For example, it transpires that the Golani weapons on exhibit, which include a tripod of rifles topped by an upside-down battle helmet, are American made—M16s, in fact. One may legitimately wonder whether the M16 is so categorically incompatible with McDonald's "M" or whether it is indeed even possible to cherish the former and disavow the latter. It seems plausible to assume that the kind of economic, strategic, and technological symbiosis that exists between Israel and the United States cannot be dissociated from the cultural makeup of the country at the receiving end—in this case, Israel. The attachment to America's material culture precludes the kind of rejection of America's symbolic culture that the bereaved parents attempted.

Furthermore, to the chagrin of the bereaved, the army actually invited McDonald's, as well as other fast-food chains, onto military bases. Soldiers are provided with magnetic cards crediting them with a daily meal of their choice from a food court. The convenience is aimed at discouraging them from wandering about street-side food stands or shopping malls just outside the bases, but it obviously dovetails the wholesale privatization policy spreading through Israel.[11]

This example of McDonaldization, however, was dressed in exalted social justification: officers declared that it alleviates the socioeconomic gaps evinced by the habit of soldiers from better-off families to circumvent the military kitchen and dine off base (Barzilai 2000). And so, in an ironic twist, the flagship of American capitalism was summoned to the rescue of the Israeli army's egalitarian ethos. Thus it seems that even when the "receiving culture" endeavors to resuscitate what is perceived as its own original social values, in the context of globalization, the practice is filtered through the medium of the "transmitting culture."

Under these circumstances, when the then-state-president Ezer Weizman—legendary combat pilot of yore and a successful businessman who imported cars from Southeast Asia to Israel—castigated McDonald's and the Americanization of Israeli society, his rhetoric rang hollow: "We must look to our own Jewish and Israeli identity," he proclaimed, "especially as we are being inundated with Americanism." The Israeli people, according to the president, were to be wary of three "M"s: McDonald's, Michael Jackson, and Madonna (Ma'ariv 1995, 5). His stance was echoed by several leaders from the national-religious sector. But Omri Pedan, McDonald's franchiser, aptly reminded the president that the Israel Air Force, which Weizman had helped found, does not reject American Phantoms and F-15 aircrafts, adding,

> McDonald's is one of the most positive meeting grounds between Israeli and American culture, a culture which boasts democracy, freedom, an enlightened constitution and, which, among other things, provided the world with such international brands as "Coca-Cola," "Levi's" and "McDonald's." (Ma'ariv 1995, 5)

The voice of McDonald's was in this case representing more authentically the attitudes of Israelis toward the United States. Although the image of America in the world in the beginning of the 2000s was tarnished, to say the least, Israelis continue to project a warm attitude toward it. In a poll taken in 2003,

Israel topped the list of twenty countries, with 79 percent of respondents holding a favorable view of the United States—higher than England (70 percent) and much higher than the rest of the list (Pew Research Center for the People and the Press 2003).

What is valid for France, as expounded by Fantasia's study of McDonaldization, is valid also for Israel: "Attempting to defend traditional cultural forms against 'cheap commercialism' while simultaneously encouraging 'market forces' as the only logical arbiter of human affairs is a losing game" (Fantasia 1995, 233).

There is an additional aspect to the Golani Junction affair. The land where Golani Junction is located is state-owned land, and, like many other lands in Israel, it was once in the possession of local Palestinian villagers. This history refuses to vanish altogether, and its buried traces occasionally surface. One such occasion was the opening of the McDonald's branch. When construction work began in 1994, Musalach Atir Aduyi, a Palestinian Israeli citizen, recalled that a portion of the land had been confiscated from him a decade earlier, on the pretext of "public interest"—a common official euphemism for a procedure of land confiscation from Arab citizens. To his surprise, some ten years later, public interest suddenly donned the guise of a McDonald's restaurant. The matter was brought to court, where Aduyi was compelled to part with his land in the name of "public needs." Land, once his, is now graced by a McDonald's branch and bedecked with the banner of the Golani Brigade.

The McDonaldization of Israel does, in fact, pertain to the larger land issue in Israel in the neoliberal phase. The shift from state to market, from national to private ownership, and from public to business management entails the "defrosting"—another euphemism—or privatization of land as well. Some of the recently built malls and other shopping centers edging highways are located on land formerly zoned for agriculture and leased to cooperative settlements with the goal of national capturing of the land and farming development. In the 1990s some of these lands turned into highly lucrative real estate for business developers. In a creeping process on the ground and in the law books, it became possible for asset holders—members of kibbutzim and cooperative settlements—to have the land they hold on lease rezoned for commercial use and even to acquire the title for it. This enabled the veteran Jewish elites, mostly associated with the Labour establishment, to preserve its landed assets even after there was no longer any justification for the historical, national, original leasehold.

A number of social advocates, including associations such as Adalla, an Israeli Arab legal association, HaKeshet Ha-Mizrachit, an Israeli Mizrachi protest movement, and other organizations concerned with human rights, equity, and environmentalism took legal and public action to retain public assets in the public domain or ensure a more equitable distribution (see Yiftachel and Kedar 2000, 85–94; Yona and Saporta 2000; Yiftachel 2006). In regard to other tracts of land, which have become commercial real estate sprouting malls, the process of change of title and confiscation that eventually facilitated, inter alia, the establishment of McDonald's branches has by now sunk into oblivion, covered by layers of cement and glitzy shrines of consumerism (for the case of the Dizengoff Mall in the midst of Tel Aviv, see Berger 1999).

The case of the McDonald's branch at Golani Junction, as we have seen, thus involved both small and big losers: in the territorial contest between Jewish and Palestinian nationalism over the piece of land on which McDonald's stands, Jewish nationalism won. But in the cultural contest between American consumerism and Jewish nationalism, American consumerism won: the local branch is one of the most thriving in Israel, serving throngs of soldiers, including Golani's own. The one concession made is symbolic—McDonald's was forced to remove its large "M" from atop the pole, and the Golani insignia replaced it.

The Golani affair once again points to the conclusion that the relations between the global and the local are neither only a one-way nor only a two-way street but a composite of two levels: the Friends of Golani won recognition at the symbolic level, but the "friends of McDonald's," so to speak, won the day at the structural level. Although the McDonald's banner lost its place atop the pole to Golani, the McDonald's system has infiltrated military bases and, literally, soldierly guts, as well as lands allocated for cooperative agriculture. The McDonald's logic, the logic of commercialization and rationalization, has pierced the tissue of Israeli society, whereas the perpetuation of the symbols of Israeli nationalism has become, perhaps, merely ritualistic.

ONE WAY OR TWO WAY?

On the basis of the case discussed previously, how, then, are we to conceive the relations between global commerce and local idioms? The literature on the global–local interface presents myriad cases. Analyzers of these cases part between those who assign more weight to globalization, which is regarded as fostering cultural uniformity or homogeneity, and those who assign more weight to localization, which is regarded as preserving cultural particularity, or cultural differences, or heterogeneity. The former group predicts the Americanization of the national and other cultures; the latter group predicts the resilience of local cultures and a variety of fusions between the global and the local. These two approaches have earned several appellations: homogenization is also labeled as *cultural imperialism*, *McDonaldization*, and *saturation* (see, respectively, Tomlinson 1991; Ritzer 1995; Hannertz 2000); heterogenization is also labeled as *Creolization*, *hybridization*, and *indigenization*, as well as *maturation* (see Hannertz 2000; Bhabha 1994). For the sake of simplicity, we shall call the former a "one-way" approach, that is, the effect is considered as emanating from the global to the local, and call the latter a "two-way" approach, that is, the effect is considered as an interchange between the global and the local. The question is ostensibly of empirical evidence, yet a theoretical elaboration must come first.

The most prominent exponent of the one-way approach is the aforementioned George Ritzer in his 1995 book *The McDonaldization of Society*. Ritzer, more than anyone else, is responsible for rendering the brand name McDonald's into a verb referring to an epochal process: McDonaldization. For Ritzer, globalization is sweeping and it generates unequivocal homogenization, based on technological efficiency or what Max Weber defined as instrumental rationalization. McDonald's is the epitome of modernity in its Weberian sense: "McDonald's and McDonaldization do not represent something new, but rather the culmination of a series of rationalization processes that had been occurring throughout the twentieth century" (Ritzer 1995, 31). The principles of McDonaldization are efficiency, calculability, predictability, and control. McDonaldization is analogous to previous manifestations of a similar tendency, such as Taylorism and Fordism, along with their standardization, routinization, deskilling, and homogenization of production and consumption (Ritzer 1995, 24–27). From this perspective McDonaldization is an advanced version of the prevalent rationalization of the lifeworld, a process destined to annul all sorts of communal, local, or premodern "nonsystem" cultures. It is not difficult to discern here the footprints of both liberal and Marxist critiques of modernization.

Implicit in this analytical approach to McDonaldization is a humanistic critique about the sacrifice of the unique, the personal, the communal, the spontaneous, and the free dimensions of human life. Ritzer's Weberian approach has been taken to task for what was perceived as an overemphasis on rationalization and a consequent lack of attention to both material commodification (a Marxian critique) and symbolic reification (a postmodern critique; see Kellner 1999). But all in all, whether McDonaldization is conceptualized primarily in Weberian (rationalization), Marxian (commodification), or Baudrillardian (consumerization) terms, it is perceived as an expression of overwhelming globalization that undermines local cultures.

It is surprising, or not, that the one-way approach has also another variant, a neoliberal version. It concurs with the former critical interpretation that the globalization of consumerist capitalism is historically all encompassing but considers the development to have democratic implications rather than being just a crass digression from local autonomy and authenticity. All societies aspire to reach this stage of development, which is thus rendered as "the end of history" (in the Hegelian sense of the abolition of negations). Francis Fukuyama, a major advocate of this view, argued that in the aftermath of the fall of the Berlin Wall there remains no other alternative. While Fukuyama outlined the pretentiously Hegelian historiosophical skeleton of democratic capitalism, Thomas Friedman provided a colorful account of its daily intricacies (Fukuyama 1992; Friedman 1999).

To recapitulate, the variously motivated, but analytically uniform, versions of the one-way approach to global–local relations hold that the proliferation and penetration of the global into the local generate cultural homogenization and the erosion of the locals' distinctive "difference." The literature offers another view that is contrary to this one-way approach to globalization and McDonaldization, which we call here the two-way approach. This view considers globalization only as a single vector in two-way traffic, the other vector being localization. Localization suspends, refines, or diffuses the intakes from globalization, so that traditional and local cultures do not dissolve; they rather ingest global flows and reshape them in the digestion.

Anthropologist Arjun Appadurai, for one, asserts that it is impossible to think of the processes of cultural globalization in terms of mechanical flows from center to periphery. Their complexity and disjuncture allow for a chaotic contest between the global and the local that is never resolved. In his view, "The central feature of global culture today is the politics of the mutual effort of sameness and difference to cannibalize one another and thus to proclaim their successful hijacking of the twin Enlightenment ideas of the triumphantly universal and the resiliently particular. ... Both sides of the coin of global cultural processes today are products of the infinitely varied mutual contest of sameness and difference on a stage characterized by radical disjunctures between different sorts of global flows and the uncertain landscape created in and through these disjunctures" (Appadurai 1996, 34). Anthropologist Ulf Hannertz estimates that in the course of time, the process of absorption of the global by the local, with the local domesticating the global—what he calls "maturation"— would override what looks at first glance like saturation of the local culture by the global (Hannertz 2000). Anthropologist Daniel Miller is perhaps the most outspoken advocate of the two-way approach to globalization–localization. He considers local consumers as active agents who construct their identity through their intakes from global goods:

> Estonians, Trinidadians and Philippines all seek to lay claim
> to what may be regarded as the modernity style of Coca-Cola
> or Marlboro cigarettes, but in all three cases they have devel-
> oped mechanisms for disaggregating the qualities symbolized
> by Western goods into those that they are able to desire to
> accept as against those qualities that they see as evil or at least
> inauthentic to themselves. (Miller 1998, 18)

Miller strongly believes in the "ability of groups to use the variable objectifications available in a range of commodities to create much more subtle and discriminatory process of incorporation and rejection than that allowed for in simple models of Americanization or globalization" (Miller 1998, 18).

Ronald Robertson is another advocate of the two-sided approach, which he beautifully describes in terms of "the universalization of particularism and the particularization of universalism" (Robertson 1997, 73). Yet he, like Miller and others in this school, tends to disregard the enormous power disparities between the global corporations and local communities. Against this pristine notion, Stuart Hall, the cultural studies luminary, offers a more prescient view. Although adhering to the two-way view and insisting on reciprocity and locality, he does not lose sight of the overwhelming power of the "global post-modern which is trying to live with, and at the same moment, overcome, sublate, get hold of, and incorporate difference" (Hall 1997, 33). He is fully cognizant of the (still) inferior potency of local resistance, even though he sticks to the belief that "the old dialectics [of domination and resistance] is not at an end. Globalization does not finish it off" (Hall 1997, 39).[12]

This type of mistake is evident in an ethnographic study of McDonald's conducted in Southeast Asia by a team of anthropologists. They argue overall that even though McDonald's transformed local customs, customers were nonetheless able to transform McDonald's in their areas into local establishments; this led them to conclude that McDonald's "does not always call the shots" (Watson 1997a, 7). They claim that, in the realm of popular culture, it is no longer possible to distinguish between the local and the external. Who is to say, they challenge, whether Mickey Mouse is Japanese or Ronald McDonald is Chinese; perhaps this attests to a "third culture" that belongs neither to one nationality nor to the other but constitutes rather a transnational culture (Watson 1997a; in particular, Watson 1997b). This ethnographic discussion stresses the variety of supplements McDonald's has included in its menu to accommodate various local cultures.[13] Applying this approach to our case study, we can consider the new falafel, for instance, a manifestation of maturation, Creolization, or hybridization of McDonald's. The new falafel assimilated some of McDonald's practices but accommodated them to local traditions and tastes.

The two-way approach to the global–local encounter is usually portrayed as critical and espoused by radical social scientists, because it empowers the sustainability of local cultures and fosters local identities. Yet it also appears in a conservative variant. The paradigmatic manifestation is that proposed by Samuel Huntington in his *Clash of Civilizations* thesis (Huntington 1996). According to Huntington, the world after the cold war is characterized by a lack of ideological conflicts on one hand but a rise of cultural conflicts on the other. The fault lines between groups are identity boundaries over which struggles are waged. Huntington assumes the existence of relatively fixed historical civilizations, thereby rejecting the postmodern conception of fluid identities. Nevertheless, he shares the postmodern position as to the significance of cultural identity as the defining core of any given society. Furthermore, despite the apparent contrast with the two-way approach, he endorses one of its basic assumptions—the fundamental distinction between, on one hand, the economic and technological influences of globalization and, on the other, the Western historical values that define its distinctive cultural identity. Different societies can, therefore, adopt certain components of the global effect, say, technology or certain goods, and yet reject others, say, liberal values.

* * *

Having discussed the controversy between the one-way approach and the two-way approach, we may turn now to the question of homogenization versus heterogenization in global–local relationships and suggest a different resolution to it, as follows: (1) both perspectives are valid, (2) yet they apply to discrete societal levels, and (3) the one-way approach addresses one level of social reality—the structural–institutional level, that is, patterns and practices that are inscribed into institutions and organizations—and the two-way approach addresses another level—the symbolic–expressive level of social reality, that is, the level of explicit symbolization. Finally, (4) a global–local structural–symbolic model is proposed here, in which the one-way structural homogenization process and the two-way symbolic heterogenization process are structurally intertwined yet symbolically differentiated.

Whereas each of the rival perspectives on the global–local encounter is attuned to only one level of social reality, we propose that globalization be considered as a process that is simultaneously one sided and two sided but in two distinct societal levels. In other words, on the structural level globalization is a one-way street whereas on the symbolic level it is a two-way street. In Israel's case, for instance, this would mean that, symbolically, the falafel and McDonald's coexist side by side, but structurally, the falafel is produced and consumed either as an industrialized–standardized (McDonaldized) meal, or as a gourmet meal. In the affair of the Golani Junction, the McDonald's "M" sign on the pole was substituted by the brigade's olive tree insignia, yet military bases and public lands were partially McDonaldized.

Thus the two-way approach to globalization, which highlights the persistence of cultural difference, points at an undeniable empirical outcome. On the symbolic level it accounts for the diversity that does not succumb to homogeneity—in our case, the falafel once again steams from the pita, the Israeli hamburger is larger than other national McDonald's specimens (and is also kosher for Passover; on this, see Ram 2003), at Golani Junction the brigade's banner rather than the logo of a fast-food chain graces the flagpole, Israelis have their choice of a *combina* meal that suits their social habits (just as Egyptians are offered McFalafel), and so on. On the symbolic level the difference that renders the local distinctive has managed to linger on. At the same time, on the structural level this great leveler of sameness of all the locales does prevail: the falafel has become McDonaldized, the military has privatized food provisioning, the Air Force "M" can hardly be told apart from the McDonald's "M," and so on.

The logic of the argument can be illustrated through the example of national flags. On the explicit level each of the world's 190 or so national flags is unique in terms of its symbolic makeup (colors, figures, etc.), a uniqueness that makes it recognizable and appealing to the relevant groups. But on an implicit level all flags share the same code of "national flagness," so to speak: not only do they consist of a piece of colored cloth on a pole but, more important, they lend their followers a sense of common national identity.[14] The same holds for McDonaldization. The common language that is formed in institutions and practices is the practical language of commercial, instrumental, technological social organization, of the commodification and instrumentaliza- tion of social relationships. This practical language prevails even as it tolerates—or at points encourages—diverse expres- sive–symbolic manifestations.

The distinction we draw between the structural and the symbolic levels, wherein the former is globally homogenized whereas the latter is locally heterogenized, was already implied in two different, but not entirely unrelated, contemporary-classical analyses, one by Dean MacCannell and the other by Herbert Gans. MacCannell proposed the concept of "staged authenticity"—a commercially manufactured touristic authenticity, which incorporates the "other" within the modern Western middle-class order (MacCannell 1976/1989). Gans proposed the concept of "symbolic ethnicity"—a nostalgic allegiance of (third-generation) immigrants to the country of origin of their ancestors, a putative "ethnic revival," which in fact attests to their acculturation and assimilation in the new country (Gans 1996). In these cases "modernity" and "America," respectively, display the same fundamental characteristic we dissect here in globalization; that is, deep-seated structural uniformity shrouded with symbolic diversity.

An even stronger structuralist argument regards symbolic differences not merely as tolerated but indeed as functional to structural sameness in that they are purported to conceal the structure's underlying uniformity and thus to respond to the particular identity needs of various communities. A more materialistic version would even regard symbolic differentiation as a method of promoting consumer niches. In other words, the variety of local cultural identities licensed under global capitalist commercial expansion disguises the uniform formula of capital, thereby fostering the latter's legitimacy and even sales. It is in this vein that Fredric Jameson contends that the kaleidoscope of identities and styles that characterizes postmodern culture is in fact an expression of the new—post-Fordist—production system. The oft-changing, oft-fragmenting cycles of postmodern consumption well suit the technologically driven cycles of production, constantly creating new markets and constantly marketing new inventions. Postmodern diversity, therefore, divulges the uniform cultural logic of post-Fordist capitalism (Jameson 1998).[15]

Transnational corporations are quick to take advantage of multiculturalism, ethnography, and postcolonialism and to exploit to their benefit genuine concerns of cultural differences. It is worth quoting in this regard at some length a former Coca-Cola marketing executive:

> We don't change the concept. What we do is maybe change the music, maybe change the execution, certainly change the casting, but in terms of what it sounds like and what it looks like and what it is selling, at a particular point in time, we have kept it more or less patterned. … [Our activity] has been all keyed on a local basis, overlaid with an umbrella of the global strategy. We have been dealing with various ethnic demographic groups with an overall concept. Very recently … the company has moved to a more fragmented approach, based on the assumption that the media today is fragmented and that each of these groups that are targeted by that media core should be communicated to in their own way with their own message, with their own sound, with their own visualization. (Ohmann 1996, 6–7)[16]

The case of Israel presented here has shown a number of instances of the process whereby global commodities appropriate local traditions. Let us recap with the example of the new falafel. McDonaldization did not bring about a one-way demise of the falafel, and it even contributed to its revival, vindicating, as it were, the two-way perspective. Yet the falafel's new lease on life is modeled after McDonald's, that is, a standardized, mechanical, mass commodified product on one hand, or responds to it in a commercial, "gourmetized," and "ethnicitized" product on the other hand. In both cases global McDonaldization prevails structurally, although it may give symbolic leeway to the local.

Rick Fantasia's deduction about the commercialized standardized croissant in France is equally applicable to our case, namely, that "the medium [of the social organization of fast food] is the message, and not simply the exchange of equivalent cultural 'tastes'" (Fantasia 1995, 234). Although from the end user's or individual consumer's perspective the particular explicit symbolic difference may be a source of emotional gratification, from the perspective of the social structure, the system of production and consumption, the fundamental outcome of globalization is the exact opposite—namely, implicit structural homogenization.

In its broadest sense here, McDonaldization represents a robust commodification and instrumentalization of social relations, production, and consumption and therefore an appropriation of local cultures by global flows.

Karl Marx defined the fetishism of commodities as the process in which human societal productive relations are concealed behind associations between produced objects. Intersubjective relations are thus objectified, whereas associations between commodities are expressed as relations between subjects; that is, human relations become limited to an abstract monetary exchange, whereas commodities come to serve as representations of identities (Marx 1967, 71–83). Such fetishism of commodities is epitomized by the example of McDonald's in Israel—just one more case in the general drift toward "glocommodification," that is, structural global homogenization accompanied by symbolic diversification.

Six

Postnationalization

In addition to bifurcating Israel's political culture (Chapter 4) and popular culture (Chapter 5), globalization also affects Israel's national culture. The current chapter addresses the challenges posed to Israeli nationalism in the context of globalization. In the two recent decades, Jewish–Israeli mainstream nationalism—Zionism—is challenged by two opposite perspectives: a postnationalist perspective, which tilts toward global cosmopolitanism, and a neonationalist perspective, which tilts toward local tribalism. Benjamin Barber's concept in *Jihad versus McWorld* receives once more an illustrious vindication in the case of the schizophrenic effects of globalization on Israeli national identity (Barber 1995).

Whereas Zionism meant to create a synthetic Jewish–Israeli national identity, the new trends challenge the compounding hyphen and aim at the creation of either a civic Israeli identity or an ethnic Jewish identity, which drift in opposite and mutually hostile directions (on the distinction between the two forms of nationalism, civic and ethnic, see Brubaker 1992). Thus in the global era, Israeli identity splits and becomes simultaneously more universalist and more particularistic, more constitutional and more tribal. We choose to refer to these two trends as post-Zionism and neo-Zionism, respectively, even though we are aware that in simple quantitative terms most of the majority group in Israel still defines itself as Zionist and Jewish–Israeli. We maintain, however, that the trends that we depict here in ideal-typical manner transgress the conventional discourse and redefine its boundaries.

This chapter addresses, then, the identity struggle between three different paradigms of collective identity in contemporary Israel—the Jewish–Israeli national identity and the two new rival perspectives, the Jewish neonational identity and the Israeli postnational identity. The controversy between these options is dissected here to its constituting dimensions: the spatial dimension, the temporal dimension, and the boundary dimension of the collectivity and, hence, its national metanarrative.

The current political–cultural rivalry in Israel is thus a matter not of routine politics but rather of profound issues of identity, memory, and constitution. Usually this rivalry takes the form of culture wars, but at times there is a danger of it spilling into a barely contained civil war, as was gleaned at in the assassination of Prime Minister Yitzhak Rabin in 1995 or in the clashes between the Jewish settlers and the security forces in the occasion of the pullout from Gaza in 2005.

A response to a journalist query by Shimon Peres, the Labour candidate for prime minister in the 1996 elections, after his loss to the Likud candidate Binyamin Netanyahu, attests to this emerging Jewish–Israeli rift, which is usually denied in the conventional discourse: "*Question:* What had happened in the elections? *Peres:* We lost … ; *Question:* Who are we? *Peres:* We, these are the Israelis; *Question:* And who won? *Peres:* All those who do not share Israeli mentality; *Question:* Who are they? *Peres:* Call it the Jews" (Ben Simon 1997, 13). This paragraph reveals a not-so-well-renowned aspect of Israeli nationality, which we highlight and reframe here.

JEWISH–ISRAELI NATIONALISM

Zionism, modern Jewish nationalism, emerged in eastern Europe in the last third of the nineteenth century. It emerged in conjunction with the modernization of Jewish society and with the concurrent wave of Jewish mobility, migration, and identity shifts. In its first decades Zionism was a marginal trend. Only a trickle of Jews emigrating from eastern Europe in the beginning of the twentieth century (2 percent, according to common estimation) made their way to Palestine, and those who stayed there established the nucleolus of the new Israeli society. The Zionist immigrants, who have drizzled into Palestine since 1881, constructed a cultural barrier between them and their (mostly) east European Jewish communities of origin. They were rebels who renounced their Shtetl (Jewish small-town) communities and defied the rabbinical authorities and constituted their own identity in contradistinction to Diaspora Jews: they discarded Jewish religiosity and turned secular, they discarded European Jewish jargon (Yiddish) and revived the Hebrew language, and they labeled themselves "Hebrews" (Ivrim) rather than "Jews." What is commonly translated to English as "the prestate Jewish community" in Palestine was self-termed in Hebrew "the Hebrew settlement" (*HaYishuv Ha'Ivri*). In the spirit of the youth movements in Europe at the turn of the century, these young immigrants tended also to equate their own biographical age with the depicted youth of the national movement and compare it to the old ways of life of their Jewish progenitors. In the early decades of the twentieth century, a native-born ever-young "Sabra" cult would emerge out of this approach (Almog 2000). These immigrants were not simply absentminded about their Jewish past; on the contrary, they made an intent effort to be discharged from what they saw as a burden. In materialistic terms they have also discarded the typical occupational structure of European Jewry and passed through what one of their ideological inspirations, Dov Ber Borochov, had termed "productivization" and "proletarization." This self-reconstruction of their individual and collective identity was functionally required to the tasks ahead of them: the conquest of land and of labor and the construction of organizational and economic infrastructure of a new society. Of course not everybody was really personally immersed in the new identity, but this was the parlance of the leading vanguard, that is, the Labour Movement's pioneers (on prestate Zionist political thought, see Sofer 1998).

One literary protagonist, called Yudke, from a novel by author Haim Hazaz, had given an emblematic expression to the historical consciousness of the new Hebrews: "I object Jewish history," he claimed, "I object it, I mean, I don't accept it ... I don't respect it!" What Yudke objected to was "edicts, vilifications, persecutions, and martyrdom, and repeatedly, edicts, vilifications, persecutions, and martyrdom, and repeatedly, and repeatedly." What Yudke was willing to remember from Jewish history were only "great actions and stories, heroes, brethren, fighters and conquerors. In a word, a world full of bravery" (Hazaz 2005, 150–51). In a very loaded sentence, Yudke literally kicked history out of the court: "Guys, we do not have history! Since the day we were dispelled from our country we have been a people with no history. You are dismissed, go play football." Meaning, Jewish, or rather Hebrew, spirit and identity is linked to Eretz Israel, not to Diasporic Judaism. Zionism leaps over two millennia of Diaspora and links itself directly with the old biblical era. David Ben Gurion, the state's founder, related to Israel as the "Third Temple." This was the structure of Zionist memory and forgetfulness in a nutshell. And Yudke's conclusion was that Zionism was not a continuation of Judaism but a rebellion against it. In Yudke's stoned words,

> Zionism starts from where Judaism is destructed. Zionism is not a continuation, not a remedy, nonsense, it means dislocation and destruction, it is the opposite of what used to be … the end … it almost doesn't have a share with the people, an absolutely non-popular movement … a nucleus of a different people … the Land of Israel is no more Judaism. Already by now, let alone in future times … [Zionism] is not a continuation, it is different, unique in itself, almost a non-Jewish matter, almost entirely non-Jewish. (Hazaz 1952/2005, 160–62)

In retrospective it seems that Yudke was too hasty to conclude that "the Land of Israel is no more Judaism"; today, given the territorial fetishism of most religious Jews in Israel, it seems that for them Judaism is no more but "the Land of Israel" (on the political culture of religious nationalism in Israel, see Lustick 1988). Yet Yudke did express the mainstream ethos of secular Zionism of his time, for which Zionism was conceived as a revolution in Jewish history and culture rather than as a linear continuation of it. The Hebrew culture created in Palestine before the state era was a far cry from the Jewish culture elsewhere. Jews immigrating to Palestine were resocialized quickly into it, and their Sabra offspring contrived a native ethos founded on the triad of settlement, communality, and soldiering. They spoke exclusively Hebrew and were ignorant of Halacha, and they were oblivious to the culture of their parents, let alone of their grandparents. Regarding Diaspora, theirs was a pure culture of amnesia. They disregarded the Diasporic Talmud and pondered the biblical stories (Ram 2003; Shapira 1998), they disregarded Jewish names and chose for their offspring new Hebrew names (Weitman 1988), they disregarded the moderate rabbis of Yavneh and remembered the rebellious Bar Kochva, who was ignored in Jewish tradition (Zerubavel 1995), and they reluctantly related to the Holocaust but reverted the ghetto rebels (the commemoration day of the Holocaust is labeled "Commemoration Day for the Holocaust and Heroism," referring to the underground groups with whom only the native imagination could identify) (Zertal 2005; Zuckermann 1993). This admixture of remembrance and forgetfulness has constituted the Israeli national ethos, as it has grown out of Zionist culture during the prestate era and has shaped three or four cohorts of Israelis: the immigrant pioneers, the Hebrews settlers, the Sabra natives, and the Israelis of the state era (Raz-Krakotzkin 1994; Almog 2000). The following excerpt from the autobiographical memories of the author Yoram Kaniuk bluntly demonstrates the cultural wall mentioned previously that was erected in Palestine between Jews and Israelis:

> I was born in Tel Aviv ... I was taught that we were born from
> the sea ... we learnt that we did not have a history ... we called

ourselves Hebrews, Eratz Israelim (people of the Land of Israel),
not Jews. Our teachers proudly called us Sabras. In our view,
and in the view of our teachers who had immigrated from
East Europe, Jews were ridiculous figures from the stories of
Mendelie the Book Seller and Peretz … there were the "Jews,"
and in the other side there were we. (Kaniuk 1987, 4)

There was a group of young intellectuals who took this ethos
to its extreme conclusions. They called themselves "the Hebrew
Youth" and were labeled by others as "Canaanites," to mark
the ancient pre-Jewish anchorage of their imagined identity.
In their view the new Hebrew people emerging in Israel were
descendants of the ancient Hebrews, not of the Diaspora Jews.
Diaspora Jewry represents a distortion of the original Hebrew
culture. From an independent nation planted in its homeland,
the Hebrews turned into a dispersed and repressed people. The
Hebrews had been a people of toil and fight; the Jews had turned
into a people of prayer and commerce. Yoantan Ratosh, the
leading spirit of the Canaanites, had put it most sharply when
saying, "The old entanglement of Judaism can not be untied—
it can only be cut." Two millennia of Jewish history were to be
overcome to return the golden age of youth and agility (on the
Canaanim, see Shavit 1987). This marginal movement of intellectuals would not have deserved the attention it had received
(here and in Hebrew culture) had it not been given an explicit
and lucid pronunciation to the implicit and more ambiguous
trends of mainstream Zionist nationalism. David Ben Gurion
evinced a blank demonstration of this at an event in 1943
when a Holocaust survivor gave public testimony, perhaps for
the first time in Palestine, about the horrors underwent by
Jews under the Nazi regime. The testimony was given in the

Yiddish language, and Ben Gurion's reaction was swift: "We do not speak a foreign language here." New historians spilled a lot of ink in recent years over the issue of the emotional and cultural alienation between Israelis and Holocaust survivors, which was perhaps the most tragic expression of the same cultural barrier discussed here (Zertal 2005).

* * *

The Holocaust, and the absorption in Israel of Holocaust survivors since 1945, was indeed a watershed in the shaping of Israeli national identity. It contributed toward the gradual "Jewishization" of Israeli culture since the 1950s; that is, a gradual return of the imaginary internal "repressed." This was only one factor, though, in the identity shift. During the 1950s yet another demographic change had made the former "Hebrew project" come to a halt: the arrival to Israel of a massive wave of Jewish immigrants from Muslim countries. In a very short period, from 1949 to 1952, the ethnic complexion of Israel was radically transformed. The Hebrew settlers had lost their claim for exclusivity. The new immigrants from Europe, the Middle East, and North Africa had not been cultivated in a Zionist hothouse. They brought with them to the new country collective identities rich with a variety of components—traditional, Jewish, and other—but with very little component, if at all, of Zionism, let alone Hebrewism. To draw them quickly into the new national fold, the young state and the (by now) old elite had turned, somewhat reluctantly, toward the wider common denominator of all Jewish groups, namely, Jewish tradition. And so, although the new immigrants were integrated into Israel, their presence contributed to the transformation toward a new blend between Hebrewism and Jewishness. Thus Israeli "civil religion" had turned, as students of it Charles Liebman and Eliezer Don Yehiya noted, from an outright rejection of Jewish tradition to a selective adoption of elements from it (Liebman and Don Yehiya 1983). The Eichmann trial, which took place in 1961, is a benchmark in the destruction of the cultural wall between Israeli identity and Jewish history.

Yet this return to Judaism was not only caused by internal reasons. The Palestinians were the major antagonists of the emergent state of Israel and obviously were its major victims. The reinforcement of the Jewishness of Israel since the 1950s should be understood also within the context of the Israeli–Arab conflict. This conflict reached a climax in the 1948 war, which for Israel was a war of independence but for the Palestinian Arabs was a war of destruction. Some four hundred villages of them were destroyed, and some seven hundred thousand of them went to exile (Morris 1989). In fact, and despite the distinction drawn between Hebrew and Jewish identities, the Hebrews could have never relinquished Judaism in entirety. Jewish tradition supplied them with the legitimization needed for their project of colonization and with a definition of their group boundary. And so the label "Jewish" would come to mean more and more, and more than anything else, "non-Arab." So the justification for the invasion of a foreign country, the acquisition of the land, and the displacement of part of its Arab inhabitants necessitated that even secular Jews turn for justification to the Bible and to Jewish continuity and solidarity (Kimmerling 1994). And so it came to pass that between the late 1940s and early 1970s, mainstream Israeli–Jewish identity had come to be founded on two major pillars: the Holocaust on one hand and the Israeli–Arab wars on the other hand (Oron 1993).

Thus to being Jewish was added in Israel a novel meaning of being a non-Arab (as Ian Lustick [1999] lucidly put it). Another layer of collective memory and forgetfulness was thus augmenting Israeli collective identify. The liberal and left conscience of Israel has started to anxiously recollect the suffering inflicted by Israelis on Palestinians. Within this memory culture of the Left are included a novel by S. Yizhar (1949) about an Israeli soldier who participated in the expulsion of Arab villagers, a novel by A.B. Yehoshua (1968) relating to the ruins of Arab villages underneath Israeli planted woods, and a book by David Grossman (1993) that documents the fate of the "present absentee," a specially Orwellian official term referring to Arab inhabitants of Israel whom the state recognizes de facto but refuses to recognize de jure as citizens. Yet mainstream culture turned its back to the Palestinian issue and was willing to view it only "through the viewfinder of the gun" (Ben-Eliezer 1998).

The memory of the Palestinians and the 1948 disaster was eradicated not only from the canonical texts of history and from school textbooks (Firer 1985) but also from the landscape, which was de-Arabized. Remnants of Arab villages were either given to Jewish immigrants or destroyed, and their lands were dispersed among Jewish settlements. Arab names of places were eradicated and Hebrewized (Suleiman 2004, 137–217), and archaeological sites from Arab periods were disregarded (Abu El-Haj 2001).

One typical case of the Israeli ambivalent national consciousness is the Arab village of Tsuba, near Jerusalem. As art curator Tali Tamir (1995) put it, Tsuba lies at the heart of a prolonged paradox of seeing and blindness. The remnants of the houses in Tsuba are by now covered by thick forest. Public authorities have marked the area with signposts, which relate to the view of the natural landscape, to the liberation of the area during the War of Independence, and to the archaeological sites in it. No Palestinian village is mentioned. Since the 1970s Tsuba has attained a special status in the history of Israeli art. The water-color paints of it by Yosef Zaritsky are recognized as emblematic to the "concept of Israeli landscape": "an embodiment of the dazzling Eretz-Israeli light, an exposed and unmediated encounter with nature, an open surveillance of the seasons of the year, light and shade, sunrise and sunset" (Tamir 1995).

Zaritsky's paintings are abstract and lyrical and sensitive to areas, tempos, and color patches but blind to details, especially disturbing details such as remnants of desolated houses. During the early 1990s another painter was absorbed by Tsuba, Larry Abramson. Abramson was dazzled by the duplicity of the view in front of him: the Israeli planted forest on the surface and the ruins of the Palestinian village underneath. His paintings aimed to offset those of his predecessor and to expose the painful genealogy of the area. The paintings, like the site, are multilayered: as each landscape painting reached completion, having gained the saturated state of a full oil painting on canvas, Abramson pressed a sheet of newspaper to it. After the sheet had been pressed to the surface, it was peeled away, taking the upper layers of paint with it. Abramson was left with two parallel products: the peeled painting, damaged and impaired, but still bearing the picture of the village, and the sheet of newspaper bearing the reversed mirror image, the stripped-off layer, the traces of the painting. As Tamir comments, "The mechanical abstraction that Abramson obtained by means of the application and the peeling of the newspaper is an abstraction without glorification. ... The illuminated radiance in Zaritsky's watercolors is replaced here by a murky and muddy coloration, gray-brown in hue, spotted with patches of olive-green. ... In the final state the paintings themselves have turned into something like remains of paintings." This state is metaphoric, of course, for the remains of the abandoned villages that are seen and not seen. For Abramson the Israeli landscape cannot be innocent, as it was to Zaritsky. By exposing the "double map," Abramson recollects the memory of the forgotten, perhaps hoping to reinclude the dispelled, at least symbolically.

The de-Arabization of the land, the obliteration of the Arab memory, and in general the escalation of the Israeli–Arab conflict generated yet another painful consequence. Whereas Jewish immigrants from Europe were expected and encouraged to forsake their pasts and traditions when they assimilated into the new Hebrew or Israeli culture, Jewish immigrants from the Middle East and North Africa were compelled to forsake their very identities. The Jews from Europe were "non-Arabs" in the first place, yet the identity of Jews from the Muslim societies was in part Arab. And to be an Arab in the Jewish state would have meant to be an enemy. To be entirely dissociated from the enemy, these Jews were redefined as *Edot HaMizrach* (literally, oriental communities) and had to drop anything Arab about them—names, languages, music, literature, family patterns, and lifestyle. Anything contaminated with Arabism had to be concealed (Shenhav 1996; Shohat 1989).

This was the paradigm of Zionist–Israeli national identity, with all its inherent ambiguities and inconsistencies, in its Hebrew (pre-1948) and Israeli (post-1948) stages. As said, with the passage of time, especially from the 1960s onward, crucial transformations have started to take place in the patterns of memory and forgetfulness. These transformations are attributed to the changes in the complexion of Israeli society and to changes in its balance of power. In the prestate era the Jewish community was quite small (around six hundred thousand people in the War of Independence of 1948) and quite homogeneous, especially in terms of ethnic origins, and even though it was composed of several social sectors, all were united around a potent nation-building center (Horowitz and Lissak 1979). The creation of the state even strengthened the hegemonic center, yet it was preceded and immediately followed by waves of immigration of both Jewish refugees from Europe and Jews from North Africa and the Middle East, which in three years more than doubled the number of the Jewish population and transposed its ethnic and cultural complexion. As said previously, the immigrants of the late 1940s and early 1950s were not Hebrews or Israelis by socialization or upbringing, and in most cases they were not even Zionists. They were rather refugees moving overnight from the Diaspora to Israel.

In 1967 another forgotten group reemerged on the Israeli public agenda: the Palestinians. The occupation of the Palestinians since 1967, many of whom were refugees from 1948, reminded the Israelis of the past they wished to put behind them. The Palestinian rebellions, the first intifada, which started in 1987, and the second intifada, which broke in 2000, brought the issue to the headlines. And finally, in the 1980s yet another sort of disruption emerged that challenged national identity: an upcoming middle-class stratum, whose members are repugnant toward any form of collectivistic and traditional sanctifications. In response to all these trends that started to crack the solid facet of the national (i.e., Hebrew–Israeli) identity, a new group of faithful adherents and staunch defenders of it had emerged, *Gush Emunim*, which mingled old Judaism with new Hebrewism to design the new mold of the settlers' religious nationalism (Zertal and Eldar 2004).

Thus the scene of national identity and historical consciousness in Israel in the 1990s became much more heterorganic and conflictual than it had ever been before. Zionism, modern Jewish nationalism, has emerged in eastern Europe since the last third of the nineteenth century. As said, it arose in the midst of a gigantic flux in Jewish identity and an enormous wave of Jewish mobility and immigration. In its first decades Zionism was a minority trend, which remained in the margins of the flux, mobility, and immigration. Only a drizzle of the Jews who emigrated from eastern Europe had made their way to Palestine, and those who stayed established the nucleolus of the new Israeli society there. The Holocaust of European Jewry, on one hand, and, on the other hand, the emergence of an influential and prosperous Jewish community in the United States and the establishment of the state of Israel in 1948, marked a new and different phase in modern Jewish and Israeli history.

By the 1990s the old, nineteenth-century national paradigm had passed its peak. In terms of world Jewry, the state had exhausted the potential of immigration (the last waves arrived from the Soviet Union and from Ethiopia), and in terms of Jewish Israelis, the very success of the state had made it a taken-for-granted reality rather than an aspiration. Alongside the nation-state paradigm there emerged the two conflicting paradigms in the era of globalization: Jihad versus McWorld, an ethno-Jewish nationalist paradigm, and an Israeli civic–liberal paradigm. It is as if the hyphen conjoining Israeli–Jewish identity had broken down, and "civic Israelis" and "ethnic Jews" had started to drift in opposite and mutually hostile directions. On one hand, Israeli political culture has became ever more universalistic and globalistic, and, on the other hand, Jewish political culture in Israel has become ever more particularistic and localistic. We shall now turn to an examination of the ethnic and civic paradigms of collective identity and memory, focusing on the emblematic manifestations of each.

JEWISH NEONATIONALISM

Let us start with the Jihad version of the Jewish national identity. The neo-Zionist ethno-Jewish paradigm reinterprets Zionism and Judaism and fuses both together in a new mold. From secular Zionism it adopts the territorial stipulation, the centrality of the territory in the national project; from Orthodox Judaism it adopts the imperative of the Jewish codex, the Halacha, as the common denominator of the community and the expectation for messianic redemption. Fusing the two, the territory and the community become religiously sanctified. Thus Judaism has transmuted into a nationalist-territorial cult. The land and the nation have turned into the first principles of the religion. It is not, as commonly assumed, a process in which Israeli nationalism is becoming more and more religious; quite on the contrary, it is a process in which Jewish religion is becoming more and more nationalistic. In fact, except for some ultra-Orthodox enclaves, Judaism in Israel has been totally transposed from a religion of a nation to a nationalistic religion.

This new creed of messianic Zionism was contrived in the prestate Jewish community in Palestine by Rabbi Avaham Yitzhak HaCohen Kook, at the time the chief rabbi of the Jewish community. Kook differed from most orthodox rabbinical authorities of his time in his embrace of secular Zionism. Three major religious approaches toward Zionism prevailed then and have continued to shape the religious attitude toward Zionism up to now (Ravitsky 1996). The first approach is the ultra-Orthodox approach, according to which Zionism is a blasphemy, because it is not for flesh and blood to quicken the steps of the messiah. The second approach is the pragmatic approach, according to which Zionism does not have any sacred value, positive or negative, but may have a practical utility in rescuing Jews, which of course deserves support. This was the approach that guided the mainstream of religious politics in Israel until 1967. The third approach is messianic-nationalism, which was formulated by Kook. According to this approach, Zionism, in fact secular Zionism, is not only endorsed for pragmatic reasons but rather endorsed on religious grounds. The actual Zionist process of immigration, conquest, and settlement is interpreted as only the first stage in the upcoming transcendental redemption. Secular Zionists are unconsciously engaged in a larger divine scheme.

Although up to the Six Days' War of 1967 this interpretation of Zionism was dormant, it persisted in several religious-national educational and youth centers. It burst into the public arena only after the 1967 war, especially after the 1973 October war. Whereas the former war stimulated the sense of Israeli omnipotence, the latter war revived the anxieties of being on the verge of annihilation. This emotional and cultural seesaw was the background to the emergence of Gush Emunim (Block of Faithful), the avant-garde of the Jewish settlers in the West Bank and other occupied areas. During the 1970s and 1980s it turned out that Gush Emunim had been just the tip of a national-religious iceberg, which included some of the big right-wing political parties and substantial sections of Israeli establishment (Sprinzak 1981, 1991).

The political culture and political practice of Gush Emunim have received already extensive research attention (in addition to the previously mentioned works, see Aran 1987; Feige 2002; Lustick 1988; Zertal and Eldar 2004). In the context of the current study, what interests us is the historical imaginary and historical consciousness of Gush Emunim, or its particular blend of memory and forgetfulness. One of the most lucid expressions of this paradigm of collective memory is provided by a book by Harlod Fisch (1978) titled *The Zionist Revolution: A New Perspective*. Fisch was a professor and former rector in Bar Ilan University, one of the establishers of the Movement for Greater Israel after 1967 (literally, the Movement for the Complete Land of Israel), and a member of the delegation of Israel in the United Nations (in the Menachem Begin era).

Whereas painter Larry Abramson is agonized by the double map of Israel and by the fact that under the surface of Israeli genealogy a Palestinian layer is submerged, Fisch is troubled by another duplicity: the "double calendar" (1978, 79–96). He is troubled by the fact that Israeli chronosophy consists of two layers: a Jewish layer and a universal layer. Whereas Abramson's work implies that the inclusion of the forgotten "other" is essential for the healing of the Israeli collective consciousness, Fisch is interested in the further exclusion of the "other" and cleansing of universal humanism from the Israeli collective consciousness.

The double chronosophy is expressed symbolically in such texts as the Declaration of Independence of Israel, where both Jewish particular ancestry and the recognition of the "family of nations" are mustered as vindications of Israel's right for existence. The document carries two dates that attest to this duplicity: the Hebrew date, 5th Iyar 5708, and the civil date, May 14, 1948. This calendrical ambiguity reveals the fundamental duplicity of Zionism, which from the ethno-nationalistic point of view has to be curtailed. There are two Zionist perceptions, maintains Fisch: on one hand is "political Zionism," for which national sovereignty is considered a solution for the persecution of Jews and for which Zion is merely "the place where Jews would go to end their abnormal condition in the world" (Fisch 1978, 78), and on the other hand is "Zionism of Zion," for which Zionism is considered "to be the fulfillment of Judaism in acknowledgement of the mystery; ... a return to transcendent tasks and origins" (79). Zionism, then, should be purified from its pragmatic tendencies and be elevated to an arcane spiritual state.

The itinerary of Jewish history is seen as a process of setting free Jewish chronosophy from its duplicity, until the foreign calendar is finally discharged and Zionism returns to an uncorrupted Jewish essence. This journey of Zionism from a contaminated state to a cleansed state has evolved through three "moments of truth."

The first such moment is the Holocaust. What it revealed was the treachery of humanity and the impossibility of progress and enlightenment. The ultimate conclusion from the Holocaust is that Jews cannot live and endure among gentiles. There is no life for Jews in the foreign calendar: "In the cataclysm of the war years the hope of the emancipation, that which gave it its spiritual content, had largely burned away. It may be that Israel was not ready for the Jewish Messiah, but there would be no non-Jewish Messiah either. The sting had, so to speak, been taken out of the non-Jewish calendar" (Fisch 1978, 87). The second moment of truth is the Six Days' War of 1967. Here, according to Fisch, a contrary truth was revealed: not the poverty of the foreign calendar but rather the full glory and meaning of the Jewish calendar, "which binds us to a past echoing with ancestral obligations and a future of promise and redemption" (Fisch 1978, 87). The conquest of vast areas of the assumed biblical land has suddenly made the imagined past embodied in Jewish tradition into a vivid reality. The Six Days' War, like other historical events, is not considered by Fisch as a historical affair but rather as a miraculous occurrence through which the past becomes the key to the future:

It was a truly religious moment, the experience of a miracle, of sudden illumination. And what was illuminated was the significance of Jewish existence. We were suddenly living in the fullness of our own covenant history. It is here that we should locate the special metaphysical character of the Six Day War. The outcome of the war did not only call in question the armistice lines set up in 1949 between the divided halves of Palestine; it also challenged the lines which divided the Israeli people from within, the lines which divided their Jewish past from their contemporary existence in the twentieth century. The Six Day War revealed a new dynamic in the Jewish calendar. It was as though archeology had come alive, or rather as though the past had become a key to the future. (Fisch 1978, 87)

The symbolic meaning of the Hebrew appellation of that war is obvious: just as the universe was created in six days, so was the Land of Israel emancipated in six days. And so, in this way, a history of flesh and blood, in this case of war in a tragic literary sense, is extracted from mundane actuality and turned into metaphysics and, indeed, eschatology. The third moment of truth is the 1973 October war. Once more the Hebrew appellation of that war is particularly loaded: the War of Atonement. Hence, so Fisch says, "It is no good talking about the October War":

> Every Jew, every Israeli knows in his bones that this was the War of the Day of Atonement. It was the war that "made one": it made us not only one people, but a people subject to a special destiny, to special stresses, to special existential perils, a people with one calendar which stretches back from Creation through the agonies and storms of the present, through a wilderness where only the pillar of fire and the column of smoke mark the path to the future. … Launched on Yom Kippur, at the most sacred hour of the Jewish year, it was a challenge to the Jewish calendar and all that it stood for, namely, the whole historical pilgrimage of the Jewish people, its covenant destiny. A metaphysical shudder, as it were, passed through the body of Israel. (Fisch 1978, 92, 94)

The historical lesson from these three moments is evident: only one calendar remains, the Jewish calendar. In this neo-Zionist calendar the present does not have a validity of its own; it is just a temporary linkage between the ancient past and the messianic future. Individual lives do not have a validity of their own either; they are just temporary fillers of the eternal collective. Hence Zionism is not a political option in its own sake but rather a passing moment in a lengthy and predetermined destiny. Pragmatic secular Zionism is ignorant of the role it plays in providential history. It misleads the youth to consider Israel as a regular state, one among many, as if being Israeli is similar to being French or Dutch. But it is fortunate that the unfolding moments of truth expose the falsehood of this supposed normalcy.

In the calendar espoused by Jewish ethno-nationalism, the Palestinians receive the status of a "nonnation," which "represents the inverted image of Israel. It thus hardly exists in its own right" (Fisch 1978, 153). "The Palestinian national identity was invented as a kind of antithesis, a parody of Jewish nationhood" (152). Speaking about Palestinian nationality, Fisch says, "There is an element of fantasy in all this. Of course refugees had local patriotism; those who had fled from Acre had a feeling for Acre; those who fled from Jaffa a feeling for Jaffa, and so forth. ... But does this add up to a corporate nationality? And does this constitute a claim for sovereignty? ... To construct a nationality and a claim to sovereignty on such basis would be a work of fiction" (151). In the Hebrew version of the book, we find also that Arab hostility to Israel is nothing but the continuation of the war of the Nazis against the Jews.

ISRAELI POSTNATIONALISM

Let us pass now to the other end of the spectrum—the McWorldist identity. In 1988, a few months after the outburst of the first intifida (the Palestinian rebellion against Israeli rule) and in direct connection to this event, Professor Yehuda Elkana published in the *Haaretz* daily a short list titled "In Praise of Forgetting" (Elkana 1988). Elkana was a professor of the history of science and ideas at Tel Aviv University and a known sympathizer of the Israeli peace movement. In this article

Elkana portrayed some of the fundamental principles of the civic paradigm of Israeli national consciousness, the opposite of the ethnic paradigm, which was presented earlier.

The opening sentence is stunning: "As a ten year old boy I was transferred to Auschwitz and passed through the Holocaust." This guarantees that the forgetfulness of Elkana is not a product of obliviousness or negligence but rather an intentional forgetfulness. Thereafter Elkana draws dryly the lessons of that dreadful experience: Nazi brutality was not exclusively German, there were others; such behavior may happen again, and in any nation, Jews not exempted; and such brutalities may be prevented by proper education and political context.

The direct trigger to Elkana's piece was a sequence of so-called exceptions in the behavior of Israeli soldiers toward the rebelling Palestinians, or in other words repeated acts of brutal treatment of Arab Palestinians by Israeli Jews. One of the peaks of these practices at the time was the burial under piles of ground of four living persons from the village Salem. The Israeli press reported on "the covering of Arabs by gravel" and on one military personnel, major sergeant Sharli Danino, who smiled during the whole event. What may reduce Israelis to such a low level of baseness and cruelty? asked Elkana. His response: "A profound existential anxiety which is fed by a certain interpretation of the Holocaust lessons." The intensive and extensive inculcation of the Holocaust in Israeli consciousness paralyzes the positive creative potential in the country and in fact presents the greatest threat to the future of Israel. Prime Minister Menachem Begin (the leader of Israel's nationalist right wing until the 1980s) led the attack on the Palestinians in Lebanon in early 1982 under the banner of the comparison of Yasser Arafat to Adolf Hitler. He avenged in the Middle East the murder of his parents and their community in Poland by the Nazis. A Jewish Holocaust and a Palestinian disaster (the 1948 expulsion) are intermixed into an untangled note. Writes Elkana, "It is for the first time now that I understand the severe consequences of our doings when during decades we have sent each and every child in Israel to repeatedly visit *Yad VaShen* [memorial of the Holocaust in Jerusalem]. How did we expect that children would process this experience? We have proclaimed in an unthoughtful mind and with stiff hearts and without explaining—REMEMBER! What for? What are children supposed to do with the memories? For very many of them the horror images may be internalized as a call for hate. 'Remember' may be interpreted as a call for a blind prolonged hatred" (Elkana 1988, B1).

Two lessons were extracted from the Holocaust, explains Elkana. One lesson is "it should never happen again," and the other is "it should never happen again to us." The latter lesson has been wildly disseminated in the Israeli educational system (Firer 1989). Elkana does not reject the former lesson on behalf of the latter, or the other way around. He rejects the very notion of living by the "historical lesson" and especially of such a terrible calamity as the Holocaust: "Any life lesson or life perception the source of which is the Holocaust is a disaster ... a disaster for a society which wishes to live in a relative calm and relative security as all societies." Elkana does not rule out altogether the function of collective or national history as such, not even the constructive role of myth. He draws a dichotomous distinction, however, between two kinds of collective approaches to the past: a democratic approach and a Fascistic approach. This significant observation deserves a full citation:

The very existence of democracy is endangered when the memory of past victims takes an active part in the democratic process. The ideologues of Fascist regimes understood this very well. It is not incidental that the research on Nazi Germany focuses upon political myths. The leaning on the lessons from the past for the construction of the future, the mobilization of past sufferings as argument in current politics, are equal to the participation of the dead in the living democratic process. Thomas Jefferson, a founding father of American Democracy, has explicitly indicated in his writings that democracy and consecration of the past cannot endure together. Democracy is the cultivation of the present and the future; the cultivation of memory and the immersion in the past undermine the foundations of democracy. (1988, B1)

If we wish to lead normal peaceful lives, Elkana tells his fellow Israelis, we must forget; we must "stand by life, and devote ourselves to the construction of our future; we must stop dealing day and night with symbols, ceremonies and lessons of the Holocaust. We must uproot the dominance of the 'remember' imperative in our lives" (1988, B1).

The position of Elkana is idiosyncratic, but it nevertheless exposes the historical orientation of post-Zionism, namely, its preference and commitment to the present and future rather than to the past. A different post-Zionist option is raised by Moshe Zuckermann, who studied the applications of the Holocaust memory in Israeli political discourse (Zuckermann 1993). In contradiction to Elkana, Zuckermann considers forgetfulness as morally hollow, and he draws a different line between past, present, and future. Whereas the common historical consciousness in Israel reflects the dictum "this should never happen again to us," Zuckermann urges that especially the "us" who had been the ultimate victim of racism and bigotry ought to live by the dictum "this should never happen again to anybody." Thus, in this post-Zionist version, the past should shed light—or in this case a shadow—on the present and future, but the lessons of the past ought to be universalistic rather than particularistic.

The civic national paradigm emerged in Israel in the 1980s. During the 1990s it broke out into the public arena. The controversy between two leading identity paradigms—the ethnic and the civic, the neonationalist and the postnationalist—in fact reflects the major schism in Israeli political culture since the 1990s, the schism between neo-Zionism and post-Zionism. An explication of this schism will conclude our discussion.

* * *

Neo-Zionism and post-Zionism are expressions of the split of the national identity in the global era. Neo-Zionism is the Israeli Jihad. It emerged with the decline of state nationalism in the 1970s. Its constituency consists largely of the Jewish settlers in the territories and their many supporters in the so-called national camp throughout the country. It is represented by a variety of right-wing parties, including the national-religious party (Mafdal) and the Likud Party and at different points in time other—religious and secular— extreme right-wing parties, such as Tozemt (Juncture), Moledet (Homeland), or Israel Beiteinu (Israel Our Home), and in a somewhat different version also the Shas party. From the neo-Zionist perspective, "the Biblical Land of Israel"—an elastic concept, changeably identified with all areas under Israeli military control—is more fundamental to Israeli identity than is the state of Israel and its territory (as defined by the

1948 green-line borders). The motherland is conceived of as a superior end, the state as an instrument for its attainment and control. The culture of neo-Zionism is an admixture of Zionist and Jewish ingredients, where in place of the discord between the two, which characterized classical nationalism, secular nationalism is conceived of as a stage in an immanent religious revival. The political allegiance of neo-Zionism is to an ostensible "Jewish people," conceived as a unique spiritual-ethnic community, rather than to Israeli nationality, in its prosaic sense of a political community defined by common citizenship. Legal (and practical) affiliation in the collectivity is considered secondary to the ostensible ascriptive national brotherhood. Neo-Zionism is thus an exclusionary, nationalist, and even racist and antidemocratic political–cultural trend, striving to heighten the fence encasing Israeli–Jewish identity. It is fed by, and in turn feeds, a high level of regional conflict and a low level of global integration. Conflict vindicates its alarming messages, and global integration may wear its grip on the national mind.

Post-Zionism is the Israeli McWorld. It started to emerge in the 1980s, in conjunction with the economic liberalization of Israel. Its constituency consists of the new middle classes, typically concentrated in the country's coastal area, especially in the one-hundred-kilometer stretch between the city of Tel Aviv (where a quarter of the population resides) and the city of Haifa. This trend grants more esteem to individual rights than to collective glory. In blunt contrast to the neo-Zionist perspective, the post-Zionist perspective considers the collectivity to be a tool to the welfare of the individual. In its historical horizon the present ("quality of life") is much more esteemed than the past ("history"), and the near future (the children) is more meaningful than the remote past (ancestors). It is expressed in movements such as Yesh Gvul (literally, "there is a border/limit"), New Profile, Black Laundry, the anarchists and others, which challenge the most sacrosanct pillar of Israeli civil religion—the military. These movements represent either soldiers who refuse to serve in the occupied territories or civilians who refuse any military service at all. These movements, small as they are, are only the outspoken cases of a wider trend among Israel's middle and upper classes to remove themselves from nationality on behalf of more individualized life prospects (on this, see Levy 2003a, 2003b).

Post-Zionism is, then, a trend of libertarianism and openness, which strives to lower the boundaries of Israeli identity and to include in it all relevant "others." It is fed by, and in turn it feeds, a lower level of regional conflict and a higher level of global integration of Israel. Conflict mobilizes nationalistic feelings and thus disables it; global integration draws people to cosmopolitan culture and thus is suitable to it.

We should emphasize that the traits of both neo-Zionism and post-Zionism are not entirely foreign to classical Zionism. In fact, these are two diametrical accentuations of Zionist traits. Their novelty is precisely in their one-sided accentuation. Neo-Zionism accentuates the messianic and particularistic dimensions of Zionism, whereas post-Zionism accentuates the normalizing and universalistic dimensions of it. In their opposing ways both trends indicate the transition toward a postnationalist Israeli collective identity in the global era. The nationalist stage was an imperative of the era of modernization, in which priority was given to territorial colonization, nation building, and state formation. Tens of years later, a variety of internal and external pressures, which are generated by globalization,

233 **Postnationalization**

wear nationalism and enhance the emergence of postnational alternatives and neonational reactions. Neo-Zionism and post-Zionism are labels for these dawning alternatives. Neo-Zionism elevates to an exclusive status the ethnic dimension of Jewish nationalism, and post-Zionism elevates to an imperative status the civic dimension of Israeli citizenship.

It is this ground shaking of the dominant nationalist ethos, Zionism, that generates the transformation of the Israeli collective identity and historical consciousness. What takes place is a scrambling of the unilinear and teleological national metanarrative by a variety of supranarratives (post-Zionist cosmopolitanism), subnarratives (empowered marginalized or excluded groups: women, Palestinians, Mizrachi Jews, Orthodox Jews, Russian Jews, Ethiopian Jews), backlash narratives (neo-Zionist ethnicity), and subsidiary narratives (bourgeois liberal). Diverse social categories, the voice of whom had been until recently tangential, take a stand in the public arena, articulate their own versions of identity and of history, and retell it. Their truths diverge naturally or, more correctly put, historically from the hegemonic truth. Just as in the end of the nineteenth century and the first half of the twentieth century, Zionism was busy inventing for itself a tradition and composing for itself a historical narrative, so today in the postnationalist era, a variety of groups in Israel are busy deconstructing that particular version of nationalist history and reconstructing their own histories. The new politics of identity and memory refurbishes drastically the tissue of the Israeli national consciousness.

Conclusion:
Israel as Studied by the Globalization Paradigm

According to the bifurcation thesis that is presented in the onset of this book and further elaborated throughout it, in the global era of McWorld versus Jihad, Israeli society undergoes simultaneously two dialectically opposing yet complementing processes of "marketization" and of "tribalization." Furthermore, in Israel's particular case this dialectical tension is expressed inter alia in a growing antagonism between its Israeli facet of civic identity and its Jewish facet of ethnic identity. Whereas the official Zionist ideology of Israel purports to depict it as a Jewish and democratic nation-state, this book documents and analyzes how globalization bifurcates the Jewish-democratic ostensible unison and splits up the "Jewish" and the "democratic" dimensions along opposing directions: a Jewish-Jihad trend—which is termed "neo-Zionism"—and an Israeli-McWorld trend—which is termed "post-Zionism." Moreover, it is part and parcel of the bifurcation thesis of this book that this split is compatible to a significant extent with the new class polarization of Israeli society, in the sense that some portions of the winners of globalization tend to become more global whereas some portions of the losers of globalization tend to react more locally.

The book documents, first, the radical socioeconomic transformation that Israel undergoes in the global era, when its economy undergoes a postindustrial revolution, its society undergoes a bourgeois revolution, and its culture undergoes a consumerist revolution (Chapter 1). The book also discusses the implications of these radical socioeconomic transformations—foremost of them the emergence of a new social polarization between the winners and the losers of globalization. The book documents the ascendance of a new business elite and professional stratum committed to neoliberalism and a privatization code; the predicament of the middle classes, part of which descends down and part of which ascends up; and the plight of the working classes, who lose their jobs, status, income, and political representation. The book maintains further that this new class polarization is partially congruent with the political polarization in Israel, especially with regard to the Palestinian territories and to the nature of Israeli nationalism. The tie is created through the evolvement of a material interest in national reconciliation (or rather in the termination of open violent hostilities) and civic constitutionalism by portions of the dominant classes, which is countered by symbolic politics of national escalation by portions of the lower classes, which is fueled and then exploited by rightwing populist elites (Chapter 2). All these socioeconomic transformations and their social, cultural, and political ramifications are then associated in this book with the new social formation called "post-Fordism," which in turn is related to globalization. The book shows how technological changes facilitate a radical change in the class balance of power that obtained in the previous era of Fordist national capitalism and thus generate a transition toward a post-Fordist transnational capitalism (Chapter 3).

After laying this foundation for the analysis of the globalization of Israel, the book moves next to the analysis of changes of major dimensions of Israel's politics and culture: it analyzes the Americanization of Israeli political culture (Chapter 4), the McDonaldization of Israel's popular culture (Chapter 5), and the postnationalization of Israel's collective memory (Chapter 6). Each of the chapters highlights anew the bifurcation, which generates a two-pronged result—McWorld versus Jihad.

* * *

In face of the untenable ambiguities of mainstream Zionism (Israel as Jewish and democratic) and the ethnic racism of Jewish neo-Zionism (Israel as a Jewish state), the concept of post-Zionism (Israel as a liberal state; see Ram 2006; Silberstein 1999) has emerged since the 1990s as a genuine alternative to the current identity and structure of Israel. Post-Zionism serves today as a fulcrum for an emerging array of studies of Israeli society and its critique, both analytically and normatively. Post-Zionists argue that the actual social, cultural, and political realities of the country invalidate the claim about the rapport between the Jewish and the democratic dimensions of Israel. They maintain that these two dimensions are in fact adversarial and that each slides in an opposite direction, thus creating two opposing alternatives for the future of Israel— either to transmute into an ethnic Jewish state or to transmute into a liberal state of its citizens.

Ever since the 1990s Israel has become simultaneously more of a market society and more of a tribal society, more neoliberal and more neofundamentalist, more post-Zionist and more neo-Zionist. The contingent result of the struggle between McWorld and Jihad in globalized Israel is yet to be seen.

Notes

INTRODUCTION

1. On globalization as paradigm, see Mittleman (2004b), and on critical globalization studies, see Mittleman (2004a).

2. The literature on globalization has acquired a magnitude beyond any one scholar's sight. I found special use in the following survey books and anthologies, in which the reader might find detailed references to the relevant topics: Axford (1995); Dicken (2003); Held et al. (1999); Scholte (2000); O'Meara, Mehlinger, and Krain (2000); and Murray (2006).

3. The Marxist school is quite voluminous by now. Foci of its creation include the *Monthly Review* journal, the *Socialist Register*, and the *New Left Review*. Among the books in this school are Amin (1997); Appelbaum and Robinson (2005); Bauman (1989); Falk (1999); Harvey (1989, 2005); Hoogvelt (2001); Klein (2002); Petras and Veltmeyer (2001); Robinson (2004); Sklair (2002).

4. On globalization and (American) imperialism, see Harvey (2003), Panitch and Gindin (2004), Pieterse (2004), Stewart-Harawira (2005), and Wallerstein (2003).

5. On concepts such as information, networks, and complexity in this regard, see Castells (1996), Urry (2003), Mattelart (2003), and Barney (2004).

6. Cited respectively in Robertson (1995) and in http://www.oup.com/ elt/teachersites.

7. On postmodernism and postcolonialism in the global context, see Jameson (1991), Lash and Urry (1994), Loomba et al. (2005), and Wallerstein (2006).

8. On the global–local problematic, see Pieterse (2003) and Wilson and Dissanayake (1996).

CHAPTER 1

1. For a cogent yet more qualified assessment of the social and economic globalization of Israel, see Shalev (1999).

2. Israel's Central Bureau of Statistics information and communication technologies include manufacturing industries that produce electronic components, electronic communication equipment, and equipment for control and supervision, and services industries that provide telecommunication services, computer and related services, research and development services, and start-up companies (CBS 2003a,1).

3. Measured in 1995 prices.

4. Measured in 2002 prices.

5. Measured in 1995 prices.

6. For an indispensable account of the high-tech sector, see *Statistilite No. 36* (CBS 2003a) and *Bank of Israel Annual Report 2004* (pp. 105–9). For a comprehensive and incisive analysis of the economic, social, political, and cultural conditions favorable to the development of the high-tech sector and its success and an account of the history of this sector, see Fontenay and Carmel (2002/2004).

7. Bior (2003) and The Manufacturers Association of Israel (2006).

8. An IVC (Israel venture capital) online database. See http://info.babylon.com/gl_index/gl_template.php?id=48294.

9. See http://72.14.209.104/search?q=cashe:DtOdbYYsY6wJ: www.lahav.ac.il/.

10. The source of the former estimate is Dolev (2003); the source of the latter estimate is research cited in a Tel Aviv University site: http://72.14.209.104/search?q=cashe:DtOdbYYsY6wJ: www.lahav.ac.il/. I could not locate the research.

11. These were, in descending order, Teva, Poalim Bank, Leumi Bank, Check Point, Amdocs, Discount Bank, IDB, Mizrachi, and Fibi Holdings.

12. The CBS defines "Israeli multinational enterprise" as a group of business companies that includes a "parent company" in Israel and subsidiaries abroad in which the parent company has hold of more than 50 percent of the subsidiaries. "Foreign controlled affiliate" is a company in Israel of which 50 percent or more is owned by a foreign parent group (CBS 2006d).

13. Data is for 2003 and does not include the companies from the diamond industries and financial corporation (CBS 2006d, Tables 3.2.1, 3.2.2, 3.2.3, 1.2.2).

14. Data is for 2003 and does not include the companies from the diamond industries and financial corporation (CBS 2006d, Table 3.1.1, 3.1.2, 3.1.3).

15. On the role of the Bank of Israel in the transition from a welfare-state policy to a free market economy in Israel, see Maman and Rosenhek (forthcoming).

16. Achdut et al. (2006). Here are the results for the ten brackets of income: lower decimal NIS −643, 2nd decimal NIS −458, 3rd decimal NIS −312, 4th decimal NIS −111, 5th decimal NIS −27, 6th decimal NIS +114, 7th decimal NIS +255, 8th decimal NIS +404, 9th decimal NIS +674, and upper decimal NIS +1,246.

17. The struggle over the welfare state takes place both on the level of personal benefits (administered by the ministry of Labour and Social Welfare and the National Insurance Institute) and on the level of public services such as health and education.

18. On these welfare models, see Esping-Anderson (1990, 26–33); for further discussion, see Pierson (2001, 171–81) and Doron (2003a, 2003b).

19. On the privatization trends in Kibbutzim, see Rosner and Getz (1996), Rosner (2000), Cohen (2004, 2006), and Cohen and Ashkenazi (2004).

20. The travel statistics tap the number of departures even if the same individual has multiple departures, so that the number of departures does not indicate the number of individuals who travel.

21. Noam Yuran names "the new stateliness" no less aggressive and racist than the old one, drawing on a "fantasy" that can be defined as local, Jewish, and neonationalist (Yuran 2001).

22. For presentation of the telecommunication market in Israel, see Ministry of Communication: Telecom in Israel, http://www. moc.gov.il/moc/doa_iis.dll/Serve/item/English/1.2.1.1.html.

CHAPTER 2

1. The source of the data is General Gidon Schaffer, former chief of personnel in the army, cited in Harel (1998).

2. The fifteen families are as follows: Ofer, Arison, Borowitz, N. Dankner (IDB), Hamburger, Wertheimer, Zisaphel, Levayev, Federman, Saban, Fishman, Shachar-Kaz, Shtrauss, Shmletzer, and Teshuva. Among the five hundred corporations, the first ones are Teva, Electricity, Bank HaPoalim, Israel Chemicals, Bank Leumi, Amdox, Bezeqe, Zim, Aviation Industry, and Selcum.

3. Heading the list in the economic journal *The Marker* of the five hundred wealthiest Israelis in 2003 are Ethan and Steph Wertheimer (US$2.5 to 3 billion), Sheri Arison (US$2.4 billion), Morris Kahn (US$1.5 billion), the Ofer family (US$1 billion), and Benny Steinmatz (US$1 billion) (*The Marker* 2003).

4. For journalistic depiction see Chen (1998b) and Petersberg (2003, 2004).

5. Figures are based on Results of Elections for 16th Knesset, pp. 346–47, Table XVII/19 (published by the Government of Israel, Jerusalem), and *Statistical Yearbook of Jerusalem No. 20* (2002/2003) (edited by Maya Choshen, Jerusalem Institute for Research and Jerusalem Municipality).

6. For a like-minded analysis of the nature of "capitalist peace" and the popular reaction to it, see Peled (1995), Peled and Shafir (1996), Shafir (1998), Shafir and Peled (2002), Ben-Porat (2006), and Ram (2000). For a similar comparative analysis of Israel, Palestine, and Jordan, see Bouillon (2004).

7. By associating Barak with the Left, we do not by any means express our own categorization but only reflect the commonly perceived classification. This goes as well for all the Left and Right distinctions we report here.

CHAPTER 3

1. On the tensions but also compatibilities between distribution and recognition, see Fraser and Honneth (2003).

2. In the United States, state-induced redistribution of income is very low. The difference between market income inequality and disposable income inequality as measured by the effect on the Gini coefficient is only 22 percent, compared to 32 percent on average in other rich Western countries (Brandolini and Smeeding 2006, 5, Figure 2).

3. For the trends in inequality, see also Bradshaw and Wallace (1996) and Wilterdink (1999). For the United States, see also U.S. Census Bureau (1994), Braun (1997), Schmitt (1999), and Morris and Western (1999). For OECD countries, see Atkinson (2002).

4. Britain evinces the highest level of inequality, with the government intervention only worsening the situation. Italy is exceptional in this set of data in that its level of inequality is on a decrease.

5. Because of the size of China's population, it has a unique effect on world inequality statistics. On one hand its economy has seen exceptional growth rates since the 1980s, and in this regard it contributes to international equalization as measured by the distribution of GDP among states. Yet on the other hand its internal income distribution became considerably more unequal, and in this regard it contributes to the global rise of

inequality when measured among individuals or households. India plays a similar role with a bit more moderate impact (Kaplinsky 2005, 45). Further intricacies of the statistical measures and the consideration of different results reached by various researchers are beyond the scope of this book. Readers interested in interpretation and references are invited to consult the useful overview in Kaplinsky (2005, 26–51).

6. For instance, the rate of poor families is reduced from 32.2 percent by market income to 18 percent by disposable income; likewise, the rate of poor individuals is reduced from 31.2 percent to 19.5 percent (Achdut and Cohen 2001, 53, Table 4). Likewise, the share of income of the two upper deciles of income earners is reduced from 52.9 percent of the national market income to 41.8 percent of the national disposable income, although the share of the two lower deciles increases from 1.3 percent in market income to 6.7 percent in disposable income (Achdut and Cohen 2001, 76, Table 17).

7. Thus, company tax on profit was reduced from 61 percent in 1986 to 36 percent in 1996; national insurance payments by employers were reduced from 15.65 percent in 1986 to 4.93 percent in 1996; and employers tax (private sector) was reduced from 7 percent in 1986 to 0 percent in 1992 (Swirski and Konnor-Atias 2001, 13).

CHAPTER 4

1. On the Americanization of politics and the decline of political parties in Israel, see also Lehman-Wilzig (1995), Bar (1996), Caspi (1996), Koren (1998), and Aronoff (2000).

2. This does not necessarily mean that there are no ideological divisions in the U.S. public but that they are not fully articulated politically and rather remain on the level of moral or ethical "culture wars" (Davidson 1991). Not that all differences between the Democratic and the Republican parties, or between Republican and Democratic presidents, in recent years are entirely insignificant, yet by and large the differences

are more of sensibility and nuance rather than of substance and program. On this situation in American politics, see Ginsberg and Shefter (1990) and Katznelson, Kesselman, and Draper (2002, 133–76).

CHAPTER 5

1. A number of other encounters between McDonald's and local Israeli culture are examined elsewhere. They include McDonald's encounter with Israel's Orthodox Jewish sector, with the extreme Right and extreme Left, and with Israel's up-and-coming business and middle classes (see Ram 2003).

2. The exclusive franchise of McDonald's in Israel is Aloniel Ltd., owned by Israeli businessman Omri Padan. Burger King was franchised locally to Rikamor, owned by international Jewish businessman Meshulam Riklis.

3. According to one estimate 55 percent of the overall volume of fast dining out in Israel is accounted for by hamburger chains. Thirty-eight percent is accounted for by Italian fast food, especially pizza; the chains are American (the franchises are Israeli)—Pizza Hut and Domino's Pizza. The remaining 7 percent is split among other fast-food chains: Nandos roasted chickens, Subway sandwiches, and Dunkin' Donuts pastries (Barabash 2000).

4. In 2003 the Burger King chain faced losses, and its outlets are offered for sale. The bidders are McDonald's and Burger Ranch.

5. On the Americanization of consumption in Israel, see Avraham and First (2003). On other aspects of Americanization, see Abramson and Troen (2000).

6. On the habitus as a nexus of predispositions and tastes that define social categories, see Bourdieu (1984).

7. In 1999 Israelis, per capita, consumed an average of 343 calories a day from meat, as compared to only 143 in 1960. Other figures for the respective periods are 28 grams of meat protein, compared to less than 12, and almost 25 grams of meat fat, compared to a little more than 10 (Central Bureau of Statistics

2000, Table 11.11). Among its other world accomplishments, in meat consumption Israel ranks high—eleventh place— with an annual per capita average of more than 20 kg. The record holder is Argentina with 63 kg, followed by Uruguay with 52 kg, and the United States with 45 kg (MHR Viandes Magazine 2000).

8. The ultimate symbiosis between McDonald's and the falafel was achieved in the latter's native land, the neighboring country of Egypt. At the start of 2002, McDonald's there came out with a new product, "McFalafel," falafel balls in a bun (Walla News 2002b).

9. "Today's American soldiers," my dentist told me, "are the Coca-Cola bottles in my refrigerator!" This was before the war in Iraq.

10. As if to vindicate Thomas Friedman's book, whose title juxtaposes the olive tree with the Lexus car (Friedman 1999).

11. The tendency peaked with the handing over of guard duty at Jewish settlements in the occupied West Bank from the military to private security companies (Walla News 2002a); for an analysis of this trend in military affairs, see Levy (2003a; 2003b).

12. Positing localization as a counterbalance to globalization, rather than as an offshoot, part of the cultural-studies literature is indeed rich in texture and subtlety when depicting the encounters of global commerce with local popular cultures and everyday life, for instance Oncu and Weyland (1997) and Kandiyoti and Saktanber (2002). Yet this literature is at its best in "twisting the stick in the other direction," from the top-down political-economic perspective to a bottom-up cultural perspective, but it falters when attempting to replace wholesale the top-down approach with a bottom-up one, without weighting the relative power of the top and the bottom.

13. In Turkey, McDonald's serves yogurt (ayran); in Italy it serves cold pasta and espresso; in Japan, Taiwan, and Hong Kong it serves a Teriyaki burger; in the Netherlands it serves

a vegetarian burger; in Norway it serves salmon sandwiches (McLaks); in Germany it serves sausages and beer; in England it serves Chicken McTikka for Indian cuisine enthusiasts, that is, the accommodation of the global to the local Indian who has become indigenous; in France it serves a cheese assortment; in India it serves a veggie burger or lamb burger; in Israel it serves a larger charcoal-grilled burger and a combina burger for the "guys to share"; and so forth.

14. Benedict Anderson aptly remarked on the contradiction of the self-perceived uniqueness common to all nationalities (Anderson 1991).

15. If this is the case, those observers who intend to "give voice" to the "other" and the "subaltern" by highlighting the "Creoloization" or "hybridization" of consumer goods may in fact unwittingly achieve an opposite effect. These include multiculturalists, who consider the variety of postmodern identities an arena of cultural differences; advocates of identity politics, who consider the postcolonial discourse a basis for subversion and resistance; and ethnographers, who consider everyday rituals as the arena of autonomic interpretation. Exclusive attention to explicit symbolism from below at times diverts attention from implicit structures from above. See a lucid exposition of this view in Tetzlaff (1991).

16. Mattel, the manufacturer of the famed Barbie doll, provides another example of the global commodification of local identities. The company decided to diversify the doll's wardrobe with various "folk customs." Barbie, who in 1959 began life as a slim, American blonde, in the 1980s became multiracial and multinational. A million Barbie dolls are sold each week in 140 countries (Varney 1998, 162, 164), some of which are supposed to embody in color and form, garments, and accessories the local feminine style. But as Wendy Varney aptly observes, the local versions of Barbie are mere shallow fabricated images of the texture of local life, which is crushed underneath the global marketing press. As local identity is lost, multinational

Barbies and their counterparts become the only available signifiers of local cultures. Hence, ironically, the Barbie doll, like other global commodities, offers a surrogate identity, a substitute for the absence of a creation of their own (Varney 1998). For a similar analysis of different cases of commercial appropriation of the postmodern and postcolonial discourse on difference, see Ono and Buescher (2001), who decipher the commodification of native American women in the movie *Pocahontas*, and Shugart, Waggoner, and Hallstein (2001), who analyze the appropriation of feminist themes in the media.

Bibliography

Sources in Hebrew are identified as such at the end of the bibliographical item. All citations from daily newspapers such as *Haaretz, Ma'ariv, Yedioth Ahronoth, Ynet News, Walla News,* and so forth are translated from Hebrew (unless marked otherwise).

Abramson, Glenda, and Ilan Troen, eds. 2000. The Americanization of Israel. Special issue, *Israel Studies* 5 (1).

Achdut, Leah. 2006. *National Insurance Institute of Israel—Annual Survey 2005.* Jerusalem: National Insurance Institute of Israel. (Hebrew)

Achdut, Leah, and Rafaela Cohen. 2001. Poverty and Inequality in Income Distribution. In *National Insurance Institute of Israel—Annual Survey 2000.* Jerusalem: National Insurance Institute of Israel. (Hebrew)

Achdut, Lea, Rafaela Cohen, and Miri Endwald. 2003. Poverty and Income Inequality. In *National Insurance Institute of Israel—Annual Survey 2003.* Jerusalem: National Insurance Institute of Israel. (Hebrew)

Achdut, Lea, Miri Endwald, Zvi Sussman, and Rafaela Cohen. 2006. *Social Aspects of the State's Budget 2001–2006.* Jerusalem: National Insurance Institute of Israel.

Adiram, Yechezkel. 1996. The Producer of the Likud Jingle Sues Offira Yssefi for NIS 400,000. *Yedioht Ahronoth,* May 5, 1996, 7.

Advertiser. 1998. *Workshop on Americanization.* Alma: College of Hebrew Culture. Private transcript. April 24, 1998.

Aglietta, Michael. 2001. *A Theory of Capitalist Regulation: The US Experience*. London: Verso.

Aharoni, Yair. 1991. *The Israeli Economy: Dreams and Realities*. New York: Routledge.

———. 1998. The Changing Political Economy of Israel. *Annals of the American Academy for Political and Social Sciences* 555:127–46.

Aldrich, John R. 1995. *Why Parties?* Chicago: University of Chicago Press.

Alexandrowicz, Ra'anan. 2003. *James's Journey to Jerusalem*. Film.

Alfasi, Nurit, and Tovi Fenster. 2004. The National City and the Global City: Tel Aviv and Jerusalem in the Age of Globalization. *Israeli Sociology* 6 (1): 39–67. (Hebrew)

Allen, John. 1996. Post-Industrialism/Post-Fordism. In *Modernity: An Introduction to Modern Societies*, ed. Stuart Hall, D. Held, D. Hubert, and K. Thompson, 533–63. Cambridge: Blackwell.

Almog, Oz. 1991. Monuments to the Fallen in Wars in Israel: A Semiological Analysis. *Megamot* 34:179–210. (Hebrew)

———. 1993. *The Sub-Culture of Gallei Zahal*. Ramat Efal: Yad Tanenkin. (Hebrew)

———. 1998. From Conquering the Mountain to Conquering a Goal: The Revolution of Professional Sport in Israel. *Mifne* 23:32–38. (Hebrew)

———. 1999. From Our Rights over the Country to Civic Rights and from a Jewish State to Legality: The Judicial Revolution in Israel and Its Cultural Implications. *Alpayim* 18:77–132. (Hebrew)

———. 2000. *The Sabra: The Creation of the New Jew*. Berkeley: University of California Press.

———. 2004. *Farewell to Srulik: Changing Values among the Israeli Elite*. Haifa: Haifa University and Zemorah Bitan. (Hebrew)

American Political Science Association. Task Force on Inequality and American Democracy. 2004. *American Democracy in an Age of Rising Inequality*. www.apsanet.org/imgtest/taskforcereport.pdf.

Amin, Samir. 1997. *Capitalism in the Age of Globalization: The Management of Contemporary Society*. London: Zed Books.

Appadurai, Arjun. 1996. Disjuncture and Difference in the Global Cultural Economy. In *Modernity at Large: Cultural Dimensions of Globalization*, 27–47. Minneapolis: University of Minnesota Press.

Appelbaum, Richard P., and William I. Robinson, eds. 2005. *Critical Globalization Studies*. New York: Routledge.

Aran, Gideon. 1987. From Religious Zionism to a Zionist Religion: The Origins and Culture of Gush Emunim; A Messianic Movement in Modern Israel. PhD diss., Hebrew University of Jerusalem.

Arian, Asher, and Michal Shamir. Various years. *The Elections in Israel*. Albany, NY: SUNY Press.

Arlozorov, Merav. 2004. We Broke the Organized Labour in Israel. *Haaretz*, May 5, 2004, C1.

Aronoff, Myron Joel. 2000. The Americanization of Israeli Politics and Realignment of the Party System. *Israel Studies* 5 (1): 92–127.

Atkinson, Tony. 2002. *Income Inequality and the Welfare State in a Global Era*. Kingstone, Ontario: Queen University: School of Policy Studies, the J. Douglas Gibson lecture. http://www.queensu.ca/sps/the_policy_forum/distinguished_lectures/the_douglas_gibson_lecture/02Lecture.pdf.

Avraham, Eli, and Anat First. 2003. "I Buy American": The American Images as Reflected in Israeli Advertising. *Journal of Communication* 53 (2): 282–99.

Axford, Barry. 1995. *The Global System: Economics, Politics and Culture*. Cambridge, MA: Polity.

Azaryahu. 2005. *Tel Aviv, the Real City: A Historical Mythography*. Beer Sheva: Ben Gurion Research Institute, Ben Gurion University Press. (Hebrew)

———. 1996. Look How Bibi Looks; Look on Peres. *Ha'ir*, August 28, 1996. (Hebrew)

Bank of Israel. 1995. *Bank of Israel Annual Report 1994*. Jerusalem: Bank of Israel.

———. 1998. *Bank of Israel Annual Report 1997*. Jerusalem: Bank of Israel.

———. 2000. *Foreign Workers in Israel*. Spokesperson, December 18, 2000. http://www.bankisrael.gov.il/press/msgs/977134290/001218a.htm.

————. 2002. *Bank of Israel Annual Report 2001*. Jerusalem: Bank of Israel.

————. 2004a. *Bank of Israel Annual Report 2003*. Jerusalem: Bank of Israel.

————. 2004b. *The Centralization in the Financial Sector in Israel*. Spokesperson, June 30, 2004.

————. 2005. *Bank of Israel Annual Report 2004*. Jerusalem: Bank of Israel.

Banting, Keith, and Will Kymlicka. 2003. Multiculturalism and Welfare. *Dissent* 50 (4): 59–66.

Bar, Aliza. 1996. *Primaries and Other Methods of Candidate Selection*. Jerusalem: Israel Institute for Democracy and HaKibbutz HaMeuchad. (Hebrew)

Barabash, Roni. 2000. DBI: Sales of Fast Food in 2000 about Billion NIS. *Haaretz*, October 24, 2000, C4.

Barnea, Nachum. 1996. Peres Gave, Bibi Has Taken. *Yedioth Ahronoth*, May 31, 1996, 6.

Barney, Darin. 2004. *Network Society*. Cambridge, MA: Polity.

Baruch, Gili. 2002. Silicon Wadi: Hi Tech in the Identity Discourse of the New Class in Israel. Master's thesis, Department of Behavioural Sciences, Ben Gurion University. (Hebrew)

Barzel, Bina. 1996. This Is How the Election Slogan of Bibi [Binyamin Netanyahu] Was Created. *Yedioth Ahronoth*, April 8, 1996, 10.

Barzilai, Amnon. 1997. IDF in Search of Youth. *Haaretz*, November 19, 1997, B2.

————. 2000. Armor against Inequality: Hamburger to Each Soldier. *Haaretz*, September 11, 2000, A6.

Bassok, Moti. 2003. The Ministry of Finance against the Monopolies. *Haaretz*, November 12, 2003, C1, C8.

Baudrillard, Jean. 1988. *Selected Writings*. Stanford, CA: Stanford University Press.

————. 1992. Transpolitics, Transsexuality, Transaesthetics. In *The Disappearance of Art and Politics*, ed. W. Stearns and W. Chaloupka, 9–26. New York: St. Martin's.

Bauman, Zygmunt. 1989. *Globalization: The Human Consequences*. New York: Columbia University Press.

Bell, Daniel. 1976. *The Coming of Post-industrial Society: A Venture in Social Forecasting*. New York: Basic Books.

———. 1994. The Coming Post-industrial Society. In *Social Stratification: Class, Race and Gender*, ed. D. Gursky, 687–97. Boulder, CO: Westview.

Ben Ami, Shlomo. 1998. *A Place for All*. Tel Aviv: HaKibbutz HaMeuchad. (Hebrew)

Ben David, Dan. 2003. Israeli Workforce in International Perspective. *The Economic Quarterly (HaRiv'on LeKalkala)* 1 (3): 73–90. (Hebrew)

Bendlak, Jacque. 2004. *Wage Income Averages by Settlement and Various Economic Factors 2000–2001*. Jerusalem: National Insurance Institute of Israel. (Hebrew)

Ben-Eliezer, Uri. 1998. *The Making of Israeli Militarism*. Bloomington: Indiana University Press.

———. 2004. Post-modern Armies and the Question of Peace and War: The Israeli Defense Force in the "New Times." *International Journal of Middle East Studies* 36 (1): 49–70.

Benhabib, Seyla. 2004. *The Rights of Others: Aliens, Residents and Citizens*. Cambridge, UK: Cambridge University.

Ben Israel, Ruth. 2000. Social Justice in the Post-industrial Era: Distributive Justice in the Division of Work. In *Distributive Justice in Israel*, ed. Menachem Moutner, 309–40. Tel Aviv: Ramot. (Hebrew)

Ben-Porat, Amir. 1998. The Commodification of Football in Israel. *International Review for the Sociology of Sport* 33 (3): 269–76.

Ben-Porat, Guy. 2006. *Global Liberalism, Local Populism: Peace and Conflict in Israel/Palestine and Northern England*. Syracuse, NY: Syracuse University Press.

Ben-Porat, Guy, and Amir Ben-Porat. 2004. (Un)Bounded Soccer: Globalization and Localization of the Game in Israel. *International Review for the Sociology of Sport* 39 (4): 421–36.

Ben Simon, Daniel. 1997. *A New Israel*. Tel Aviv: Arye Nir Publishers. (Hebrew)

Ben-Tzruya, Haim. 1993. The Impact of the Peace Process on Economic Trends in the Israeli Economy: Quantitative Estimates. http://www.mfa.gov.il/MFA/Archive/Peace%20Process/1993/Impact%20of%20the%20Peace%20Process%20on%20Economic%20Trends%20in.

Benvenisti, Miron. 2004. [Naomi Shemer] Daughter of Extinguished Tribe. *Haaretz*, July 7, 2004, B1.

Ben-Yehuda, Nachman. 1995. *The Massada Myth: Collective Memory and Mythmaking in Israel*. Madison: University of Wisconsin Press.

Berger, Tamar. 1999. *Dionysus at Dizengoff Center*. Tel Aviv: HaKibbutz HaMeuchad. (Hebrew)

Bernheimer, Avner, and Rinat Golan. 1998. Five Years to the Turnabout: How Channel 2 Made Rating the New Code of Israeli Society. *Yedioth Ahronoth-Shiva Yamim*, September 18, 1998.

Bezeq, Israeli Communication Cooperation. 1996. *Statistical Annual 1995*. Jerusalem: Government Printer.

Bhabha, Homi. 1990. *Nation and Narration*. New York: Routledge.

——. 1994. *The Location of Culture*. New York: Routledge.

Bior, Haim. 2002. Who Is Strong Enough to Strike. *Haaretz*, November 4, 2002, C8.

——. 2003. The Industrialists: 20 Textile Plants Closed in 2003. *Haaretz*, March 12, 2003, C6.

——. 2004a. President of Manufacturers Federation: The Increase of Minimum Wage Will Cause the Closing of 300 Plants. *Haaretz*, September 20, 2004, C6.

——. 2004b. Rachlevski Will Publish Report on Low Wage in Public Service. *Haaretz*, March 3, 2004, C3.

——. 2004c. Research: The Great Number of Unionized Employees—A Contributor to Strikes. *Haaretz*, May 24, 2004.

Bouillon, Markus E. 2004. *The Peace Business: Money and Power in the Palestine–Israel Conflict*. London: I. B. Tauris.

Bourdieu, Pierre .1984. *Distinction: A Social Critique of the Judgment of Taste*. Cambridge, MA: Harvard University Press.

Bradshaw, York W., and Michael Wallace. 1996. *Global Inequalities (Sociology for a New Century Series)*. CA: Pine Forge Press.

Brandolini, Andrea, and Timothy M. Smeeding. 2006. Patterns of Economic Inequality in Western Democracies: Some Facts on Levels and Trends. *Political Science and Politics* 39:21–26.

Braun, Denny. 1997. *The Rich Get Richer: The Rise of Income Inequality in the U.S. and the World.* Chicago: Nelson-Hall Publishers.

Breitberg-Semel, Sarah. 1993. Tiranit's Youth. *Studio* 44:14–17. (Hebrew)

Brodet, David. 2004. *Recommendations Regarding the Higher Education.* Jerusalem: Israel Democracy Institute. (Hebrew)

Bureau of Statistics and the U.S. Bureau of Census (a Joint Project). 2000. *Annual Demographic Survey.* http:/ferret.bls.census.gov/macro/032000/quint/15_000.html.

Capgemini and Merrill Lynch. 2004. *World Wealth Report.* http://www.microsoft.com/industry/financialservices/capitalmarkets/wealthmgmntabstract.mspx.

———. 2005. *World Wealth Report 2005.* http://download.microsoft.com/download/0/a/c/0ac6ccc1-993b-488c-bb61-524efca5d669/Capgemini_wealthmgmnt.pdf.

Caspi, Dan. 1996. American-Style Electioneering in Israel: Americanization versus Modernization. In *Politics, Media and Modern Democracy,* ed. D. L. Swanson and P. Mancini, 173–92. Westport, CT: Praeger.

———. 2006. Americanization Hit the IDF. *Ynet News,* July 28, 2006.

Caspi, Dan, and Yehiel Limor. 1999. *The In/Outsiders: The Mass Media in Israel.* Cresskill, NJ: Hampton Press.

Castel-Bloom, Orli. 1996. The Complete Prison: On the Emotional State of the Photos. In *Tiranit Barzilai 1995* (Exhibition Catalogue). Tel Aviv: Tel Aviv Museum. (Hebrew)

Castells, Manuel. 1996. *The Rise of the Network Society (The Information Age, I).* Oxford, UK: Blackwell.

———. 1997. *The Power of Identity (The Information Age, II).* Oxford, UK: Blackwell.

Central Bureau of Statistics. 1996a. *Time Use in Israel 1991/2*. Publication No. 1029. Jerusalem: CBS (Hebrew)

———. 1996b. *Motor Vehicles in Israel*. Publication No. 1065. Jerusalem: CBS (Hebrew)

———. 1997. *Tourism 1996*. Publication No. 1067. Jerusalem: CBS (Hebrew)

———. 1998a. *Jubilee Publications (No. 3)—National Accounts*. Jerusalem: CBS. (Hebrew)

———. 1998b. *Statistical Abstract of Israel 1998*. Report No. 49. Jerusalem: CBS. (Hebrew)

———. 2000. *Statistical Abstract of Israel 2000*. Report No. 51. Jerusalem: CBS. (Hebrew)

———. 2001. *Information and Communication Technologies 1990–2000*. Publication No. 1164. Jerusalem: CBS. (Hebrew)

———. 2003a. *Information and Communication Technologies in Israel 1990–2002*. Statistilite No. 36, composed by Galia Yohay and Nurit Yaffe. Jerusalem: CBS. (Hebrew)

———. 2003b. *Statistical Abstract of Israel 2003*. Report No. 54. Jerusalem: CBS. (Hebrew)

———. 2005. *Statistical Abstract of Israel 2005*. Report No. 56. Jerusalem: CBS.

———. 2006a. *Household Expenditure Survey 2004*. Jerusalem: CBS.

———. 2006b. *Household Expenditure Survey 2005*. http://www.cbs.gov.il/hodaot+2006n/15_06_158b.pdf.

———. 2006c. *Statistical Abstract of Israel*. Report No. 57. Jerusalem: CBS.

———. 2006d. Multinational Enterprises in Israel, 2002–2003. http://www.cbs.gov.il/hodaot2006n/09_06_021e.pdf

Chen, Shoshana. 1998a. A Short History of Gorging. *Yedioht Ahronoth*, April 10, 1998, 20–21.

———. 1998b. And They Live Happily Ever After. *Yedioth Ahronoth—Seven Days*, April 13,1998, 48–54.

Clark, Nichols Terry, and Seymour Martin Lipset, eds. 2001. *The Breakdown of Class Politics: A Debate on Post-industrial Stratification*. Baltimore: Johns Hopkins University Press.

Cohen, Amiram. 2004. About Third of the Kibbutzim Undergo Privatization Procedures. *Haaretz*, March 11, 2004.

———. 2006. Kibbutz Homes Go Private in Death Knell to Communal Life. *Haaretz*, February 22, 2006.

Cohen, Amiram, and Eli Ashkenazi. 2004. Survey: Kibbutz Wage Gaps as High as 700 Percent. *Haaretz*, October 25, 2004, A1, A6.

Cohen, Erik. 1995. Israel as a Post-Zionist Society. In *The Shaping of Israeli Identity: Myth, Memory and Trauma*, ed. R. Wistriech and D. Ohana. London: Frank Cass.

Cohen, Stuart. 1995. Israel's Defense Force: From a "People's Army" to a "Professional Force." *Armed Forces and Society* 21:237–54.

Cohen, Yinon, Yitchak Haberfeld, Guy Mundlak, and Ishak Saporta. 2003. Unpacking Union Density: Membership and Coverage in the Transformation of the Israeli Industrial Relations System. *Industrial Relations* 42 (4): 692–711.

Condor, Yaakov. 1997. *Foreign Labourers in Israel*. Jerusalem: National Insurance Institute of Israel. (Hebrew)

Crotty, William. 2006. Party Origins and Evolution in the United States. In *Handbook of Party Politics*, ed. Richard Katz and William Crotty, 25–33. London: Sage.

Dahan, Momi. 2001. The Rise of Earning Inequality. In *Israeli Economy 1985–1998: From Government Intervention to Market Economy*, ed. Avi Ben Basat. Jerusalem: Falk Institute. (Hebrew; English edition by MIT Press, 2002)

Dan and Bradstreet. 2006. *Ranking Tables Dans 100 2006*. http://www.dbisrael.co.il/duns100heb/art14.asp.

Davidson, James Hunter. 1991. *Culture Wars: The Struggle to Define America*. New York: Basic Books.

Dicken, Peter. 2003. *Global Shift: Reshaping the Global Economic Map in the 21st Century*. 4th ed. New York: Guilford.

Dolev, Gilai. 2003. Life after the Purchase. *Yedioth Ahronoth*, August 8, 2003.

Dori, Zviya. 1998. *Industry in Israel 1997*. Jerusalem: Ministry of Industry and Trade.

Doron, Abraham. 1999. The Welfare State in Israel: Developments in the 1980s and 1990s. In *Public Policy in Israel*, ed. David Nachmias and Gila Menahem. London: Routledge. (Hebrew)

———. 2003a. The Israeli Welfare Regime: Changing Trends and Their Social Effects. *Israeli Sociology* 5 (2): 417–34. (Hebrew)

———. 2003b. The Welfare State in an Era of Contractions: A Look at the Beginning of the 21st Century. *Society and Welfare (Hevra U-Revacha)* 23 (3): 275–94. (Hebrew)

Downs, Anthony. 1957. *An Economic Theory of Democracy.* New York: Harper and Row.

Durkheim, Emile. 1947. *The Division of Labor in Society.* Glencoe, IL: Free Press.

Duverger, Maurice. 1959. *Political Parties.* London: Methuen.

D. Y. 1998. Golani Junction—Memorial and McDonald's. *Haaretz,* February 22, 1998, B6.

Dyer-Witheford, Nick. 1999. *Cyber-Marx: Cycles and Circuits of Struggle in High Technology Capitalism.* University of Illinois Press.

Eckstein, Shlomo, Shimon Rozevich, and Ben Zion Zilberfab. 1998. *Privatization of Public Enterprises in Israel and Abroad.* Ramat Gan: Bar Ilan University. (Hebrew)

Elkana, Yehuda. 1988. In Praise of Forgetting. *Haaretz,* March 2, 1988, B1.

Ellman, Michael, and Smain Laacher. 2003. *Migrant Workers in Israel: A Contemporary Form of Slavery.* The Euro-Mediterranean Human Rights Network and the International Federation for Human Rights. http://www.fidh.org/IMG/pdf/il1806a.pdf.

Ellwood, Wayne. 2001. *The No-Nonsense Guide to Globalization.* London: Verso.

Esping-Andersen, Gosta. 1990. *The Three Worlds of Welfare Capitalism.* Princeton, NJ: Princeton University Press.

———. 1996. *Welfare State in Transition: National Adaptations in Global Economies.* Thousand Oaks, CA: Sage.

Falk, Richard. 1999. *Predatory Globalization: A Critique.* Cambridge, MA: Polity.

Fantasia, Rick. 1995. Fast Food in France. *Theory and Society* 24:201–43.

Faux, Jeff, and Lawrence Mishel. 2001. Inequality and the Global Economy. In *On the Edge: Living with Global Capitalism*, ed. Will Hutton and Anthony Giddens, 93–111. London: Vintage.

Felsenstein, Daniel, Eike W. Schamp, and Arie Shachar. 2003. *Emerging Nodes in the Global Economy: Frankfurt and Tel Aviv Compared*. Dordrechet: Kluwer.

Filc, Dani. 2004. Post-Fordism's Contradictory Trends: The Case of the Israeli Health Care System. *Journal of Social Policy* 33:417–36.

———. 2005. The Health Business under Neo-liberalism: The Israeli Case. *Critical Social Policy* 25 (2): 180–97.

———. 2006. *Populism and Hegemony in Israel*. Tel Aviv: Resling. (Hebrew)

Filc, Dani, and Uri Ram, eds. 2004. *The Power of Property: Israeli Society in the Global Age*. Jerusalem: Van Leer Institute and HaKibbutz HaMeuchad. (Hebrew)

Fisch, Harold. 1978. *The Zionist Revolution: A New Perspective*. London: Weidenfeld and Nicolson.

Fishbein, Einat. 1998. The Depressive Sector. *Ha'ir*, November 20, 1998, 46–51. (Hebrew)

Fletcher, Eileen. 1999. Transportation, Roads, Environment, and Social Justice in Israel. Tel Aviv: Adva Center.

Florida, Richard. 2003. *The Rise of the Creative Class: And How It's Transforming Work, Leisure, Community and Everyday Life*. New York: Basic Books.

Fontenay, Cathrine de, and Erran Carmel. 2002/2004. Israel's Silicon Wadi: The Forces behind Cluster Formation. In *Building High-Tech Clusters: Silicon Valley and Beyond*, ed. T. Bresnahan, and A. Gambardella. Cambridge: Cambridge University Press. http://www.mbs.edu/home/defontenay/IsraelSiliconWadiJune2002.pdf.

Fox-Piven, Frances, ed. 1991. *Labor Parties in Postindustrial Societies: Europe and International Order*. Oxford: Oxford University Press.

Frenkel, Michal, Yehuda Shenhav, and Hannah Herzog. 2000. The Cultural Wellsprings of Israeli Capitalism: The Impact of Private Capital and Industry on the Shaping of the Dominant Zionist Ideology. In *The New Israel: Peacemaking and Liberalization*, ed. Gershon Shafir and Yoav Peled, 43–70. Boulder, CO: Westview.

Friedman, Thomas L. 1999. *The Lexus and the Olive Tree*. New York: Farrar, Straus, and Giroux.

Fukuyama, Francis. 1992. *The End of History and the Last Man*. New York: Free Press.

Gabai, Yoram. 2003. Economic Leadership and Globalization: Israel 2003. *Management: The Magazine of Israeli Executives* 153 (4): 12–18. (Hebrew)

Galil, Yair. 2003. Yad Eliyahu on the Hudson. *Panim* 25:24–30. (Hebrew)

Galili-Zucker, Orit. 2004. *The Tele-politicians: New Political Leadership in the West and Israel*. Tel Aviv: Tel Aviv University, Ramot. (Hebrew)

Gans, Herbert. 1996. Symbolic Ethnicity. In *Ethnicity: Oxford Readers*, ed. John Hutchinson and Anthony D. Smith, 146–55. Oxford: Oxford University Press.

Gaoni, Yael. 1999. Telad: Friday Will Be Winning Day. *Haaretz*, September 1, 1999, C7.

Gavison, Yoram. 1998. Delta—The Main Customer Is in Troubles. *Haaretz*, November 16, 1998, C9.

Giddens, Anthony. 1990. *The Consequences of Modernity*. Stanford, CA: Stanford University Press.

Ginsberg, Benjamin, and Martin Shefter. 1990. *Politics by Other Means: The Declining Implications of Elections in American Politics*. New York: Basic Books.

Goldstein, Tani. 2005. 15 Families. *Ynet News*, August 21.

Gottlieb, Daniel. 2002. The Impact of Non-Israeli Labourers on Employment, Income and Inequality 1995–2000. *The Economic Quarterly (Ha-Riv'on Lekalkala)* 4:694–736. (Hebrew)

Gould, Eric, and Omer Moav. 2006. *The Israeli Brain Drain*. Jerusalem: Shalem Center, The Institute for Economic and Social Policy Social Policy. http://www.shalem.org.il/Admin/FileServer/df4b061c96-a6fbceb95026260cb4de8a.pdf.

Government Companies Authority. 2002. *Report 2001*. Jerusalem: Government Companies Authority.

————. 2003. Basic Policy Guidelines of the Government. *Haaretz*, 2003, A8, A14.

Green, Sagi. 1998. The Virtual Israel: Sand, Plastic and Bereavement. *Haaretz*, September 20, 1998, 4.

Greenwood, Naftali. 1998. *Israel Yearbook and Almanac—Jubilee Edition*. Jerusalem: IBRT Translation/Documentation.

Grinberg, Lev. 2001. Social and Political Economy. In *Trends in Israeli Society*, vol. I, ed. E. Yaar and Z. Shavit, 585–704. Tel Aviv: Open University. (Hebrew)

Grossman, David. 1993. *Sleeping on a Wire: Conversations with Palestinians in Israel*. New York: Farrar, Straus and Giroux.

Grunau, Reuven. 2003. *Globalization: Israeli Economy in the Shadow of Global Economic Processes*. Position Paper No. 36. Jerusalem: Israeli Democracy Institute. (Hebrew)

Gvirtz, Yael. 1996. Everything We Were Barred from Knowing up to Now. *Yedioth Ahronoth*, May 31, 1996, 20–21.

Habermas, Jürgen. 1984. *The Theory of Communicative Action, Vol I*. Cambridge, MA: MIT Press.

————. 1987. *The Theory of Communicative Action, Vol. II*. Cambridge, MA: MIT Press.

————. 1989. *The Structural Transformation of the Public Sphere: An Inquiry into a Category of Bourgeois Society*. Cambridge, MA: MIT Press.

Hall, Stuart. 1997. The Local and the Global: Globalization and Ethnicity. In *Culture, Globalization and the World System*, ed. A. D. King, 19–39. Basingstoke: Macmillan.

Hannertz, Ulf. 2000. Scenarios for Peripheral Cultures. In *Culture, Globalization and the World System*, ed. A. D. King, 107–28. Minneapolis: University of Minnesota Press.

Harding, Sadndra. 1998. *Is Science Multicultural?* Bloomington: Indiana University Press.

Harel, Amos. 1998. Military Personnel Chief: 45% of Each Cohort Do Not Conscript. *Haaretz*, September 7, 1998. (Hebrew)

Harrison, Bennett. 1994. *Lean and Mean: The Changing Landscape of Corporate Power in the Age of Flexibility*. New York: Guilford.

Harvey, David. 1989. *The Condition of Postmodernity: An Enquiry into the Origins of Cultural Change*. Cambridge, MA: Blackwell.

———. 2003. *The New Imperialism*. New York: Oxford University Press.

———. 2005. *A Brief History of Neoliberalism*. New York: Oxford University Press.

Hazaz, Haim. 2005. *The Sermon and Other Stories*. New Milford, CT, and London: Toby Press.

Held, David, and Anthony McGrew. 1999. Globalization. In *Oxford Companion to Politics*. http://www.polity.co.uk/global/globocp.htm.

Held, David, Anthony McGrew, David Goldblatt, and Jonathan Perraton. 1999. *Global Transformations: Politics, Economics and Culture*. Stanford, CA: Stanford University Press.

Hirschl, Ran. 1998. Israel's "Constitutional Revolution": The Legal Interpretation of Entrenched Civil Liberties in an Emerging Neo-liberal Economic Order. *American Journal of Comparative Law* 46 (3): 427–52.

Hobsbawm, Eric. 1996. *The Age of Extremes: A History of the World 1914–1991*. London: Abacus.

Hobsbawm, Eric, and Terence Ranger, eds. 1983. *The Invention of Tradition*. Cambridge, MA: Cambridge University Press.

Hoogvelt, Ankie. 2001. *Globalization and the Postcolonial World: The New Political Economy of Development*. Baltimore: Johns Hopkins University Press.

Horesh, Hadar. 2004a. The Number of Internet Surfaces in Israel Doubled. *Haaretz*, June 24, 2004, C3.

———. 2004b. 40% of Households Are Connected to the Fast Internet. *Haaretz*, April 21, 2004, C7.

Horkheimer, Max. 1975. Traditional and Critical Theory. In *Critical Theory*, 188–244. New York: Continuum.

Horowitz, Dan, and Moshe Lissak. 1989. *Troubles in Utopia: The Overburdened Polity of Israel*. Albany, NY: SUNY Press.

Huntington, Samuel P. 1998. *The Clash of Civilizations and the Remaking of World Order*. New York: Simon and Schuster.

Inglehart, Ronald. 1997. *Modernization and Postmodernization*. Princeton, NJ: Princeton University Press.

Jameson, Fredric. 1991. *Postmodernism, or, The Cultural Logic of Late Capitalism (Post-contemporary Interventions Series)*. Durham, NC: Duke University Press.

———. 1998. *The Cultural Turn: Selected Writings on the Postmodern 1983–1998*. London: Verso.

Jessop, Bob. 1994a. Post-Fordism and the State. In *Post-Fordism*, ed. Ash Amin, 251–79. Oxford: Blackwell.

———. 1994b. The Transition to Post-Fordism and the Schumpeterian Workfare State. In *Towards a Post-Fordist Welfare State?* ed. Roger Burrows and Brian Loader, 13–37. London: Routledge.

———. 2002. *The Future of the Capitalist State*. London: Polity.

Kandiyoti, Deniz, and Ayse Saktanber. 2002. *Fragments of Culture: The Everyday in Modern Turkey*. Piscataway, NJ: Rutgers University Press.

Kaniuk, Yoram. 1987. A Cruel Junction. *Politika* 17:2–8. (Hebrew)

Kaplinsky, Raphael. 2005. *Globalization, Poverty and Inequality: Between a Rock and a Hard Place*. Cambridge, MA: Polity.

Kapra, Michal, and Ofer Shelach. 1998. Descends 98. *Ma'ariv—Saturday Supplement*, August 7, 1998, 2, 4, 8.

Katz, Elihu, and Hadas Hess. 1995. Twenty Years of Television in Israel: Do They Have a Long Term Impact? *Zmanin: Historical Quarterly* 52:80–91. (Hebrew)

Katz-Freiman, Tami. 1996. The Artists: Catalogue. In *Desert Cliché: Israel Now—Local Images*, ed. Amy Cappellazzo and Tamy Katz-Freiman, 94–110. Miami Beach, FL: The Israeli Forum of Art Museums and the Bass Museum of Art.

Katznelson, Ira, Mark Kesselman, and Alan Draper. 2002. *The Politics of Power: A Critical Introduction to American Government*. Belmont, CA: Wadsworth.

Kav La'Oved. 2004. *Update on Trafficking in Persons for Forced Labour in Israel: A Kav La'Oved Newsletter.* http://www.kavlaoved.org.il/ katava_main.asp?news? news_id=976&sivug_id=21.

Kearney, A. T./Foreign Policy magazine. 2004. Measuring Globalization. *Globalization Index 2004.* http://www.foreignpolicy.com/issue_ marapr_2004/ countrydetail.php.

Kellner, Douglas. 1999. Theorizing/Resisting McDonaldization. In *Resisting McDonaldization*, ed. B. Smart, 186–206. London: Sage.

Kemp, Adriana, David Newman, Uri Ram, and Oren Yiftachel, eds. 2004. *Israelis in Conflict: Hegemonies, Identities and Challenges.* Sussex: Sussex Academic Press.

Keren, Michael. 1995. *Professionals against Populism: The Peres Government and Democracy.* Albany, NY: SUNY Press.

Keynes, John Maynard. 1936/1997. *The General Theory of Employment, Interest, and Money.* Amherst, NY: Prometheus Books.

Kim, Hanna. 1996a. Likud Marketing Peace; Labor Marketing Security. *Haaretz*, March 23, 1996, B1.

———. 1996b. One Big Right-Wing. *Haaretz*, April 29, 1996.

Kimmerling, Baruch. 1994. Nationalism and Democracy in Israel. *Zmanim: Historical Quarterly* 50–51:116–31. (Hebrew)

Kipnis, Baruch A. 2004. Tel Aviv, Israel—A World City in Evolution: Urban Development at a Deadend of the Global Economy. *Dela* 21:183–93.

Kipnis, Baruch A., and Tamar Noam. 1998. Restructuring of a Metropolitan Industrial Park: Case Study in Herzeliyya, Israel. *Geografiska Annaler. Series B. Human Geography* 80 (4): 215–27.

Kirchheimer, Otto. 1966. The Transformation of the Western Party System, in J. LaPalombara and M. Weiner, eds. *Political Parties and Political Development*, pp. 177–200.

Kirchheimer, Otto. 1969. *Politics, Law and Social Change: Selected Essays.* New York: Columbia University Press.

Klein, David. 2003. The Constrains of Globalization: Challenges to the Management of Social Policy in Israel. In *Bank of Israel, Publications. The Bank Israel Governor.* Jerusalem.

Klein, Naomi. 2002. *No Logo: No Space, No Choice, No Jobs.* Picador.

Kleingbail, Sivan. 2005. The Power-Centers Get Stronger. *The Marker*, June 28, 2005, 15.

Kleinman, Ephraim. 1996. The Political Economy of Israel: Etatism on a Crossword. In *Israel Towards 2000*, ed. Moshe Lissak and Baruch Knei-Paz, 196–212. Jerusalem: Magnes Press. (Hebrew)

Kondor, Ya'akov. 1997. *Foreign Workers in Israel*. Jerusalem: National Insurance Institute. (Hebrew)

Koren, Alona. 1999a. Five Families Dominate 40% of the Stock Exchange Value. *Haaretz*, August 2, 1999, C8.

———. 1999b. High Profitability in Textile. *Haaretz*, March 15, 1999, C8. (Hebrew)

Koren, Ella. 1998. Labour Immigrants in Israel: Foreign to Reality or Epitomizing It? *The Other Side (MeZad Sheni)* 2:28–30. (Hebrew)

Kotan, Asnat. 2000. And We Have Falafel. *Ma'ariv-Business*, 9–10.

Kristal, Tali, and Yinon Cohen. 2005. *Decentralization of Collective Agreements and Rising Wage Inequality in Israel*. http://www.ccpr.ucla.edu/israc28/final%20papers/decentralization_Kristal_Cohen.pdf.

Kurt, James. 1999. Military–Industrial Complex. *The Oxford Companion to American Military History*, 440–42. Oxford: Oxford University Press.

Kuzar, Ron. 2001. *Hebrew and Zionism: A Discourse Analytic Cultural Study*. New York: Walter de Gruyter.

LaPalombara, Joseph, and Myron Weiner, eds. 1966. *Political Parties and Political Development*. Princeton, NJ: Princeton University Press.

Lash, Scott, and John Urry. 1987. *The End of Organized Capitalism*. Madison: University of Wisconsin Press.

———. 1994. *Economies of Signs and Space*. London: Sage.

Lehman-Wilzig, Sam. 1995. The 1992 Media Campaign: Towards the Americanization of Israeli Elections? In *Israel at the Polls 1992*, ed. Daniel Elazar and Samuel Sandler, 251–80. Lanham, MD: University Press of America and Jerusalem Center for Public Affairs.

Leibes, Tamar. 1999. Israeli Broadcast Programming as a Reflection of Society. *Kesher* 25:88–97. (Hebrew)

Lemish, Dafna. 2000. "If You Are Not Here—You Don't Exist": Advertising as a Peeping Hole to Israeli Society. In *Fifty Years: Reflection of a Society*, ed. H. Herzog, 539–59. Tel Aviv: Tel Aviv University, Ramot. (Hebrew)

Levi-Faur, David. 2000. Change and Continuity in the Israeli Political Economy: Multi Level Analysis of the Telecommunications and Energy Sectors. In *The New Israel: Peacemaking and Liberalization*, ed. Gershon Shafir and Yoav Peled, 161–88. Boulder, CO: Westview.

———. 2001. *The Visible Hand: State-Directed Industrialization in Israel*. Jerusalem: Yad Ben Zvi. (Hebrew)

Liebman, Charles S., and Eliezer Don Yehiya. 1983. *Civil Religion in Israel: Traditional Judaism and Political Culture in the Jewish State*. Berkeley: University of California Press.

Lifshitz, Yaacov. 2003. *The Economics of Producing Defense: Illustrated by the Israeli Case*. Springer.

Likud. 2003. *Party Program towards the 16th Knesset*. http://www.knesset.gov.il/elections16/heb/lists/plat_16.htm.

Limor, Yechiel. 2003. Mass Media in Israel. In *Trends in Israeli Society*, vol. II, ed. E. Yaar and Z. Shavit, 1017–1123. Tel Aviv: Open University. (Hebrew)

Lipson, Nathan. 2006. The Richest 500. *The Marker*, June 2006.

Loomba, Ania, Frederick Cooper, Kelwyn Sole, and Laura Chrisman, eds. 2005. *Postcolonial Studies and Beyond*. Durham, NC: Duke University Press.

Lustick, Ian. 1980. *Arabs in the Jewish State: Israel's Control of a National Minority*. Austin: University of Texas Press.

———. 1988. *For the Land and the Lord: Jewish Fundamentalism in Israel*. New York: Council on Foreign Relations.

———. 1999. Israel as a "Non-Arab" State: The Political Implications of Mass Immigration of Non-Jews. *Middle East Journal* 53 (3): 101–17.

Lyotard, Jean-Francois. 1984. *The Post-modern Condition: A Report on Knowledge*. Minneapolis: University of Minnesota Press.

Ma'ariv. 1995. Following the Arad Disaster: President Weizmann—Israel Should Beware McDonald's, Michael Jackson and Madonna. *Ma'ariv*, June 21, 1995, 5.

MacCannell, Dean. 1976/1989. *The Tourist: A New Theory of the Leisure Class*. New York: Schocken Books.

Maman, Daniel. 1997. The Elite Structure in Israel: A Socio-historical Analysis. *Journal of Political and Military Sociology* 25 (1): 25–46.

———. 1999. The Social Organization of the Israeli Economy: A Comparative Analysis. *Israel Affairs* 5 (2–3): 876–1021.

———. 2002. The Emergence of Business Groups: Israel and South Korea Compared. *Organizational Studies* 23 (5): 737–58.

Maman, Daniel, and Zeev Rosenhek. Forthcoming. *The Politics of Neoliberal Institutions: The Central Bank in Israel*. Jerusalem: Van Leer Jerusalem Institute and HaKibbutz HaMeuchad. (Hebrew)

Mamon—*Yedioth Ahronoth*. 2003. The Israelis Who Made It. April 16, 2003.

The Manufacturers Association of Israel. 2006. *The Textile and Fashion Branch 2005*. http://www.industry.org.il/Publications/Item.asp?ArticleID=2736& CategoryID=3211&Archive=0.

Maor, Dafna. 2004. Eight Israeli Companies are in the Big 2000 List of Forbes. *Haaretz*, March 29, C3.

The Marker. 2003. The 500 Rich Israelis. April 27, 2003.

The Marker. 2006. The 500 Wealthiest Israelis. April 2006.

Marshall, T. H. 1963. Citizenship and Social Class. In *Sociology at the Crossroads and Other Essays*. London: Anchor.

Marx, Karl. 1967. *Capital*. Vol. I. New York: International Publishers.

———. 1847/1963. *The Poverty of Philosophy*. New York: International Publishers.

Marx, Karl, and Friedrich Engels. 1848/1998. *The Communist Manifesto*. London: Verso.

Mattelart, Armand. 2003. *The Information Society: An Introduction*. Thousand Oaks, CA: Sage.

May, Christopher. 2002. *The Information Society: A Sceptical View*. Cambridge, UK: Polity.

McSweeney, Dean. 1990. Is the Party Over? Decline and Revival in the American Party System. In *Explaining American Politics*, ed. Robert Williams, 144–66. New York: Routledge.

Meiri, Shmuel. 1998. Rotlevy: 1500 Textile Workers Were Fired in 1998. *Haaretz*, October 28, 1998, C3. (Hebrew)

Meital, Shlomo. 1997. Why Israel Does Not Have an International Competitiveness Capability. *Executive*, December/January, 6–10. (Hebrew)

Melman, Yossi. 1992. *The New Israelis: An Intimate View of a Changing People*. New York: Birch Lane Press.

MHR. 2000. *Viandes Magazine 2000.* www.mhr.viandes.com

Michels, Robert. 1962. *Political Parties: A Sociological Study of the Oligarchic Tendencies of Modern Democracy*. New York: Free Press.

Miller, Daniel. 1998. Why Some Things Matter. In *Material Cultures: Why Some Things Matter*, ed. D. Miller, 3–21. Chicago: University of Chicago Press.

Ministry of Education, Government of Israel. 2005. *Report of The National Task Force for the Advancement of Education in Israel* (The Dovrat Report). http://cms.education.gov.il/Educationcms/units/Ntfe/HdochHsofi/DochSofi.htm

Ministry of Finance, Government of Israel. 2003. *Economic Trends in Israel.* http://www.mof.gov.il/research_e/trends2003e.pdf.

Ministry of Finance, Government of Israel. The Supervisor of the Financial Market, Insurance and Savings. 1997. *Annual Report 1996.* Jerusalem.

Ministry of Industry, Trade, and Labor, Government of Israel. 2004. *The Traditional Industrial Branches*.

———. 2005. *The Israeli Economy at a Glance.* http://www.tamas.gov.il/NR/exeres/20905A78-4041-4E0B-9D2B-B837847832Db.htm.

———. 2006. *Business Climate: Israel's Competitiveness.* http://www.investin-israel.gov.il/CmsTamat/InvestInIsrael/Inv_PrintVersion.aspx?guid= {1C6C4252-64E1-4996-8BF8-50E0B791CE94}.

Mitchell, Timothy. 2002. McJihad: Islam in the U.S. Global Order. *Social Text* 20 (4): 1–18.

Mittelman, James. 2004a. Critical Globalization Studies. In *Whither Globalization? The Vortex of Knowledge and Ideology*, 34–44. London: Routledge.

——. 2004b. Globalization: An Ascendant Paradigm? In *Whither Globalization? The Vortex of Knowledge and Ideology*, 21–33. London: Routledge.

Mizrachi, Yonathan, Noa Bar, Irit Katsernow, and Nachman Oron, eds. 2005. *E-Readiness and Digital Divide Survey, Israel 2005*. Jerusalem: Ministry of Finance.

Morris, Benny. 1989. *The Birth of the Palestinian Refugee Problem, 1947–1949*. Cambridge: Cambridge University Press.

Morris, Martina, and Bruce Western. 1999. Inequality in Earnings at the Close of the Twentieth Century. *Annual Review of Sociology* 25:623–57.

Mosse, George L. 1990. *Fallen Soldiers: Reshaping the Meaning of the World Wars*. New York: Oxford University Press.

Murray, E. Warwick. 2006. *Geographies of Globalization*. New York: Routledge.

Myre, Greg. 2006. Giving Galilee a Foothold in Industry. *New York Times*, May 18, 2006.

Nachshon, Udi. 1995. We the World. *Yedioth Ahronoth—Seven Days*, December 15, 1995, 15, 18, 20.

Nadiv, Ronit. 2003. *Employment through Manpower Contractors Labour Contractors: Israel 2000*. Jerusalem: State of Israel, Ministry of Labour, Authority for Manpower Planning. (Hebrew)

Nasi, Jonathan. 1999. Foreigners Hold 50% of Ownership of the Big Companies. *Haaretz*, February 22, 1999, C2.

Nativ. 2004. *Index 1988–2004*. Merkaz Ariel. (Hebrew)

Newman, I. Bruce. 1999. *The Mass Marketing of Politics: Democracy in the Age of Manufactured Markets*. London. Sage.

Newsweek. 1998. Where Wired Is a Way of Life. November 9, 1998, 38–43.

Nimni, Ephraim, ed. 2003. *The Challenge of Post-Zionism: Alternatives to Fundamentalist Politics in Israel*. London: Zed Books.

Nitzan, Jonathan, and Shimshon Bichler. 2002. *The Global Political Economy of Israel*. London: Pluto Press.

O'Donnell, Guillermo. 1979. *Modernization and Bureaucratic-Authoritarianism: Studies in South-American Politics*. Berkeley: University of California Press.

Offe, Claus. 1984. *Contradictions of the Welfare State*. London: Hutchinson.

————. 1985. *Disorganized Capitalism: Contemporary Transformation of Work and Politics*. Cambridge, MA: MIT Press.

Ohmann, Richard. 1996. *Making and Selling Culture*. Hanover, NH: Wesleyan University Press.

O'Meara, Patrick, H. D. Mehlinger, and M. Krain, eds. 2000. *Globalization and the Challenges of a New Century: A Reader*. Bloomington: Indiana University Press.

Oncu, A., and P. Weyland, eds. 1997. *Space, Culture and Power: New Identities in Globalizing Cities*. London: Zed Books.

Ono, A. Kent, and D. T. Buescher. 2001. Deciphering Pocahontas: Unpacking the Commodification of a Native American Woman. *Critical Studies in Media Communication* 18:23–43.

Ophir, Adi, ed. 1999. *50 to 48: Critical Moments in the History of the State of Israel Essays and Chronicle*. Jerusalem: Van Leer Institute and HaKibbutz HaMeuchad. (Hebrew)

————. 2001. *Working for the Present: Essays on Contemporary Israeli Culture*. Tel Aviv: HaKibbutz HaMeuchad. (Hebrew)

Oron, Yair. 1993. *Israeli–Jewish Identity*. Tel Aviv: Sifriyat Poalim. (Hebrew)

Panitch, Leo, Colin Leys, Gregory Albo, and David Coates, eds. 2000. *Working Classes: Global Realities. Socialist Register 2001*. New York: Monthly Review Press.

Panitch, Leo, and Sam Gindin. 2004. *Global Capitalism and American Empire*. London: Merlin Press.

Parsons, Talcott. 1951. *The Social System*. Glencoe, IL: Free Press.

Peled, Yoav. 1994. Luxurious Diaspora: On the Rehabilitation of the Concept of Diaspora in Boyarin and Raz-Karkotzkin. *Theory and Criticism* 5:133–40. (Hebrew)

———. 1995. From Zionism to Capitalism: The Political Economy of Israel's Decolonization of the Occupied Territories. *Middle East Report*, May–June/July–August, 13–17.

———. 2006. Zionist Realities: Debating Israel–Palestine. *New Left Review* 38:21–36.

Peled, Yoav, and Gershon Shafir. 1996. The Roots of Peacemaking: The Dynamics of Citizenship in Israel, 1948–1993. *International Journal of Middle East Studies* 28:391–413.

Perel, Moshe. 1997. The Ten Best Executives in Israel. *Ma'ariv*, April 21, 1997.

Peri, Smadar. 1998. The Peace Underwear. *Yedioth Ahronoth—Seven Days*, January 6, 1998, 36–39, 41, 43, 66.

Peri, Yoram. 1988. From Political Nationalism to Ethno-Nationalism: The Case of Israel. In *The Arab–Israeli Conflict: Two Decades of Change*, ed. Yehuda Lukcas and Abdalla M. Battah, 41–53. Boulder, CO: Westview.

———. 1996. The Radical Social Scientists and Israeli Militarism. *Israel Studies* 1 (2): 230–66.

———. 2004. *Telepopulism: Media and Politics in Israel*. Stanford, CA: Stanford University Press.

Peri, Yoram, and Neubach Amnon. 1984. *The Military–Industrial Complex in Israel*. Tel Aviv: International Center for Peace in the Middle East. (Hebrew)

Petersberg, Ofer. 2003. Happy in the Penthouse. *Yedioth Ahronoth—Seven Days*, March 27, 2003, 71, 72, 76.

———. 2004. The Most Expansive in the Country. *Yedioth Ahronoth—Seven Days*, December 24, 2004, 14–15.

Petras, James F., and Henry Veltmeyer. 2001. *Globalization Unmasked: Imperialism in the 21st Century*. London: Zed Books.

Pew Research Center for the People and the Press. 2003. Views of a Changing World, June 2003. *The Pew Global Attitudes Project*. http://people-press.org/reports/pdf/185.pdf.

Pierson, Paul. 2001. *The New Politics of the Welfare State*. London: Oxford University Press.

———. 2006. *Beyond the Welfare State? The New Political Economy of Welfare*. London: Polity.

Pieterse, Jan Nederveen. 2003. *Globalization and Culture: Global Mélange*. Lanham, MD: Rowman and Littlefield.

———. 2004. *Globalization or Empire?* London: Routledge.

Plocker, Sever. 1996. Dan Shohat and Biege Meridor. *Yedioth Ahronoth*, September 27, 1996.

———. 1998. Buying and Selling the State over Lunch. *Yedioth Ahronoth*, June 13, 1998, 20–21.

Rabad, Achiya. 2006. Shitrit Boasts: We Cut Ourselves Off from All Ideologies. *Ynet News*, March 26, 2006.

Rabin, Eitan. 1996a. An Investigating Commission on the Issue of IDF and Motivation. *Haaretz*, November 10, 1996, B3. (Hebrew)

———. 1996b. Let Others Go Fighting. *Haaretz*, October 15, 1996, B3.

Raday, Frances, and Gil Noam. 2004. Labour Unions and Collective Bargaining in Israel—A View to the 21st Century. *Mishpatim* 34 (1): 39–90. (Hebrew)

Rae, Nicol C. 2006. Exceptionalism in the United States. In *Handbook of Party Politics*, ed. Richard Katz and William Crotty, 196–203. London: Sage.

Ram, Uri. 1993a. The Colonization Perspective in Israeli Sociology: Internal and External Comparisons. *Journal of Historical Sociology* 6:327–50.

———. 1995b. Zionist Historiography and the Invention of Modern Jewish Nationhood: The Case of Ben Zion Dinur. *History and Memory* 7 (1): 91–124.

———. 2005. *The Globalization of Israel: McWorld in Tel Aviv, Jihad in Jerusalem*. Tel Aviv: Resling. (Hebrew)

———. 2006. *The Time of the "Post": Nationalism and the Politics of Knowledge in Israel*. Tel Aviv: Resling. (Hebrew)

———. 2006. Post-Zionism: The First Decade. *Israel Studies Forum* 20 (2): 22–45.

Ravitsky, Aviezer. 1996. *Messianism, Zionism and Jewish Religious Radicalism*. Chicago: Chicago University Press.

———. 1997. Religious and Seculars Israelis: A Post-Zionist Cultural War? *Alpayim* 14:970–80. (Hebrew)

Raz-Krakotzkin, Amnon. 1994. Exile within Sovereignty: Toward a Critique of the "Negation of Exile" in Israeli Culture. Parts I and II. *Theory and Criticism* 4:23–56 and 5:113–32. (Hebrew)

———. 2001. History Textbooks and the Limits of Israeli Consciousness. *Journal of Israeli History* 20 (2–3): 155–72.

Red Herring. 2000 (September Issue).

Reich, Robert. 1992. *The Work of Nations: Preparing Ourselves for the 21st-Century*. New York: Vintage.

Reily, Miri. 2003. Escaping from Recession into the Mall. *Haaretz— Real Estate Supplement*, October 26, 2003, 6.

Regev, Motti, and Edwin Seroussi. 2004. *Popular Music and National Culture in Israel*. University of California Press.

Riain, Sean O. 2000. States and Markets in an Era of Globalization. *Annual Review of Sociology* 26:187–213.

Ritzer, George. 1995. *The McDonaldization of Society*. London: Sage.

———. 2003. *The Globalization of Nothing*. Thousand Oaks, CA: Pine Forge Press.

Robertson, Ronald. 1995. Glocalization: Time–Space and Homogeniety–Hetrerogeneity. In *Global Modernities*, ed. M. Featherstone, Scott Lash, and Ronald Robertson, 25–44. London: Sage.

———. 1997. Social Theory, Cultural Relativity and the Problem of Globality. In *Culture, Globalization and the World System*, ed. A. D. King, 69–90. Minneapolis: University of Minnesota Press.

Robinson, William I. 2004. *A Theory of Global Capitalism: Production, Class, and State in a Transnational World*. Baltimore, MD: Johns Hopkins University Press.

Robinson, William I., and Jerry Harris. 2000. Toward a Global Ruling Class? Globalization and the Transnational Capitalist Class. *Science and Society* 64:11–54.

Rolnik, Guy. 1998a. Breathing High Air. *Haaretz*, April 26, 1998, C2.

———. 1998b. The Peace Process Is Halted but Dov Lautman Accelerated. *Haaretz*, April 26, 1998, C1.

———. 1999. Dov Lautman: Person of the Year. *Haaretz*, January 1, 1999, C7.

Rolnik, Guy, and Nathan Lipson. 1997. The Growth Decade 1988–1997. *Haaretz, Economy—Special Supplement*, December 15, 1997. (Hebrew)

Roniger, Luis. 1999. Individualism within the Jewish Public in Israel in the 1990s. In *Between the Me and the Us: Construction of Identity and Israeli Identity*, ed. Azmi Bashara, 109–27. Jerusalem: Van Leer Institute and HaKibbutz HaMeuchad. (Hebrew)

Roniger, Luis, and Michael Feige. 1992. From Pioneer to Freier: The Changing Models of Generalized Exchange in Israel. *European Journal of Sociology* 33 (2): 280–307.

Rosenblum, Doron. 1996. Blind People Perceive an Elephant. *Haaretz*, April 5, 1996, B1.

Rosenblum, Sarit. 2004. The End of the Junk? McDonald's Surrender: Healthy Meals in Israel. *Ynet News*, June 24, 2004.

Rosenfeld, Henry, and Shulamit Carmi. 1976. The Privatization of Public Means, the State Made Middle Class, and the Realization of Family Values in Israel. In *Kinship and Modernization in Mediterranean Society*, ed. J. G. Peristiany, 131–59. Rome: Center of Mediterranean Studies, American University.

Rosenhek, Zeev. 1995. New Development in the Study of the Palestinian Citizens of Israel: An Analytical Survey. *Megamot* 47:167–90. (Hebrew)

———. 2002. Social Policy and Nation Building: The Dynamics of the Israeli Welfare State. *Journal of Societal and Social Policy* 1 (1): 15–31.

Rosner, Menahem. 2000. *Future Trends of the Kibbutz: An Assessment of Recent Changes*. University of Haifa, the Institute for Study and Research of the Kibbutz. Publication No. 83. http://research.haifa.ac.il/~kibbutz/pdf/trends.PDF.

Rosner, Menahem, and Shlomo Getz. 1996. *The Kibbutz in Era of Changes*. Tel Aviv: HaKibbutz HaMeuchad. (Hebrew)

Schlosser, Erik. 2000. *Fast Food Nation: The Dark Side of the All-American Meal*. New York: Harper Collins.

Schmitt, John. 1999. Inequality and Globalization: Some Evidence from the United States. In *The Ends of Globalization: Bringing Society Back In*, ed. Don Kalb et al., 157–68. Boulder, CO: Rowman and Littlefield.

Schmitter, Phillipe, and Gerhard Lehmburch. 1979. *Trends toward Corporatist Intermediation*. London: Sage.

Scholte, Jan Aart. 2000. *Globalization: A Critical Introduction*. Baskingstoke: Palgrave.

Semyonov, Moshe, and Noah Lewin-Epstein. 1987. *Hewers of Wood and Drawers of Water: Noncitizen Arabs in the Israeli Labor Market*. Ithaca, NY: Cornell University Press.

Shafir, Gershon. 1989. *Land, Labor and the Origins of the Israeli–Palestinian Conflict, 1882–1914*. Cambridge: Cambridge University Press.

———. 1996. Israeli Society: A Counterview. *Israel Studies* 1 (2): 189–213.

———. 1998. Business in Politics: Globalization and the Search for Peace in South Africa and in Israel/Palestine. *Israel Affairs* 135 (2): 1023–1920.

Shalev, Michael. 1999. Have Globalization and Liberalization "Normalized" Israel's Political Economy? *Israel Affairs* 5 (2–3): 121–55.

———. 2003. *Placing Class Politics in Context: Why Is Israel's Welfare State So Consensual?* http://www.geocities.com/michaelshalev/papers.html.

Shalev, Michael, and Gal Levi. 2005. The Winners and Losers of 2003: Ideology, Social Structure and Political Change. In *The Elections in Israel 2003*, ed. Asher Arian and Michal Shamir. Albany, NY: SUNY Press.

Shalev, Michael, with Sigal Kis. 2002. Social Cleavages among Non-Arab Voters: A New Analysis. In *The Elections in Israel 1999*, ed. Asher Arian and Michal Shamir. Albany, NY: SUNY Press. (Citations are from the Hebrew version of the book, published in 2001 by the Israel Democracy Institute.)

Shamir, Ronen. 1996. Society, Judaism and Democratic Fundamentalism. In *A Jewish and Democratic State*, ed. Dafna Barak-Erez, 241–60. Tel Aviv: Ramot. (Hebrew)

Shapira, Anita. 1992. *Land and Power: The Zionist Resort to Force 1881–1948.* New York: Oxford University Press.

———. 1997d. Ben Gurion and the Bible: The Forging of an Historical Narrative? *Middle Eastern Studies* 33 (4): 645–74.

———. 1998. The Religious Motives of the Labor Movement. In *Zionism and Religion*, ed. Shmuel Almog, Jehuda Reinharz, and Anita Shapira. Waltham, MA: Brandies.

Shapiro, Yonathan. 1984. *An Elite without Successors: Generations of Political Leaders in Israel.* Tel Aviv: Sifriat Poalim. (Hebrew)

———. 1991. *The Road to Power: Herut Party in Israel.* Albany, NY: SUNY Press.

Shavit, Ari. 2005. A Truthful Agenda. *Haaretz*, November 24, 2005.

Shavit, Yaakov. 1987. *The New Hebrew Nation.* London: Frank Cass.

Shenhav, Yehuda. 1996. A Conspiracy of Silence. *Haaretz Supplement*, December 27, 1996.

Shugart, Helene A., Catherine Egley Waggoner, and D'Lynn O'Brien Hallstein. (2001). Mediating Third Wave Feminism: Appropriation as Postmodern Media Practice. *Critical Studies in Mass Communication* 18:194–210.

Shuval, J. T., and O. Anson. 2000. *Health Is the Essence: Social Structure and Health in Israel.* Jerusalem: Magnes Press. (Hebrew)

Sigan, Lilach. 1998. T.G.I. 35% of the Population Dialed Abroad. *Haaretz*, August 3, 1998, C3.

Silberstein, Laurence J. 1999. *The Postzionism Debates: Knowledge and Power in Israeli Culture.* New York: Routledge.

Simanovsky, Shlomo. 1999. Delta Galil. In *The Stock Exchange Book*, 380. Tel Aviv: Meitav. (Hebrew)

Sinai, Ruthie. 2004. The Institute for National Insurance Institute Security Report: Almost 1 in Every 3 Waged Employees Earned Less Than the Minimum Wage. *Haaretz*, October 25, 2004, 6A.

The Globalization of Israel

Sklair, Leslie. 2000. *The Transnationalist Capitalist Class*. New York: Blackwell.

———. 2002. *Globalization: Capitalism and Its Alternatives*. New York: Oxford University Press.

Sofer, Sasson. 1998. *Zionism and the Foundations of Israeli Diplomacy*. Cambridge: Cambridge University Press.

Sprinzak, Ehud. 1981. Gush Emunim: The Iceberg Model of Political Extremism. *State, Regime and International Relations* 17:22–43. (Hebrew)

———. 1991. *The Ascendance of Israel's Radical Right*. Oxford: Oxford University Press.

Spurlock, Morgan. 2004. *Super Size Me*. Film.

Starkman, Rotem, and Ido Alon. 2004. 15 Managers Sold Shares in 1.1 Milliard NIS. *Haaretz*, April 25, 2004, C1.

State Comptroller. 2001. Supervision on Employment by Manpower Contractors. In *Annual Report 51B*, 562–71. Jerusalem: Government's Publication House. (Hebrew)

Steger, Manfred. 2003. *Globalization: A Very Short Introduction*. New York: Oxford University Press.

Steinberg, Robi. 1999. In 1998 20 Hi-Tech Companies Were Sold to Foreigners for $3 Milliard. *Haaretz*, March 12th, 1999, C5.

Steinmetz, George, ed. 2005. *The Politics of Method in the Human Sciences: Positivism and Its Epistemological Others*. Durham, NC: Duke University Press.

Stewart-Harawira, Makere. 2005. *The New Imperial Order: The Indigenous Response to Globalization*. London: Zed Books.

Strassler, Nehemiya. 1998. The End of Socialism. *Haaretz*, June 1, 1998, C2–3.

———. 2003. Benjamin Netanyahu: Israeli Economy Is Centralist, Inefficient, and Corrupted. *Haaretz*, September 26, 2003, C1–2.

Suleiman, Yasir. 2004. *A War of Words: Language and Conflict in the Middle East*. Cambridge, UK: Cambridge University Press.

Sussman, Noam, and Dimitri Romanov. 2003. *Foreign Workers in the Construction Branch: Current Situation and Policy Implications*. Jerusalem: Research Department, Bank of Israel. (Hebrew)

Sussman, Zvi, and Dan Zakai. 2004. *Wage Gaps in the Israeli Civil Service during the 1990s: A Policy or a Crawl?* Jerusalem: Research Department, Bank of Israel.

Swirski, Shlomo. 1989. *Israel's Oriental Majority.* London: Zed. (Hebrew edition: 1981. *Orientals and Ashkenazim in Israel.* Haifa: Notebooks for Research and Critique.)

———. 1993. Tomorrow. In *Israeli Society: Critical Perspectives*, ed. Uri Ram, 363–51. Tel Aviv: Breirot. (Hebrew)

———. 1995. *Seeds of Inequality.* Tel Aviv: Breirot. (Hebrew)

———. 2005. *The Price of Arrogance : The Cost of the Occupation.* Tel Aviv: Mapa. (Hebrew)

———. 2006. On Economics and Society in the Days of Empire. Manuscript. Tel Aviv: Adva Center. (Hebrew)

Swirski, Shlomo, and Eti Konnor-Atias. 2001. *Israel: A Social Report 2001.* Tel Aviv: Adva Center. (Hebrew)

———. 2003. *Israel: A Social Report 2003.* Tel Aviv: Adva Center. (Hebrew)

———. 2004. *Israel: A Social Report 2004.* Tel Aviv: Adva Center. (Hebrew)

———. 2005. *Israel: A Social Report 2005.* Tel Aviv: Adva Center. (Hebrew)

Swirski, Shlomo, Yechezkel Yaron, and Eti Konnor-Atias. 1998. *Israel: A Social Report 1998.* Tel Aviv: Adva Center. (Hebrew)

Tamir, Tali. 1995. Tsuba: Abstraction and Blindness. In *Tsooba: Larry Abramson*, ed. T. Tamir. Tel Aviv: Kibbutz Art Gallery.

Taub, Gadi. 1997. *HaMered HaShafuf, Al Tarbut Tse'ira Beyisra'el* [The Dismal Rebel: On Youth Culture in Israel]. Tel Aviv: HaKibbutz HaMeuchad. (Hebrew)

Tetzlaff, David. 1991. Divide and Conquer: Popular Culture and Social Control in Late Capitalism. *Media, Culture and Society* 13:9–33.

Tilly, Charles. 1993. *Coercion, Capital and European States, A.D. 990–1992.* New York: Blackwell.

Tomlinson, John. 1991. *Cultural Imperialism: A Critical Introduction.* Baltimore, MD: Johns Hopkins University Press.

Tzoreff, Ayala. 2003. The Recession and Mistaken Marketing Policies Toppled Burger King. *Haaretz*, February 6, 2003, C1.

United Nations. 1999. *Human Development Report 1999*. New York: United Nations Development Program.

———. 2005. *Human Development Report 2005*. New York: United Nations Development Program.

Urieli, Nathi. 1989. The Cultural Dimension of Cigarettes Advertisements. Master's thesis, Department of Sociology and Anthropology, Tel Aviv University.

Urry, John. 2003. *Global Complexity*. Malden, MA: Polity.

U.S. Census Bureau. 1994. *A Brief Look at Postwar U.S. Income Inequality* (P60–191). http://www.census.gov/hhes/www/p60191.html.

———. 2000. *Income Inequality*. http://www.census.gov./hhes/income/incineq/p60asc.html.

Varney, Wendy. 1998. Barbie Australis: The Commercial Reinvention of National Culture. *Social Identities* 4:161–75.

Vinitzky-Seroussi, Vered. 2002. Commemorating a Difficult Past: Yitzhak Rabin's Memorial. *American Sociological Review* 67 (1): 30–51.

Wage and Labour Agreements Comptroller. 2004. *Report Number 10* (2002). Jerusalem: State of Israel, Ministry of Finance.

Walla News. 2001. *Israel Star Prize to "Combina" Meal of Burger Ranch*. www.walla.co.il.

———. 2002a. *Guarding in Settlement to Civil Contractors*. www.walla.co.il.

———. 2002b. *McDonald's: The Mediterranean Version; McFalafel*. www.walla.co.il.

Wallerstein, Immanuel. 1974. *The Modern World System*. Vol. I. New York: Academic Press.

———. 2003. *The Decline of American Power: The U.S. in a Chaotic World*. New York: New Press.

———. 2004. *World-System Analysis: An Introduction*. Durham, NC: Duke University Press.

———. 2006. *European Universalism: The Rhetoric of Power*. New York: New Press.

Ware, Alan. 2006. American Exceptionalism. In *Handbook of Party Politics*, ed. Richard Katz and William Crotty, 270–77. London: Sage.

Watson, James L. 1997a. *Golden Arches East: McDonalds in East Asia*. Stanford, CA: Stanford University Press.

———. 1997b. Transnationalism, Localization, and Fast Food in East Asia. In *Golden Arches East: McDonalds in East Asia*, ed. J. L. Watson, 1–38. Stanford, CA: Stanford University Press.

Wattenberg, Martin. 1998. *The Decline of American Political Parties 1952–1996*. Cambridge, MA: Harvard University Press.

Weimann, Gabi. 1999. The Bonfire of Vanity—On "Television Culture" in Israel. *Kesher* 25:98–104. (Hebrew)

Weiss, Shevach. 1997. *14,729 Missing Votes: An Analysis of the 1996 Elections in Israel*. Tel Aviv: HaKibbutz HaMeuchad. (Hebrew)

Weitman, Sasha. 1988. Surnames as Cultural Indicators: Trends in the National Identity of the Israelis, 1882–1990. In *Nekudat Tatzpit: Literature and Ideology in Eretz Yisrael in the Thirties*, ed. N. Gertz, 141–51. Tel Aviv: Open University. (Hebrew)

Wilson, Rob, and Wimal Dissanayake, eds. 1996. *Global/Local: Cultural Production and the Transnational Imaginary*. Durham, NC: Duke University Press.

Wilterdink, Nico. 1999. The Internalization of Capital and Trends in Income Inequality in Western Societies. In *The Ends of Globalization: Bringing Society Back In*, ed. Don Kalb et al., 187–200. Boulder, CO: Rowman and Littlefield.

World Economic Forum. 2006. Israel Establishes Her Place among the World's Most Competitive Economies. Press release. http://www.weforum.org/pdf/pressreleases/israel.pdf.

Wright, Erik Olin. 1982. Class Boundaries and Contradictory Class Locations. In *Classes, Power, and Conflict: Classical and Contemporary Debates*, ed. A. Giddens and D. Held, 112–29. Berkeley: University of California Press.

Yedioth Ahronoth. 2004. *Mamon Magazine*, September 29, 2004.

Yehoshua, Avraham B. 1984. *In Praise of Normalcy: Five Essays on Zionism*. Jerusalem: Schocken. (Hebrew)

Yiftachel, Oren. 1999. Ethnocracy: The Politics of Judaizing Israel/
Palestine. *Constellations* 6 (3): 364–90.

———. 2006. *Ethnocracy: Land and Identity Politics in Israel/Palestine*. Phila-
delphia: University of Pennsylvania Press.

Yiftachel, Oren, and Alexander (Sandy) Kedar. 2000. Land Power:
The Making of the Israeli Land Regime. *Theory and Criticism*
16:67–100. (Hebrew)

Yizhar, S. 1949. *The Story of Hirbet Hiz'ah and the Prisoner Stories*. Tel Aviv:
Sifriat Poalim. (Hebrew)

Yona, Yossi, and Itzhak Saporta. 2000. Land and Housing Policies in
Israel: The Limits of Citizenship Discourse. *Theory and Criticism*
16:129–51. (Hebrew)

Yuchtman-Yaar, Ephraim, and Yochanan Peres. 2000. *Between Consent
and Dissent: Democracy and Peace in the Israeli Mind*. Jerusalem, and
Lanham, MD: Rowman and Littlefield. (Citations from the
Hebrew edition, 1998.)

Yuran, Noam. 2001. *Channel 2: The New Statehood*. Tel Aviv: Resling.
(Hebrew)

Zach, Yaniv. 2000. Nouvo Falafel. *Haaretz*, November 2, 2000, D1, D4.

Zarhia, Zvi. 2004. President of Manufacturers Federation: 3% of
Business Product of Israel Was Transferred Abroad in the Last
Five Years. *Haaretz*, May 25, 2004, C4.

Zertal, Idith. 2005. *Israel's Holocaust and the Politics of Nationhood*. New York:
Cambridge University Press.

Zertal, Idith, and Akiva Eldar. 2004. *The Lords of the Land: The Settlers and
the State of Israel 1967–2004*. Tel Aviv: Kinneret, Zmora-Bitan and
Dvir. (Hebrew)

Zoref, Ayala. 2003. Vacation in Elections Day. *Haaretz*, January 12,
2003, C1.

———. 2004. The IDF Discovers That Even an Army Has to Be
Marketed. *Haaretz*, April 1, 2004, C7.

Zuckermann, Moshe. 1993. *Shoah in the Sealed Room: The Holocaust in
the Israeli Press during the Gulf War*. Tel Aviv: Moshe Zuckermann.
(Hebrew)

Index